The Journey of
Robert Monroe

Books by Ronald Russell

Focusing the Whole Brain (ed.)

The Vast Enquiring Soul

Using the Whole Brain (ed.)

Swimming for Life: The Therapy of Swimming

(and twelve other titles)

The Journey of Robert Monroe

FROM OUT-OF-BODY EXPLORER TO CONSCIOUSNESS PIONEER

Ronald Russell

HAMPTON ROADS
PUBLISHING COMPANY, INC.
for the evolving human spirit

The Journey of Robert Monroe
From Out-of-Body Explorer to Consciousness Pioneer

Ronald Russell
Foreword by Charles Tart

Cover design by Jane Hagaman

Hampton Roads Publishing Company, Inc.
1125 Stoney Ridge Road • Charlottesville, VA 22902
434-296-2772 • fax: 434-296-5096
e-mail: hrpc@hrpub.com • www.hrpub.com

If you are unable to order this book from your local
bookseller, you may order directly from the publisher.
Call 1-800-766-8009, toll-free.

Library of Congress Cataloging-in-Publication Data

Russell, Ronald, 1924-
  The journey of Robert Monroe : from out-of-body explorer to consciousness pioneer / Ronald Russell ; foreword by Charles Tart.
      p. cm.
  Summary: "The phrase 'out-of-body experience' is widely used today
because of Robert Monroe's courage to publicly recount his own expe-
riences back in the 1970s. This compelling biography delves into the
private world of Robert Monroe, the pioneer of consciousness research,
tracing his journey from a New York radio engineer to the founding of
The Monroe Institute"--Provided by publisher.
  Includes index.
  ISBN 978-1-57174-533-0 (alk. paper)
  1. Monroe, Robert A. 2. Parapsychology--Biography. 3. Psychics--
Biography. 4. Consciousness. 5. Astral projection. I. Title.
  BF1027.M65R87 2007
  133.9092--dc22
  [B]
                                        2007009146

ISBN 978-1-57174-533-0
10 9 8 7 6 5 4 3 2 1
Printed on acid-free paper in the United States

In memoriam

Robert A. Monroe
October 30, 1915–March 17, 1995

Laurie A. Monroe
April 3, 1951–December 18, 2006

CONTENTS

FOREWORD

Ron Russell has written the definitive biography of Robert A. Monroe.

But why would anyone want to read a book about Monroe? Who was he, anyway, and what did he do that we should care about?

For untold thousands of people, the answer is obvious: his work and writings have confirmed their sanity and opened their lives to some marvelous adventures and learnings. But if you're not among the readers of his books (you will be after you read this book) or a graduate of his training programs, why should you care about Monroe's life and work?

I will answer as a basic human being, someone who puzzles over life, wonders what its purpose is, tries to live in a sensible way, and faces my own and my loved ones' inevitable death. This will bother almost all of my scientist colleagues, but it gets right down to essentials.

1. You have a soul.

2. The highest scientific authorities have repeatedly told you there is no such thing as a soul.

3. In fact, they think you are stupid or crazy to even think about such a nonsensical idea as a soul.

4. Most of us have suffered and continue to suffer from having our soul, our spiritual nature, denied.

5. Bob Monroe was a sane, down-to-earth, solid, and successful American who discovered his soul and found ways to work with it that benefit all of us wounded people. He was not some arcane, distant historical figure, but someone who speaks our language.

6. A better understanding of Monroe's life, both his talents and his shortcomings, can stimulate and inspire our own personal understandings of our souls and our goals.

At the end of this foreword I will say it again in more scientifically nuanced language, but that's the gist of why you would want to read a book about Monroe's life.

Robert A. Monroe. Those of us who knew him as a friendly and informal person called him Bob. You'll learn who he was in fascinating detail in this book, but basically Bob embodied a quintessential rags-to-riches American success story, going from young man bumming around as a hobo during the Depression, to successful New York producer of radio shows (remember *The Shadow*? That was one of Bob's productions!), to businessman. (He owned the cable TV business for a moderate-size city, Charlottesville, Virginia, when I first met him.)

In spite of his no-nonsense, practical, indeed irreligious attitudes (he was repelled by the hypocrisy of so many "religious" people), Bob was "drafted" by what he realized, many years later, was a "Higher Power." At the height of his successful career, he started having what we technically call out-of-body experiences (OBEs, an abbreviation I had the honor of coining). In ordinary language, he experienced leaving his physical body behind and traveling places as a disembodied mind or soul. He worried, as any "normal" American would do, that he was going crazy. When his doctor couldn't "cure" him, he gave in to reality and started exploring his OBEs rather than rejecting them.

Bob was obsessed for years with the question of whether his experiences were real, as you or I would be if OBEs happened to us. Was his mind really traveling away from his body, or was this just some vivid, crazy kind of imagination or dream? As his experiences accumulated, he found that "real" was a tricky idea. His OBEs were sometimes partly "real"—in the sense of accurately giving him information about what was happening at a distance in the ordinary world—but there were a lot more places he visited, often more interesting places, than the ordinary world. What kind of reality did they have? Why was it happening to him? What, if anything, was he supposed to do with OBEs and the knowledge he was gaining from them?

My wife, Judy, and I met Bob in the fall of 1965, shortly after we had moved to Charlottesville so that I could take up a research position at the University of Virginia. I had looked forward to this meeting for several years, having heard about Bob's OBEs through parapsychologist Andrija Puharich (who wrote about him while protecting his identity by calling him Bob Rame). As you'll learn in this book, Puharich's writing was actually rather inaccurate from Bob's perspective and angered him, as it took some isolated instances where exposure to glue fumes preceded an OBE and made it sound like Bob was a habitual glue-sniffer. This was not a socially desirable role to be portrayed in, given the antidrug hysteria of the times—to put it mildly! Bob said nothing about this anger at the time I met him, though.

OBEs had long fascinated me and I had already done some research on them. I expected to meet an unusual person that I would be professionally interested in. Little did I know that this professional interest aspect would be a small part of a deep friendship that would span the next thirty years.

My interest in unusual areas like parapsychology, altered states of consciousness, and the nature of the mind was by choice, having been fascinated by them since I was a teenager. Bob's interest in these areas had been forced on him by his OBEs. Because our culture was ignorant, pig-headedly ignorant, prejudiced ("they must be crazy!"), and suppressive about these areas of life, Bob had been struggling to answer his questions pretty much in lonely isolation. But by 1965, cultural changes were occurring, the blossoming of what was later called New Age culture. Bob and I had many exciting conversations as we saw the world starting to open up to spiritual realities.

We discussed questions such as how we could learn more about OBEs, both scientifically and spiritually. What did they mean? Was there a soul? What did a word like *soul* mean? What parts of religion were about great truths, what parts were misleading? How could you teach other people to experience OBEs for themselves, and thus see for themselves what was real? How could the insights of spiritual experiences lead to a better world?

Since I'm a scientist, specifically a psychologist, by training, it's natural for me to ask "How do Bob's experiences, observations, and ideas fit into our official knowledge systems of religion and science?" In a formal sense, Bob was neither "religious" nor a "scientist," yet in the highest sense, he was, deeply.

If "religious" is taken to mean dogmatic and narrow aspects of religion that are, unfortunately, all too common in our world—then "religious" certainly didn't describe Bob. But insofar as "religious" means trying to fathom the meaning of life and act with integrity and kindness along the way, Bob was deeply religious. Indeed, Bob had many experiences that would traditionally be classified as mystical, the kind of deeply moving revelations that people easily get overly attached to and inflated by, and which can lead the less mature to an attitude of "I know the truth and you don't, so just believe me and do what I say!" Not Bob. He always kept a light touch about his experiences, valuing them, trying to share them, trying to help others experience them too, yet staying open to learning from life and not getting carried away by them. People tried to place him on a pedestal and make a guru out of him, but he strongly resisted this.

And if "scientist" is taken to mean an establishment authority figure who explains away all the spiritual aspects of life, and insists on rightness because of formal credentials—and there are all too many dogmatic people like that—Bob wasn't a scientist. But in the best sense of "scientist"—someone who is always curious about reality and is willing to keep testing ideas and beliefs, to experiment—Bob was a scientist. I have always thought of him as a colleague in my investigations of OBEs, of the nature of the mind, and of the meaning of life.

Bob's first attempt to share what he'd learned from his OBEs was his 1971 book *Journeys Out of the Body*. He had mixed feelings about publishing it. On the one hand, he knew that a lot of people had also experienced OBEs and were worried that this was a sign of insanity or something, and his book could reassure such people. On the other hand, Charlottesville was a conservative Southern community. Would he be shunned as some kind of crazy or heretic? When we first met, this possible rejection wasn't a real problem yet (and indeed, fortunately, never became a major problem), for while he'd hired an agent to find a publisher for his book, the agent hadn't had a single response from a publisher (I wondered, had he even tried?) in the year he'd had the manuscript.

I was incensed at this, both for realistic reasons and from the impatience of youth: the manuscript was fascinating and important! So I got a copy from Bob and sent if off to Bill Whitehead, my editor at Doubleday. I don't think Bill was particularly interested in OBEs, but Doubleday had done well with the paperback edition of my *Altered States of Consciousness* book, so, as a favor to me, he took Bob's manuscript home to glance at after dinner.

Bill found he was still reading, fascinated, at three in the morning! At this point he forced himself to put the manuscript down, for, as he told me, he had reached the chapter on how to have an OBE and he was afraid it might work if he read it! He'd absorbed quite enough mind-expanding ideas for one night.

I wrote an introduction and Doubleday published *Journeys Out of the Body*. It's still in print today and has been a major source of relief to people who have had OBEs and worried about their sanity, as well as a contribution to the scientific literature on OBEs.

Bob devoted the last thirty years of his life to sharing what he had learned with others, while he kept experimenting and learning himself. The Monroe Institute and its training programs are as great a testament to his competence and kindness as could be given. Many people who have taken courses at the Institute have had deep experiences that have markedly enhanced the spiritual aspects of their lives. His three books have had, and continue to have, an even wider reach.

I began this foreword with some provocative statements. For those who prefer more nuanced scientific language, I will rephrase my points. You can say

1. You have a soul.
Or, to sound more scientific, you can say

Human beings, both spontaneously in everyday life and under rigorous laboratory test conditions, have sometimes shown abilities to gather information, communicate, and affect physical reality in ways that go beyond anything that can be reasonably attributed to the physical functioning of the brain or body. While "soul" carries too many untestable metaphysical connotations for scientists, we need to call this "something else" something, and *soul* is the best word we've got to date.

> 2. The highest scientific authorities have repeatedly told
> you there is no such thing as a soul.
> Or

Almost all prestigious scientists, who carry enormous social authority in our culture, personally subscribe to a *philosophy* (not a science, a philosophy) of materialism. Nothing is real but physical matter and physical energies. The concept of a nonmaterial soul is inherently nonsensical to a materialist. (I think it's a serious mistake to confuse philosophy with essential science, but it's very widespread.)

> 3. In fact, they think you are stupid or crazy to even
> think about such a nonsensical idea as a soul.
> Or

Materialistic scientists have a tendency to become arrogant, like successful people in all areas of life, and look down on those who take the idea of souls seriously. At best they see belief in souls as a sign of ignorance or stupidity, at worst as a sign of insanity or a deliberate manipulation of the ignorant by schemers cloaking themselves in the garb of religion.

4. Most of us have suffered and continue to suffer from having our soul, our spiritual nature, denied.
Or

From my perspective as a psychologist, people have experiences that are real to them, involving spiritual and psychic concepts like souls or the Divine or the psychic. While a small number of these people may be stupid, ignorant, or crazy (as in any area of life), most of these experiencers are normal or above-normal people. Aside from the scientific, parapsychological evidence that at least some of these experiences are real, it's harmful to anyone to arrogantly and ignorantly invalidate their experience. This needlessly increases the suffering in the world.

5. Bob Monroe was a sane, down-to-earth, solid, and successful American who discovered his soul and found ways to work with it that benefit all of us wounded people. He was not some arcane, distant historical figure, but someone who speaks our language.
Or

There are many ways to understand ourselves better, to learn from our own and others' experiences rather than invalidating them, and one of the more successful is to hear about things from people like ourselves, people we can identify with, rather than distant authorities who are not like us. When the ideas come with practical methods to check them out—like Monroe's suggestions on how to experience OBEs for yourself—they are even more powerful than just ideas.

6. A better understanding of Monroe's life, both his talents and his shortcomings, can stimulate and inspire

our own personal understandings of our souls and our
goals.

Or

You can learn a lot from Monroe's books, where he does his best
to make sense of his OBEs and other spiritual experiences, but all of
us have our filters and biases that color our view of reality. Knowing
about Monroe's life both enriches and refines our understanding of
what he learned from his OBEs.

It's the same thing, either way.

And, as I mentioned at the beginning, Monroe's was a fascinating life, and Ron Russell has done us a great service in relating it in
such a detailed and fascinating way.

Charles T. Tart, PhD
Berkeley, California
December 2006

ACKNOWLEDGMENTS

This story of the journey of Robert Monroe would have been impossible without the assistance and cooperation of members of his family. I am happy to acknowledge the more than generous help of Laurie Monroe, Nancy (Scooter) McMoneagle and Joe McMoneagle, Penny Holmes, A. J. (Terry) Honeycutt, Lucinda Honeycutt, Emmett and Alice Monroe, Robert Monroe, and Maria Whitehead.

Others who gave most freely of their time and memories were Skip Atwater, Mark Certo, George Durrette, Leslie France, Melissa Jager, Stefano Siciliano, and Rita Warren. I am indebted to Tom Campbell and Rosie McKnight for permission to quote from their published works, and to Jim Beal, Gail Blanchette, Shirley Bliley, Marie Coble, Dr. Al Dahlberg, Ria Erickson, Mike George, Helene Guttman, Ron Harris, Dr. Fowler Jones, Franceen King, Paul King, David Lambert, Chris Lenz, Karen Malik, Darlene Miller, Dr. Suzanne Morris, Justine Owens, PhD, Joseph Chilton Pearce, Ed Pearson, Dr. Rupert Sheldrake, Rev. Shay St. John, Ray Waldkoetter, and Teresa West for their help and information.

I am grateful to Skip Atwater for permission to reprint his authoritative paper on the Hemi-Sync technology, and to Dave

Mulvey for his simplified version of the process, to Alan Alger, the Munro/Monroe clan genealogist in the United States, and to Nancy Dorman (and cats) for wonderful hospitality. Professor Joe Felser sharpened my insight into Bob Monroe's philosophy. Three dear friends who in their time contributed in different ways so much to the success of the work of the Institute, Dave Wallis, Martin Warren, and Ruth Domin, are remembered with much affection. I am also greatly indebted to the late Bayard Stockton, who kindly gave me permission to make use of *Catapult,* his biography of Robert Monroe, published by Donning in 1989.

I have been very fortunate in my editor, Frank DeMarco, and my agent, Barbara Bowen, and am happy to acknowledge their help. My thanks also to Tania Seymour and her colleagues at Hampton Roads Publishing.

Professor Charles Tart was a friend of Bob Monroe for thirty years. This book would not have been complete without his perceptive and informative—and very generous—foreword, for which I am most grateful.

It is to Jill that I owe my greatest debt. Had it not been for her insistence I would never have been to the Institute, never have taken the *Gateway* or any other program, and never have met Bob and Nancy Monroe. Her patience and perception have guided this book from the very beginning. And her memory is a lot sharper than mine!

INTRODUCTION

Flying Free

Well, there are two types of deed. One is the physical deed, in which the hero performs a courageous act in battle or saves a life. The other kind is the spiritual deed, in which the hero learns to experience the supernormal range of human spiritual life and then comes back with a message.

—Joseph Campbell, *The Power of Myth*

Bob Monroe was, on the face of it, an unlikely hero. When he set out on his hero's journey he was, as he said of himself, a fairly conventional person: a wealthy businessman with a beautiful wife and an impressive record of achievement in the highly competitive world of radio broadcasting, listed in *Who's Who in America,* president of this, vice president of that, with a host of opportunities opening before him. Actually, he wasn't all that conventional. His parents, each of them strong characters in their own right, were both members of professions with enough money in hand to help him on his way. Bob, however, chose to take a year off riding the rails as a hobo, then to embark on a series of jobs to pay his own way through college, and after that to share one large room in New York with three would-be actors while he sent off scripts for radio shows, most of which ended up in someone's bin. His great passions, indulged whenever he could, were flying and driving fast cars. They sound like expensive hobbies, but the aircraft he flew were mostly held together with string and tape and the fast cars he cobbled together himself. And he had one unusual distinction: when he found a girl he liked, he married her. Or so he said.

And then, at the height of his career, it all began to change. He became, of all unlikely things, and by chance rather than by choice, an explorer. The time came when the name of Robert Monroe was no longer associated with mass entertainment but with something quite different: the exploration of human consciousness. *Rocky Gordon* and *High Adventure* were long forgotten; now Robert Monroe was the "out-of-body man" or the "astral traveler." His first book, *Journeys Out of the Body,* became essential reading for those interested in psychic phenomena, in postdeath survival, in the extraordinary rather than the ordinary, everyday world. Scientists from various disciplines, psychologists, psychiatrists, New Age gurus, journalists, and the merely curious came to visit him in the foothills of Virginia's Blue Ridge, where he built a research laboratory on the grounds of his country home for the furtherance of his explorations. And, as it happened, the influence of certain sound frequencies on human consciousness became the focus of his investigations. He became convinced that focused consciousness contained definitive solutions to the questions arising from human experience.

What began as one man's desire to understand what had happened to himself developed into a research project, into experimental work with volunteers, into the discovery and development of a technology capable of producing identifiable, beneficial effects, into the establishment of a residential institute with its own research laboratory—all leading to a major contribution to the exploration and understanding of human consciousness.

As an explorer, Monroe sought to create a map of the territories that he personally explored. This was a long and at times difficult and dangerous task. Lines by the Welsh poet Gerard Manley Hopkins illustrate some of the perils that he had to face:

O the mind, mind has mountains; cliffs of fall
Frightful, sheer, no-man-fathomed. Hold them cheap
May who ne'er hung there . . .

At the outset he found no guidance, no track to follow. He had to face the possibility that in seeking to scale those mountains his own sanity was at risk. Yet somehow he knew he had no choice. Night after night he returned to his explorations. He began to recognize certain landmarks, to gain in confidence, to fill in more details on his map. His explorations lasted for thirty-five years. As they ended, he was convinced that he had found what he was looking for—but he had not known what he was looking for until he found it.

Early on, Monroe accepted that it was his mission to provide the opportunity for others to study his map and, if they chose, to move into the open country and make their own discoveries. He designed the tools and equipment to help them on their journeys and a safe environment for them to embark from and return to. So we who are prepared to take this opportunity inch our way forward, and the open country no longer seems forbidding as our experience becomes richer and our understanding of what Joseph Campbell called "the super-normal range of human spiritual life" gradually increases.

What was the message that Monroe brought back from his explorations? If you had asked him that question, his reply would probably have been to quote the opening sentences of the affirmation that participants in the courses he designed are asked to repeat before they begin their personal explorations. "I am more than my physical body. Because I am more than physical matter, I can perceive that which is greater than the physical world." But there is more to it than that. The audio technology that he developed as a result of his explorations trains its users to be able to move at will into different states and areas of consciousness, sharpening their perceptions and enriching their experience, and enabling them to comprehend that their physical life existence is not the only existence that is open to them.

Jill and I first met Bob in the summer of 1986. We had heard about his Institute from a somewhat unlikely married couple. He was a distinguished scholar holding a senior post in an ancient English university and his much younger wife had enjoyed many rich experiences on the West Coast of the United States. They had just returned from taking a course at the Institute and encouraged us to do the same. After much deliberation, mostly on my part, we booked in to a *Gateway* program that summer.

The countryside in the foothills of Virginia's Blue Ridge, some thirty miles from Charlottesville, was beautiful: swathes of grassland, tree-clad hills, neat houses tucked away in the woodland, a farm with cattle, a picturesque lake, turkey buzzards overhead, the Blue Ridge Mountains on the horizon. The Residential Center where the program took place was comfortable enough. We shared a sort of cabin with two berths, each fitted with a control panel equipped with headphones, switches, and colored lights. Most of the time was spent listening to a series of different exercises recorded on tape and discussing our experiences afterwards with the trainers and the rest of the group—twenty-two in all, and only five of them women. That was odd, for a start, as we had understood that women were usually in the majority on "life-changing" courses. And what about the participants, especially the seven Californians? Did they ever stop talking—did they ever stop telling you things?

So here we were—two matter-of-fact Brits amid a gang of fantasists. Or so at first it seemed. But it didn't stay like that for long. Soon we were fantasizing with the best of them. Then it happened—

it almost always does. This *wasn't* fantasizing. These experiences were real—more real than anything we had experienced before. There were no drugs, no alcoholic drinks, no hypnosis—only gently modulated sound signals and a firm and friendly voice talking you through a series of exercises and giving you space and time to explore. The mind, the consciousness, which had hitherto been occupied with the matter of daily living, the details, problems, and decisions of work and family life, now was enabled to fly free, to soar and plunge and glide, to venture into areas never imagined before, to explore and discover—and then to return to report.

When the program was finished and it was time to leave, we waited to bid Bob Monroe farewell and to thank him for an experience that, as we already suspected, would change our lives. He cut us short. "Have you got time?" he asked. "How about a drive round the New Land?" We climbed into his battered four-by-four. He put his mug of tea into a holder and started up. The fuel gauge, I noticed, stood resolutely at zero. We drove off, away from the Institute buildings and along the rough road winding its way up Roberts Mountain. Bob pointed out houses tucked away among the trees, mentioning who owned them. He stopped at one particularly splendid house and took us inside. "Eleanor's just had this built," he said. "She's away just now—she's my agent—she flies in from New York in her own aircraft. Come in, I'll show you round."

We were impressed, as no doubt he intended us to be. It was a beautiful house, open-plan, elegantly furnished, walls lined with modern paintings, huge windows overlooking a swimming pool and the forest beyond—a dream house, despite the pervasive smell of cats. Anyway, we like cats. Then we drove on, sharing the mug of lukewarm tea, the roads rougher and narrower as we neared the summit. Occasionally, Bob pointed out parcels of land for sale. "You'd have good neighbors here," he said, indicating one heavily overgrown patch. "A doctor owns the next-door plot."

Then as we continued he fell silent. Yet somehow we felt that a conversation was continuing—no longer a sales pitch but something quite different. It was as if the three of us had recognized each other and were communicating wordlessly—as if we were joining him in some orbit where words were not needed for the conveyance of thoughts, feelings, visions. Whatever was happening, our intention as we arrived back at the Center was that, no matter what the cost, as soon as we possibly could we would return not only for another program, but also for the opportunity to spend more time with Bob Monroe, whose magic already held us in thrall.

So began a friendship with Bob that lasted until his death nine years later. We returned to the Institute to take a program or to attend the Professional Seminar and the advisors meeting every year—except one. That was the year we were moving house—and early in the following year he died. In between our visits we called him frequently, especially in the months after the death of his beloved wife, Nancy, whom we had come to know and love. In those conversations his sense of desolation became apparent, and he was able to express this by telephone without the embarrassment of doing so face to face.

What was he like? Complex, contradictory, multifaceted—all those terms apply. To most of those who came to his courses he was the main attraction—here was the famous traveler into inner space who came down from his home on the mountaintop to share his experiences and his wisdom. To see and hear him, to shake his hand and ask him to sign your copy of one of his books—that was something you would never forget. And he certainly possessed charisma. He knew how to hold an audience and his sense of timing was as finely tuned as that of any professional actor. Many who met him would appreciate the comment of a journalist from a local newspaper who was sent to interview him. He admitted to being somewhat apprehensive, hearing that the man he was going to meet had been described as impatient at best and autocratic at worst. But his impres-

Bob Monroe, Gateway Program 1987

sion was different. "When I first met Bob Monroe," he wrote, "he struck me as a cross between George Gurdjieff, the Armenian mystic philosopher, and George Cleveland, who played Gramps on *Lassie*."

Bayard Stockton, whose study of Monroe was published in 1989 under the title *Catapult*, found three important strands in Monroe's life. The first was to search for his identity, a process that, he says, was "incredibly expensive, exhausting, frightening, lonely, selfish—and beneficial." The second was that through his engineering approach, "he helped to de-mystify what others refer to as the occult, the supernatural or supernormal, even the metaphysical, for many other people." The third was his success "in introducing a potent new technology in some branches of medicine, in education . . . and, conceivably, in business," adding that "his tools-of-the-mind may be far more useful than has heretofore been suspected." It is impossible to be certain that Monroe ever did figure out who he was—and that can be said, I suspect, for most of us. But the other two identifiable strands in his life have led to significant benefits, increasing year after year as the applications of his technology become more widely recognized.

As we got to know him better, and as I began to look more deeply into the story of his life, more facets of his personality were revealed. In him you could discern the competitive and sometimes ruthless businessman, the actor able to command any audience, the daredevil adventurer, sometimes pushing himself to the extremes, the wise mentor, the warm friend, and, perhaps most significant, the visionary. His judgment was not always sound and he was certainly no saint. But thousands upon thousands of people loved him.

Bob's death did not come as a shock. It was not that he had lost the will to live, but his failing health and his loneliness over his last three years, when his only constant companions were his little dog, Steamboat, and his seven cats, had drawn most of the pleasure out of his life. From his decades spent exploring the realms beyond physical life he was assured that death was simply the end of one phase of existence. You were not extinguished, nor did you stay around. You moved on.

On the Earth plane, Bob Monroe endures in the minds and hearts of those who knew him and loved him. But once he had discovered what lay beyond that plane, in those farther reaches where he had ventured and explored, there was nothing to hold him here.

CHAPTER I

Young Bob

On November 11, 1651, the sailing vessel *John and Sarah* left London docks. On board were several hundred Scottish prisoners, soldiers who had been taken by Cromwell's New Model Army at the Battle of Worcester. The English Civil War had ended with the defeat of the Royalists and the execution in 1649 of King Charles I. England was now a Commonwealth, with Oliver Cromwell at its head. The king's son, also Charles, refused to accept this. He assumed the title of king, was crowned at Scone, and raised a Scottish army with the hope of winning back the crown. The Scots had fought bravely under incompetent leadership. Many thousands were killed or captured at Dunbar in 1650, but the survivors persisted. Such was the state of Scotland at the time, divided and impoverished, that there must have seemed little left to live for.

Charles now led his army south, heading for London. They met surprisingly little opposition until they arrived at the outskirts of Worcester. For a few hours it seemed that the Scots might triumph, but the arrival of fresh English forces soon settled the matter. Charles was among the few who escaped. For the Scots this second defeat was a major disaster. Those of the clan chiefs who had not been killed were either imprisoned or exiled, and the wearing of tartan was forbidden.

Among those taken prisoner was William Munro, twenty-six years of age, son of Robert Munro of Aldie, Aberdeen, sometimes known as the Black Baron, although he was neither.

(Robert , who had fought in the German wars and had died of wounds at Ulm in 1633, was the head of the nineteenth generation of Munros, a clan whose history stretches back to Donald, son of Occaan, prince of Fermonaugh. Donald had sailed from Ireland to help King Malcolm II repel invaders from Denmark and as a reward had been granted land bordering the Cromarty Firth, north of Inverness. This land, with headquarters at the castle of Foulis, remains clan property to this day.)

William was fortunate. After being captured at Worcester, he was neither executed nor imprisoned but instead sold to the plantations on the east coast of the New World. He was consigned to Thomas Kemble of Boston, who a few years later sold him as an apprentice at the Saugus Iron Works. By 1657 William Munro must have been a free man, as his name appears in the records when he and a certain Thomas Rose were fined for not having rings in the noses of their swine.

By 1660 William was settled in Cambridge Farms, now known as Lexington, Massachusetts, in a part of the town then called Scotland. In 1690 he was made a freeman, and he held several important parish offices. In 1699 he was received into the Communion of the Church. He married three times and fathered fourteen children—four by Martha George, who died in 1672 at the age of thirty-eight, and ten by Mary Ball, who died in 1692, aged forty-one. Shortly afterwards William married a widow, Elizabeth Johnson, who died in 1714 at the age of seventy-nine. Four years later William himself died, aged ninety-two. He was buried in Lexington, Massachusetts. Eleven of his children survived and are mentioned in his will. Thus began the Munro/Monroe line in the United States.

Among William's descendants was Ensign William Munro, who built the Munroe Tavern in Lexington, which later became a historical museum. He died at age eighty-nine, having fathered thirteen children, although few survived infancy. His grandson Lemuel enlisted in the Revolutionary War in 1776 at the age of seventeen and fought at the Battle of Bunker Hill. He served in the New York State Militia in the war of 1812 and in various other campaigns. In between times he was a farmer and boot maker. In a family known for longevity he exceeded all others, dying at the age of ninety-seven. It was probably during Lemuel's lifetime that the family adopted the Monroe spelling of their surname.

Lemuel's grandson, Robert Emmett, was also a farmer. He enlisted in the 6th Michigan Cavalry in the Civil War, being called up to take the place of a conscripted man who failed to show. His wife, Jane, served as a nurse during the conflict, acquiring a reputation as a healer. To treat wounds she used a poultice of bread and hot milk. On one occasion, when treating a soldier's badly cut leg, the bread she used was moldy. The leg healed very quickly, which was regarded by the local people as miraculous. It is suggested that the mold was producing penicillin, but in any event Jane always used moldy bread after that. The couple had eight children, two of whom died in infancy. Jane died in 1915 and Robert Emmett in 1921 at the age of eighty-three. They were the grandparents of Robert Allen Monroe.

In later years, Bob Monroe's childhood was closely examined for clues that might throw light onto what happened to him in later life. But only a ray or two of that light was forthcoming.

Bob's father, Robert Emmett Jr., was born on February 11, 1883, and brought up on the Monroe family farm in Webberville, Michigan. He was the fifth of his parents' six surviving children. In his early years he seems to have developed a particularly independent cast of mind, deciding that although he was a "farm boy" he had no desire to continue in the family farming tradition. He struck out on his own, determined to make his own way in life. It may be that it was the expectation of foreign travel that impelled him to study French at the University of Michigan, from where he graduated in 1908 with an MA degree. In the same year he married Georgia Helen Jordan, from Wabash, Indiana, whom he had met at university. Georgia, content to follow her own family tradition by studying medicine, had graduated in 1906, one of only six medical graduates in that year. After a year teaching French at Georgetown University, Robert Emmett obtained a junior professorship in Romance languages at Transylvania College, Lexington, Kentucky, where the family made their home. (It makes a neat coincidence that William, founder of the Monroe line in the United States, had settled in Lexington, Massachusetts.)

Robert and Georgia had five children, all born in Georgia's family home in Wabash, where she returned to live in the final stages of all her pregnancies. There were two girls to begin with: Dorothy, born in 1909, followed two years later by Margaret, usually known as Peggy. Robert Allen was born on October 30, 1915. His sister Dorothy recalled that he weighed twelve pounds at birth. The new baby was actually christened Bob Allen, but Bob was later changed to Robert by the school authorities on the assumption that this was really his given name. A younger sister, Georgia Helen, was born in 1919, but died when less than two years old. The family was completed in 1923 with the birth of Emmett Paul.

Bob's parents were both strong characters. Theirs was a household full of books and the sound of music. His father was vigorous and purposeful, with a restless, inquiring mind and a lurking sense of fun. As a parent he seldom displayed any signs of emotion, asking few questions and allowing his children a good measure of freedom, provided they did not interfere with the smooth running of the household. Georgia, described later by Bob as an idealist, held the family together with an air of quiet authority. Both parents accepted their children for who they were, despite the fact that Dorothy and Bob both at times pushed hard against the margins of acceptable behavior. Dorothy once described her father as a tyrant because he insisted that his children follow the school and college courses that he chose. He was suspicious of her boyfriends and threatened to withhold her pocket money if she did not conform to his wishes. It was a threat that failed to work, as she was blessed with a beautiful alto voice and could earn up to fifty dollars a time singing with a local choir. There was, however, concern for Peggy, a quiet little girl very much attached to Dorothy and quite different in nature and character from her elder siblings.

Lexington at the time was a small segregated town with a population of about thirty thousand and with tobacco warehousing the only industry. The Monroes had little to do with the town itself, Robert being a college professor and Georgia that exceptional creature for the time, a female MD. Robert was a strong, single-minded character; Bob later described him as "the authority figure in my childhood—calm and sure-footed, the one who made important decisions in the family, without even questioning the needs of other members." He refused to allow Georgia to practice medicine, insisting that her prime duty was to the family. The only time she was able to make use of her training was during the years of World War I, when Robert himself was overseas.

Apart from his job and his family—who seemed for the most part quite able to look after themselves—there was nothing in the locality to attract the lively minded Robert Emmett. He was drawn to the prospects of foreign travel, especially to Europe. He volunteered for war service and was sent to France in 1917. On the strength of his linguistic skills he was attached for a time to the French army. Although he saw no action in the field, he saw plenty of it in the boxing ring, becoming an army middleweight champion boxer and a boxing instructor. After the war he was decorated by the king of the Belgians for athletic coaching he undertook for the YMCA.

On returning to civilian life, Robert found his college remuneration barely sufficient for raising a family, and for some years they continued to live in apartments rented to them by the college. However, he soon found a way of increasing his income tenfold by organizing and conducting vacation tours to Europe for three months every year. His return from these visits were exciting occasions for the children, as with a ceremonial flourish he would open his portmanteau and distribute gifts to all.

What tensions did occur within the family were often relieved by Robert Emmett's sense of humor. He was also fond of a practical joke, as when he hid young Bob in his suitcase, producing him with much ceremony at a presentation to a group of prospective tourists, or when he terrified six-year-old Bob and his friends who were telling ghost stories in a graveyard by donning a white sheet and screaming at them from between the tombstones. He was something of an entrepreneur, setting up a small pottery and selling garbage collected from the college to a pig farmer. However, he was never much of a companion for his children, being deeply involved with his own concerns, especially in drumming up business for his highly profitable European tours. From these profits he was eventually able to buy a house for the family on Ashland Avenue in Lexington.

It was Georgia, described by her son Bob as "a doing person," who supplied the visible love and support for the growing children. She was the family peacemaker, seeking always to preserve harmony when disputes arose. Georgia was also a talented musician, playing the cello in a local orchestra. Both Dorothy and Bob inherited her musical ability, while her younger son Emmett followed in her family medical tradition. Peggy, however, was never able to pursue a career and it became clear that there was no prospect of her being able to live a normal life. It was not until she was about thirty that she was diagnosed as schizophrenic and had to be hospitalized for the remainder of her years.

Bob Monroe was a quick learner—he could read and write by the age of four. He was an active and adventurous child, eager to make his own way. He was left-handed, which concerned his parents, as they thought this would put him at a disadvantage. For a time they compelled him to put his left arm in a sling, but eventually they gave up trying. Generally, they allowed him to make his own way, provided that he did his chores as required and was home in time for meals. Still only four years old he was sent to kindergarten, but after one week he decided that it was not for him. He insisted that he should start school, to which his parents agreed provided he could get there by himself. This required him to walk sixteen blocks and cross a busy road, clutching three cents in his hand for his lunch—two cents for a peanut butter bun and one cent for a cup of watery cocoa.

Young Bob Monroe had several special interests at the time. The first of these was the cinema, and whenever the opportunity arose he would take himself off to watch whatever flickering black-and-white silent films were being shown. When talking about them afterwards, he would refer to the films as if they were in color. He also greatly enjoyed swimming in the recently opened local swimming pool and would talk about the underwater lights as if they were colored also. He was much surprised to learn in later years that they were not. It was as if he was interpreting imaginatively what he observed, especially when his mind was fully involved in what was going on.

Another special interest was music, and it was this that led to Bob's involvement with the church, despite the fact that his parents rarely attended services and there was no copy of the Bible in their house. His ambition was to join the children's choir, but this necessitated becoming a member of the church. He took himself off to consult the minister and, to his consternation, found that baptism by total immersion was compulsory if he was to be allowed to join.

Having survived this experience, he was enrolled as a member of the choir. From time to time he also attended Sunday school, although he admitted to being more attracted by the oranges provided for refreshment than by the teaching he received.

Robert Emmett was not at all enthusiastic about his elder son's activities. Music, Robert Emmett insisted, was for sissies and girls, so Bob's requests to take piano lessons were firmly refused. Boxing was for boys, he declared, and he began to give his six-year-old son occasional lessons in what he thought of as the manly art. "I was a reluctant, then a willing student," Bob later recalled. This was just as well; as a contemporary of his remarked, "You had to know how to fight to establish yourself at the beginning of every school year." His boxing ability also meant that he could carry a girl's books on the walk home from school without being called a sissy.

Even so, boxing was no substitute for music. While Dorothy and Peggy were learning to play the piano, the only instrument available to their young brother was the harmonica. This he soon mastered; harmonicas became something of a passion for him, and in later years he amassed a large collection. He was also allowed to use the family wind-up Victrola that resided in a large mahogany case with a box of wooden needles. Although most of the available records did not appeal to him, he managed to borrow what he wanted from a friend, Harry Bullock, who shared his enthusiasm for such notables as Louis Armstrong, Duke Ellington, and Fats Waller. "Ain't We Got Fun" was a special favorite, as he recalled some seventy years later. Altogether his interest in music was so strong that when he attended junior high school he chose the music option, although this meant he was the only boy in a class of thirty girls.

Many of Bob Monroe's later concerns were prefigured in his childhood. In an early introduction to the entertainment world he was cast as Aladdin in a school production of *Aladdin and His Lamp*. Recalling this, his brother Emmett later suggested that the magic of the lamp may have been Bob's first contact with "the beyond." His chief interests at the time, however, lay in the world around him. Trains were a major attraction and young Bob spent much time at the local train yard, climbing on and under freight cars and locomotives and exploring the engine roundhouse. This interest was reflected later in his first successful radio production, *Rocky Gordon,* which ran for four years on NBC, with trains featuring in every program. Cars were another obsession for the growing boy, and by the age of ten Bob not only understood how their engines worked but he was also able to repair them. This was in contrast to his father, who when driving used only two gears—top and reverse. When his car broke down, which usually happened shortly after he had bought it, he would dispose of it and buy another one—any used car that was available. When Bob was thirteen his father at last acknowledged his expertise and agreed to follow his advice. From then on he became known as the professor who drove "hot cars with big souped-up engines," although to his son's despair he still preferred to drive in top gear.

Aircraft also fascinated him. Four miles outside Lexington was an airfield with one makeshift hangar. Whenever he could, Bob would hurry out to this field to watch aircraft land and take off, and he was an eager spectator at the Gates Brothers Flying Circus. On one occasion he witnessed a fatal accident when one aircraft flew too close to another. The pilot of the second aircraft lost control and severed the tail of the one ahead. The leading aircraft crashed to the ground and caught fire. The pilot burned to death. Already beginning to understand something about the principles of flight, Bob was convinced that the accident was caused by the second plane being caught in the turbulence created by the leader. The accident in no way affected his enthusiasm for flying, although none of the pilots he chatted with at Lexington ever offered him a ride.

Shortly afterwards, when Robert Emmett was on one of his trips to Europe, the rest of the family took the train to Knoxville, Tennessee, to visit one of the aunts. Bored with the conversation, Bob suddenly became aware of the noise of aircraft engines nearby. Making some excuse he found his way towards the sound, even though it meant climbing over several fences. Arriving at a field on the outskirts of the town, he was enthralled to find several aircraft practicing taking off and landing. Bob watched for a while and then noticed a stationary aircraft with the pilot standing beside it. He ran over to it, more in hope than expectation. To his delight, the pilot, seeing the youngster's eager expression, asked him if he wanted to take a ride. For Bob it was a few minutes—all too few—of sheer exhilaration, even though he was not tall enough to see out of the open cockpit. When the pilot realized this, he banked the aircraft so that Bob could identify the various features on the ground below. On landing he was bubbling over with excitement, but he managed to keep his mouth shut when he returned to the house. Surprised by this, his mother looked at him closely when he came in and asked him where he'd been. Unable to control himself he told her of his adventure and was extremely relieved when there was no rebuke. All she said was, "Well, come on and eat."

Altogether this was a wonderful time for a young and active boy. Railway yards and airfields were not closed off, cinemas had no age restrictions, roads could be crossed with impunity, caves could be explored, and no one seriously thought that danger lurked round every corner. Even though opportunities for cadging a flight occurred very seldom, Bob found a substitute in building enormous kites that, if the wind was strong enough, could lift him several feet off the ground.

Both Robert Emmett and his son escaped the embarrassment of instruction in sex education. The only mention of it was when Bob found two potato bugs, one on top of the other. He showed them to his father, asking him what they were doing. "Reproducing," was the answer, and that was that. What information Bob otherwise acquired came, as he said, from "here, there, and around the corner." Bob and his friend Harry, who had a pretty ten-year-old cousin, sometimes discussed the subject, about which each of them claimed to know more than they did. One day it was agreed that Bob and the cousin, as they were not related to each other, should retire to some secluded spot and try it out. They climbed up to a room over the garage and then paused, looking at each other. The conversation, as he later recalled, was brief.

"What do we do?"

"I don't know."

To save face, they agreed simply to say, "We did it." They waited a few minutes, arranged their clothing to make it look as if it had been hastily removed and replaced, and came downstairs. In response to Harry's eager questioning, they replied, "Fine, fine," and exchanged what they hoped were meaningful smiles.

This episode did nothing to further their sex education and innocence persisted for a while, as shown by another incident. Bob and Harry were both members of the Cub Scouts. When at camp they became intrigued by the behavior of the scoutmaster who used to select a boy to join him in his tent at bedtime so that, as he explained, they could both keep warm. Also, when the camp ended, the scoutmaster would choose a special little boy to help him clean up. This was odd, they thought, but that was as far as their thoughts went.

Some months later, however, Bob's eyes were opened wider. He had a paper route that took him into a poor area of the town populated almost entirely by blacks. His best customers were a group of white women who lived in a sizeable run-down house, but he could never understand why they kept their money in their shoes. One early morning as he approached the house he saw a familiar figure emerging from the door. It was, he realized, the scoutmaster—and before long the pieces began to drop into place.

While Bob and his father were often at odds with each other, his relationship with his mother was always harmonious. Georgia adored him, accepting whatever he did far more readily than his father. It was part of her nature to sidestep any unpleasantness, a trait that Bob himself developed in later life. He appreciated the freedom he was granted and was also grateful, as he once said, that neither of his parents ever attempted to indoctrinate their children with a heavy religious belief system that they would have had to unload in the years to come.

In some ways he had more in common with two elderly relatives than he had with his parents, One was his father's older brother, always known as Uncle Charlie. Charlie was a jack-of-all-trades, but was mostly employed as a construction worker. He enjoyed life, was full of energy, played the ukulele, and was a good storyteller. Everyone loved him. He would bundle Bob and his two sisters into his car and drive them to the Saturday movie. There he would usually fall asleep. One afternoon they saw the movie three times before he awoke. When Robert Emmett bought a new Dodge Taurus, Charlie borrowed it to see what the engine would do and promptly blew it up. Later he became a writer of a syndicated newspaper column, which required him to develop another talent—having to write poetry. Uncle Charlie reckoned he would live to be a hundred; sadly, he fell off a horse and died at the age of ninety-seven.

Another favorite relative was Bob's stepgrandmother, Minnie Jordan, his maternal grandfather's second wife, whom the family would often visit when Robert Emmett was away in Europe. Minnie practiced medicine in Wabash, with her consulting room in her home. It was just large enough to accommodate the grandchildren on their summer visits. Her laboratory was in the kitchen, all mixed up with everything else, with the result that the food was sometimes flavored with carbolic acid. As well as enjoying her company, Bob spent much of his time chatting with the pretty young girls who lived on either side, one a red-head and the other with long dark hair. However, he became temporarily disillusioned about the opposite sex when he went to a carnival in town. He was watching a group of dancing girls when he spotted a notice saying that for an extra ten cents you could see a special show in the back tent. He paid his money and for the first time he could remember he saw a naked woman. What stuck in his memory, he recalled, was not her nudity but the sight of her enormous appendix scar. There was more fun to be had swimming in the nearby creek, he said later, despite the leeches.

Things changed radically for the Monroe family when, in 1929, Robert Emmett, feeling the need for something more secure, decided to give up his tourist business, which earned him up to sixty thousand dollars in a good year, to become a full-time professor at Ohio State at a meager six thousand-dollar salary. It may be that he had some sense about what was soon to happen, as in the fall of that year came the stock market crash that wiped out the tourist business along with very much else. "It was," wrote the historian Hugh Brogan, "as if the whole fabric of modern, business, industrial America was unraveling." What did endure, however, was the steady income from the university. To supplement this income, and also possibly because he was still a Michigan farm boy at heart, Robert Emmett acquired a 370-acre farm some twelve miles from Columbus, with a lake, barns, and woodland. He stocked the farm with 150 Jersey cows, instead of the more typical Holsteins, about five hundred White Leghorns, instead of the more usual fifty or so, some eighty turkeys, and a flock of sheep, as well as an orchard and an extensive vegetable garden. Later he added about two hundred steers, which young Emmett had to look after.

As a farmer, however, Robert Emmett was notable more for enthusiasm than for expertise. The farm was not a success, being too large and too heavily stocked for the family to handle, even with the help of a full-time farmhand. Most of the chickens caught a disease and died, including one that used to perch on his shoulder as he walked around the farm. The death of this special chick distressed him greatly. Then his sons, who spent much of their spare time, not always willingly, working on the farm, sought to persuade him to buy a second-hand tractor. He would not hear of this and purchased an old white mule instead—which died within a week. Before long he was compelled to sell, and the family moved back to Columbus to a house in Oakland Park Avenue. In a second effort to bolster his income Robert Emmett invested much of the savings from his tourist business in a number of rental properties, which his two sons, again with no great enthusiasm, helped to maintain.

Bob found Columbus a cold city, very different from the small-town atmosphere of Lexington. When the family first arrived, he found himself isolated, being nearly two years younger than most of his classmates in the thousand-strong high school he attended. Most of all he wanted to join the school orchestra, which had more than fifty members, but he was initially frustrated because he was unable to read the scores. Determined to overcome this, he claimed to be a percussionist and was accepted as such, although he had to do his best to memorize the music and had to keep his eyes fixed on the conductor throughout the entire performance.

His attempts to become involved in social life also led to much frustration. Coming from a very different environment, Bob found it difficult to make friends and, lacking previous experience, was wary of encounters with girls. "Sex is evil except when legal" was the prevailing view at the time, and fear of being compelled to marry, or of contracting syphilis, were common restraints. Eventually he gained sufficient confidence to summon up enough courage to approach two or three older girls with a reputation of being easy, but they told him to go away and grow up. Still attracted by the opposite sex, however, he began to attend the Saturday night dances. On one particular Saturday he was short of two dollars to go to the dance but became convinced that he would find that amount beneath a plank in the yard. He went to look and found a plank lying on the grass—it looked as if it had been there for ages. All the same, he lifted it—and there were two dollar notes, new ones—and no possible explanation for how they were there! In later years, this became a familiar tale to participants in Institute courses.

At the age of fifteen Bob entered Ohio State College, joining the Phi Kappa Alpha fraternity. Robert Emmett had suggested that he should aim at becoming a family doctor so, for once compliant to his father's wish, he signed up for a pre-med course. This did not last long. As he later said, when he began to consider the lifestyle of those of his relatives who were family doctors—two aunts, an uncle, and his own mother—he came to realize that theirs was not the sort of life that he was looking forward to. No one at the time told him of the possibility of becoming a ship's doctor or working for an oil company, which in retrospect he thought he might have enjoyed. He decided to change course, switching to mechanical engineering, which he thought would offer more opportunities for travel and, he hoped, for adventure also. It was not only the choice, of course, that caused problems. To begin with, he found it difficult to be accepted into the social life of the college, partly because of his age and also because his father was a college professor. To this problem there was also a solution. At high school Bob had become friendly with a girl whose father ran a speakeasy in a basement near the Ohio State campus and under her guidance he had visited it once or twice. Now as a college freshman he gained a certain kind of popularity by introducing some of his fraternity colleagues to the speakeasy's delights. This assured his acceptance, and from then on he became known as "the guy that has smarts."

It was just as well for Bob that his father knew nothing of this. While Robert Emmett did not inquire closely into his elder son's activities, apart from forbidding him to accept the post of editor of the university newspaper, as he thought it improper for the son of a professor to hold this position, he was ready to accept his word and defend him against any accusations of sexual misconduct that might be leveled. Yet Bob may well have felt stifled at times by his father, though not to the same extent as his feisty elder sister Dorothy, who considered him a tyrant, always knowing better than she did about what she should do. Of the four siblings it was she who had the most difficult time, although, to her surprise, she did win his agreement that she should stay on at the University of Kentucky when the family moved to Columbus so that she could continue to play in an all-girls band. Bob's younger sister Peggy seemed to go quietly along with whatever was happening, although at times her behavior aroused Dorothy's suspicion that something was seriously amiss—a suspicion that Georgia abruptly dismissed. The two boys were more fortunate in being able to escape into their own activities, Bob being at college and Emmett having discovered a fascination for playing golf. All four of them were devoted to their mother, who made no demands on them. It was from Georgia, according to Emmett's wife, Alice, that Bob inherited his imagination and "his sense of adventure into the Unknown," while from his father came his practical and productive qualities.

Much of Bob's free time was spent haunting airfields and air shows and taking flying lessons, for which he somehow managed to pay. He experienced his first parachute jump, once managed to borrow an aircraft and fly solo to Lexington and back, and by the age of seventeen was qualified as a pilot, later obtaining a limited commercial pilot's license. While still at college he occasionally ferried airplanes from the factory to the purchaser. His enthusiasm for flying was such that he applied to join the Army Air Corps, but he was rejected because of impaired vision in one eye. Before long, however, he found himself too short of money to pay for flying time. Then while he was still wondering what action to take, the decision was taken out of his hands.

Girls were now beginning to feature in Bob Monroe's life. Once at high school he had been accused by an angry parent of taking part in an orgy, although he didn't at the time even know what an orgy was. On a trip to Europe with his father he had taken a girl out for a sail around the Bay of Naples and had almost been run down by a freighter. Then at the age of seventeen he slept with a girl for the first time—which meant, according to the standards of the place and period, that he was obliged to marry her. He put down a deposit on an engagement ring, and the two of them borrowed a car and drove across to Kentucky to find a justice of the peace. Shortly before midnight they discovered the house, but the justice they sought, so they were told, had gone fishing. They waited until four in the morning; then they decided to give it up and drive back to Columbus. Marriage, they concluded, was not an option. Bob's unintended gracefully returned the ring, which the jewelers readily accepted, especially as they insisted on retaining the deposit.

While Bob was fortunate to emerge unscathed from this adventure, this was not the case a short time later. He was paying a visit to another girl when they decided to prepare a meal. He was frying potatoes in the kitchen when the oil caught fire. He wrapped his arm in a wet towel, grabbed the pan with a pair of pliers, and threw it out of the door. The burning grease flew back into his face. He was hurried into hospital with third-degree burns. To make matters even more discouraging, while Bob was still in hospital his father had the difficult task of informing him that he had flunked out of college, having failed to obtain at least a C-plus to be able to continue.

It was several weeks before the scars were repaired and Bob no longer felt that he was, as he said, "walking around with a mummified head." Rejection from college meant that he was thrust out into the world of work, except that in Columbus, as in so many other cities throughout the United States in the Depression years, there was no work to be had—or rather, no work that young Monroe wanted to put his hand to. Living at home was now out of the question, so he decided, like many others in similar situations, to take to the road. He took on occasional jobs as a traveling salesman, selling tombstones at one time and silk hosiery at another. He hitchhiked on the railroads, jumping off wherever the fancy took him or the train happened to stop—at Cincinnati, Lexington, Louisville, St. Louis, Memphis, or Knoxville. Alighting at this last city, he recalled that this was where his aunt was living. He called on her, enjoyed a hearty meal, wandered along to the offices of the local newspaper, and was offered a job as a cub reporter on the *Sentinel*. His aunt was aware that if he took the job it would mean that she would have to accommodate this hobo—not the sort of person to respect her antique furniture—or even if she refused him he might well be living nearby and posing an occasional threat to her valued possessions. She talked him out of accepting and paid his fare home.

Bob's hobo experience lasted just over a year. To get from here to there he would hitchhike, finding that it was not difficult to travel this way, provided he looked clean. When from one manual task or other he picked up so much dirt that drivers were wary of stopping for him, he turned to riding the railroads. During this time one particular episode seemed to him in later life to have marked a turning point. He found himself in St. Louis on Christmas Eve, broke, cold, and hungry. Wandering through the streets, he came across a café, where he could see food cooking just inside the window. He stopped to inhale the tempting smell, when the owner spotted "this skinny kid" (as he described himself) and called him in, gave him a meal, and told him he could stay the night in the stockroom. Deeply moved by this spontaneous act of kindness, he began to wonder whether his life was following a worthwhile path. It so happened that the next time he visited St. Louis was in response to an invitation from the chairman of McDonald Douglas aircraft manufacturing company to join him in the boardroom.

Feeling that he had no more to learn from rough living, Bob returned to Columbus and applied to the university to be reinstated. After several requests the authorities eventually agreed, possibly owing to his father's intervention although Robert Emmett never admitted it. He refused his father's offer to pay his fees, as this was made conditional on his working on the farm during the summer vacation. Intent on keeping his independence, he sought work in town having just ten dollars, a gift from his mother, in his pocket. He soon found a job with a company manufacturing blades for circular saws. It took "the College kid," as he was known, less than five days to learn how to use an old rotary surface grinder to sharpen the blades, and he was taken on for $31.50 a week. As college fees were only fifty dollars a quarter this proved a good deal. The manager, impressed by his skill, put him on piecework, which enabled him to attend classes during the day and also to earn still more. He would begin work at five in the afternoon, complete his quota, find something to eat, and be back home in bed soon after midnight.

The second spell at Ohio State was more successful. Bob joined the Officer Training Unit, which helped to pay part of his tuition, switched courses from engineering to journalism, and worked on the college daily paper, *The Lantern.* He was nominated for the salaried editorship of the *Sun Dial,* the university's literary and humor magazine, but discovered that his father had intervened to prevent his appointment, possibly because he thought the magazine too racy for the Monroe name to be associated with it. He joined the university radio station and the dramatic and musical society, Strollers. He also revived another dramatic group, The Scarlet Mask Society, of which film director and actor Elliott Nugent and the humorist James Thurber had once been members, and helped to produce a couple of musicals. Throughout this phase, he was much influenced by one of his teachers, Professor Herman Miller, who taught drama and from whom he learned the sense of stagecraft that was to be of much benefit to him in later life.

Bob's drama career at Ohio State culminated in his being awarded second prize in Strollers' one-act play competition. Bob wrote his contribution at the last possible moment, and then dissatisfied with what he had done, retrieved his copy and rewrote it during the night before rehearsals began. The story was based on an incident in his days on the road. He had spent a night in a flophouse in St. Louis, where an old man had died in the bunk next to his. In his play Bob made the old man into a mystical figure on the point of death. An angry, cynical, resentful young man in a nearby bed heard him coughing and went over to tell him to shut up. In essence, as the dialogue made clear, the old man passed a symbolic torch to the aggressive, starving youngster, an action that totally changed his character. The play, performed before an audience of eight hundred, received a standing ovation. This first experience of communicating with an audience, Monroe later said, deeply affected his life.

Now thinking that his future might lie in drama, in his final year Bob moved to the Arts College to major in English. He took three courses in Theater Studies and was also appointed to teach freshman English to students of engineering. This involvement meant that he had to give up his part-time job. Fortunately, throughout his somewhat unorthodox university career he had managed to obtain enough credits to be awarded a degree.

Bob was now confident that his future lay in the world of entertainment. An opportunity arose, when early in 1937, he began a close relationship with Jeanette, the daughter of a local lawyer. Jeanette had recently graduated and since then had enjoyed some experience in local theaters. With their mutual interest in the stage they devised a plan to create a summer stock company that would provide students with acting and technical experience. To set this up they applied to Jeanette's father for a loan of $8,500, with the expectation that the project would in time become self-financing. The loan was forthcoming, but a complication arose. Bob heard of two empty theaters in Pittsburgh that they could use. To get to Pittsburgh, however, they had to cross the state line. The Mann Act, prohibiting the transport of women across interstate boundaries for immoral purposes, was in force at the time, and Jeanette's father also insisted that they had to marry if the project was to proceed. They had just two months to put the project together and to undergo a hastily arranged church wedding. That accomplished, off they went to Pittsburgh as man and wife with high hopes for the future.

Of the two theaters available they chose the smaller one. They rented a nearby hotel to accommodate the students that they had recruited through advertisements, and signed up two professional actors to help with the teaching. As soon as they felt the cast of students was sufficiently accomplished, they decided to put on a performance. The play they selected was *Good-Bye Again,* a popular Broadway production. On the opening night, however, only four seats were occupied in the four hundred-seat theater. After three more performances with a maximum audience of ten, they closed.

Not entirely discouraged, they determined to try again. To ensure an audience they gave out free tickets in a nearby amusement park. For one night the house was full, but over the next few days the paying audience never rose above fifty. After two weeks they had no option but to close down. Owing money they did not have, they appealed to Jeanette's father to be rescued. Her brother answered the call and drove from Columbus to move them out at night. Then as they were loading up their equipment, police flashlights went on all around them. The couple were marched across to the theater manager's office. He regarded them sadly. "Why didn't you tell me about it?" he asked. "I would have given you jobs for the rest of the season if you'd not tried to run out on me. But you've not been honest with me—so unload all that stuff and leave it here."

They returned to Columbus broke, having had to leave some three thousand dollars' worth of equipment in lieu of unpaid rent and with nothing but the clothes they were wearing. Unable to find an acceptable alternative, they moved in with Bob's parents, which they considered marginally preferable to living with the notoriously self-righteous lawyer. Bob had no money, no job, and a wife to whose father he owed $8,500. It took him seven years to repay the full amount.

Not all was gloom, however. Bob's experience with radio broadcasting at university now proved helpful and he managed to get a job at station WHK in Cleveland as a continuity writer for $31.50 a week—the same as he'd been paid for sharpening circular saw blades. The couple moved to Cleveland, where before long Bob was promoted to director of programs and became a full-fledged script writer. After six months, however, he was suddenly told he was no longer needed. (Some time later he happened to meet the station's continuity chief and discovered why he had been fired. The station manager had seen him typing with his feet on the desk folded around the typewriter. He had considered this undignified and ordered Bob to be dismissed forthwith.) In his spare time Bob had built a rear-engine car, with a chassis but so far with no body. He and Jeanette loaded it with their luggage and drove back to Columbus.

Back home, Bob completed the car and managed to trade it for a less flamboyant black Ford coupe. Then he applied for and obtained a job at seventy-five dollars a week with station WLW in Cincinnati. Here he quickly became involved in all aspects of radio production, writing programs, directing, and producing. The station had 120 hillbilly performers on its staff, together with its own orchestra. One of the programs Bob produced was a hillbilly show called *Rainbow Ridge*—a name that many years later was to become familiar to visitors to The Monroe Institute—and others included *The Boone County Jamboree* and *Moon Rover*. Some of the programs he directed were taken up by major networks such as the Mutual Broadcasting System and NBC's Blue Network.

Bob was now perfectly happy in his work, but his personal life was becoming difficult. This became apparent when Jeanette insisted on joining him in Cincinnati. He was beginning to realize that his marriage had been a major mistake. His wife was not as sophisticated as he had thought she was, or had hoped that she would become, and he had to face the fact that what they had was no more than a marriage of convenience.

Before this situation could be resolved, he was called to the office and paid off. He discovered that the station's agreement with the Radio Artists Union, of which he was a member, had required that pay be increased and that no dismissals should take place. To meet the increased pay demand, the management had decided to ignore the "no dismissals" clause and dispense with Monroe on the principle of "last in, first out." He appealed to the union, only to be told that having just signed the contract they were not prepared to take action over one guy. Bob's words to the union organizer were "You have just made a rabid antiunion person," a stand that he maintained for the rest of his life.

Back in Columbus, Bob briefly considered and rejected other employment, being convinced that his future lay in the entertainment industry. There were, he concluded, two possibilities, Hollywood or New York, and New York was nearer. Leaving Jeanette behind, he traveled to the city by bus, carrying his battered typewriter under his arm, one more youngster from the provinces seeking to make his fortune. To begin with, he obtained work with a medical doctor,

Matthew Goudiss, who had his own radio show. Goudiss took him on as a writer, paying him fifty dollars a script. This gave Bob enough to survive on for the time being, although the show was to last for only a few weeks. Finding somewhere to live in New York, however, was a major problem. He moved from one cheap lodging to another, eventually joining up with three young actors to rent a large room with a kitchenette for fourteen dollars a week. They had just one job between them: soda-jerking in a local drugstore. While the actors searched for work, Bob mostly stayed indoors, writing and answering advertisements, sending out scripts, and contributing occasional pieces to newspapers and magazines, earning a few dollars thereby, supplemented by the occasional twenty that his mother enclosed in her letters to him.

Throughout this time Bob received letters and phone calls from Jeanette, all asking when she could come to join him. He thought hard about this, he said later, but felt he could not accept her as the mother of his children-to-be. He admitted that at least some of his reasons were based on a kind of snobbery. Although she had many positive qualities, she failed to suit what he described as his "mental set" at that time, partly because "she made all the familiar grammatical mistakes." He had not spoken to her of these misgivings when she telephoned to say that she had just arrived in New York. His friend Ben Green, one of those with whom he shared accommodations, collected her from the station and took her to a hotel. Then Bob went to see her.

It was a very difficult meeting. Jeanette's family had persuaded her to come, she said, and one can only imagine how desperate she felt. But Bob was adamant. The marriage was over. He left her in her hotel room and returned to his lodgings. Ben Green came to collect her and saw her safely on a train taking her back to Columbus. It was not an episode that Bob could look back on with pride.

One other family matter affected him at this time. It came in a phone call from his sister Peggy. She had never phoned him or written to him before. Now she begged him to let her come to New York to live with him. Peggy was always quiet, unassuming, and passive, and although she did not tell him why she was asking to join him, he could understand how difficult it could be for her to continue living with her parents, two powerful individuals, and with her dominant elder sister nearby. He knew how hard it would be for her to ask for help. Yet he had barely enough money for himself to live on, and there was no way she could join the four men accommodated in one large room. While he did not refuse her outright, she was aware of his hesitation. She did not repeat her request but changed the subject, asked how he was doing, and then hung up. A month later she was diagnosed as schizophrenic. For the rest of his life her father paid for her care in a private hospital. After his death, her younger brother Emmett, now a medical doctor, took on the responsibility, providing medical services in return for her care.

Despite these deeply personal concerns, Bob found life in New York stimulating and exciting. His faith in his own ability seldom faltered and when it did so it was not for long. There were occasional spells of depression when script after script failed to be accepted, compensated for by samplings of a better life when Ben Green's brother, a sailor in the merchant marine, visited on leave with a wallet full of dollars, extra danger money for convoy duty. Off the four of them went with Ben as their banker, doing their best to spend the lot on the various delights New York high life had to offer. Then after the fun it was back to the typewriter and the mailbox for another round of attempts as the first months of 1940 passed by. So it was, until in the first year of the new decade news came from the Monroe home in Columbus. NBC had telephoned—something about a script that someone called Bob Monroe had sent in some time ago. Would he please make contact . . .

The tide had begun to turn.

Note

For much of the information in this chapter I am indebted to Bayard Stockton's biography of Monroe, *Catapult* (Donning, 1989). Bay, who was a good friend, generously gave me permission to use whatever I wished. I was deeply saddened to learn of his death shortly before this book went to press. Some information is also derived from Monroe's taped reminiscences of his childhood.

CHAPTER 2

Fame and Fortune

"It was a whirlwind of high-drive excitement, a roller-coaster of extreme highs and lows, rags to riches and back again . . . From a rooming-house west of Fifth Avenue to a home in Westchester County, in a long series of unforgettable lessons."

So Bob Monroe summarized the next stage of his life in an interview in the late 1980s. The scripts on which his success in the entertainment world was founded derived from his experiences as a hobo and dealt with the adventures of a crew of a freight train. *Rocky Gordon* was broadcast on the NBC network, five shows a week on prime time, preceding the very popular *Amos n' Andy*. Bob began by writing the scripts himself, pounding away on his old Remington typewriter, but before long he moved on to production. To enhance the realism of the show he would take recording equipment to the New York Central railyard to capture the sounds of locomotives and railway stock. A photograph of him in action with his equipment appeared in the *New York Times* in July 1940.

At the age of twenty-five Bob was now earning a thousand dollars a week. He bought himself an aircraft, a ninety-horsepower Aeronca, which he kept at Flushing Airport and used whenever he could. All this—the aircraft, the income, the absorbing job—was on the credit side; on the debit side were duodenal ulcers. While his brother, Emmett, joined the Army Air Corps after Pearl Harbor and was posted to England to fly B-24s, Bob was deeply disappointed to be graded 4F. After *Rocky Gordon* had completed its run, he sought to do what he could to support the war effort. To make use of his skills he turned back to engineering and joined a firm working on a design for a flight simulator, although it never went into production. He also wrote a monthly article on aviation for *Argosy* magazine that brought him into contact with the National Aeronautic Association, which commissioned him to produce a weekly radio show under the title of *Scramble!* This was broadcast on NBC's Blue Network, hosted by Robert Ripley (of *Believe-It-or-Not*) with a live audience. The show's objective was to catch the interest of young men in aviation, with stories of war heroes and emergency missions flown by U.S. pilots. To encourage recruitment, it also featured some of the Air Corps' generals.

Now with plenty of money in his wallet, Bob was able to indulge many of his current interests. As well as radio and entertainment in general, these included aeronautics, sailing, trains, electronics, theater, and film. He had also developed an eye for both stylish women and modern architecture. In the world of entertainment, he was beginning to make his mark. In 1943, at the age of twenty-eight, he formed his first corporation, RAM Enterprises, for the production of radio network programs. He acquired an agent, and began to produce programs for the government's coordinator of inter-American affairs. He was featured in the *New York Daily Mirror* and was interviewed more than once on the Walter Winchell show. He was recruited by Donahue & Co., a major New York advertising agency that represented MGM and Republic Pictures. Working for Donahue took him from time to time to Hollywood, where he met various leading producers, including Sam Goldwyn and L. B. Mayer. He was appointed radio production manager for Donahue with sole responsibility for placing radio commercials, and claimed to be the first such person to persuade the network to accept an advertisement for a product designed to help women with period pains. Then in 1944 E. J. Churchill, president of the Donahue agency, agreed to allow Bob to form his own company, Monroe Productions. Its first creation was a half-hour daily show for MGM entitled *Screen Test*. This was a live broadcast from a Broadway theater with each show featuring a young hopeful actor or actress in a short dramatic episode accompanied by an orchestra. The theater was always full, and after the broadcast the audience was treated to a show for their own enjoyment. Bob involved himself in all aspects of the production of *Screen Test*, which ran until 1946.

While all this was going on, Bob's personal life continued its erratic course. Since his divorce from Jeanette, he had moved out of Manhattan to a house in Mount Kisco, where he was living with Marianne, a concert pianist. Although he once described this relationship as "profound," endurance was not part of it. When it became clear to both of them that it was not going to be permanent, they separated by mutual consent. However, it was not long before his eye was caught by one of the young actresses who featured in *Screen Test*. Mary Ashworth was an attractive blonde from Boston with an exceptionally good singing voice. Mary and Bob soon became strongly attracted to each other. Then suddenly she stopped calling him and answering his calls to her. Months later he discovered that Mary's agent had warned her off, claiming that her career would suffer if she became too deeply involved with him. Mary went on to perform in several popular productions, including the *Perry Como Show,* but she never broke through into major roles. Bob was never alone for long, however, and soon after Mary withdrew he came across Frances, an attractive girl of Russian descent whom he thought might have a future as a writer. Within a short time they married and moved from Mount Kisco, eventually settling in a farmhouse in Stormville, in Dutchess County, New York.

While they were living in Dutchess County, Bob underwent an experience that—when he recalled it many decades later—seemed to have had a special significance. The well that served the farmhouse had run dry. It was an old hand-dug well, about seventy feet deep, lined with fieldstones wedged together. He could hear water running below, but something was preventing it from being pumped up. Bob thought that he should investigate so he fetched a rope, tied it to a nearby tree, and abseiled down. He found that the well was supplied by an underground stream, but the water table had dropped below the end of the feed pipe. There was just enough light for him to gather several large stones and place them in the stream until the level was sufficiently raised.

Then he looked up—and started to panic. What if he had disturbed the lining on his way down? The wall could collapse at any moment. He felt intensely claustrophobic, fearful that he might be buried seventy feet below ground. Trying to control his panic, he sat down on a rock, cupped his hands, and took several mouthfuls of the cool, fresh water. Gradually he began to relax, to feel calm and serene, peaceful. Then what he described as "the feeling of a warm intelligence" seemed to flow into him, blending into every part of him. It was as if the Earth spoke to him, sharing its strength with him, foretelling his destiny. Then gradually

Bob Monroe, Radio Chief

the warmth faded; he seized the rope, climbed safely to the top, and was amazed to find he had been in the well for more than two hours. The experience moved him greatly and the memory stayed with him for the rest of his life. (It is vividly recounted in his last book, *Ultimate Journey.*)

During the run of *Screen Test,* Bob was earning about three hundred thousand dollars a year. After the program ended, however, nothing came into view for Monroe Productions, so for several months Bob and Frances lived off his capital. He put most of his energy into flying, hiring a Navion on several weekends to fly to a gliding club at Wurtsboro, in midstate New York, which owned six sail-planes bought from the military for a knock-down price. He joined the club, which called itself The Metropolitan Air-Hopper Soaring Association, retaining his membership until 1961. Bob was also a member of the Aviation Writers Association and was one of a group to whom the Air Force loaned a DC-4 so that they might fly to a convention in Los Angeles. On the return they ran into a severe front. As the cabin was not pressurized they were unable to climb above it. The only alternative was to fly through it. Sitting at the controls Bob watched the altimeter drop two thousand feet a minute. There was chaos in the cabin behind him, with bodies and objects falling about. It was, he said later, "wild, fun, exciting," though it may not have felt like that to the passengers at the time.

This was all very well, but by the beginning of 1947 it became clear that something had to be done to restore the Monroe finances. Bob arranged an interview with the vice president of Mutual Broadcasting and offered him a show he had designed himself, together with the script, actors, and director, free of charge for a month. It was a risk but, he promised, it would cost Mutual nothing except for providing space, an orchestra, and sound effects. The show was to be broadcast on Sunday nights on the understanding that only if it was successful would Mutual pay for it. It was, and they did.

High Adventure, broadcast once a week for seven years, was a major success with the highest ratings for its time. It consisted of a series of dramas, many of them introduced by George Sanders, telling the stories of ordinary people involved in dangerous or dramatic situations. Some of these stories were later made into films, although Bob was disappointed with the results, declaring that the studios butchered them. Monroe Productions packaged other series, one starring Peter Lorre and another Madeleine Carroll. Bob also took advantage of the growing popularity of radio quiz shows, creating *Take a Number, Meet Your Match,* and *Name That Tune.* The most successful was *Take a Number,* which offered prizes up to a total value of sixty thousand dollars—a huge sum for the time—that were delivered to the winners' homes with maximum publicity. Monroe himself controlled everything in these shows, writing, directing, and producing, driving them onward with apparently inexhaustible energy.

As well as being one of the leading figures in the radio industry of the late 1940s and early 1950s, Bob Monroe was also an innovator in the field of sound. He was among the first to make use of magnetic recording tape, which he employed in the production of his radio shows. His company was also active in the early days of television, producing several shows that were sold to the networks, but the medium never really appealed to him. He was busy enough with radio anyway, at one time having twenty-eight shows broadcast every week. He devised a way of cutting costs by taping passages during rehearsals and then splicing the best takes together, adding sound effects, music, and commercials to the completed script. Bob also composed music sequences for other radio productions, in particular themes and phrases designed to evoke emotional response in the listener, a foretaste of his later efforts in the early development of Metamusic. His attempt to create a library of musical phrasings to cover a range of dramatic situations was frustrated by the powerful leader of the Federation of Musicians, who realized that such a library would deprive his members of work. Monroe responded by flying his engineers and equipment to Cuba and hiring a local orchestra for six days to record his phrasings. For much of the time they played to an audience of one—a nephew of Cuba's dictator, Fulgencio Batista, who sat listening to what was going on with his revolver by his side.

Somehow Bob found time to pursue his obsession with flying. In 1950 he joined with an experienced pilot, Edgar Wynn, to buy two war surplus aircraft, a Lockheed Lodestar and a Grumman Goose. Together they formed a company with the impressive title of Trans-American Airways. The Lodestar did three runs a week from New York to Florida and the Grumman, an amphibian, flew passengers to the New York State lakes. Trans-American lasted until Wynn was killed when an ex-Navy fighter aircraft he was piloting crashed at the Miami Air Show. Bob then sold the company, donating the profits to Ed's widow.

At about this time Mary Ashworth reentered Bob's life. During the five years since her agent had warned her off him, she had performed occasionally on Broadway as an actress and singer. She had married, given birth to a daughter, Maria, and subsequently divorced. Bob found her even more attractive than when they had first met. Frances soon joined the growing group of Monroe ex-wives and it was not long until Bob and Mary became engaged. Mary suggested that before they married it would be a good idea for two-year-old Maria and Bob to meet. Maria was staying with her grandparents in Boston. She remembers "looking down a staircase upon a handsome young man in a navy blue suit, with a moustache and incredibly endearing dimples. It was love at first sight."

Bob and Mary soon became widely known as a glamorous show business couple. Their daughter Laurie was born in New York City on April 3, 1951. Shortly afterwards the family moved to an architect-designed house in Croton-on-Hudson, Westchester County, and

Mary decided to retire from the stage to become a full-time mother. At this she proved successful, providing the young girls with what Maria and Laurie later described as "an idyllic, wondrous and magical childhood." One of their first visitors was an Irish Setter called Michael, who wandered into the garden most days. Michael helped Laurie learn to walk by allowing her to pull herself up holding his long, flowing hair. He would pace along beside her as she hung on to him while taking her first tentative steps.

The Monroes' house stood in twenty acres with a long river frontage, a log cabin, and an extensive woodland that the children loved to explore. There was also a swimming pool with underwater speakers and colored underwater lights, a childhood dream of Bob's that he was now able to fulfill. Inside the house one wall was given over to hi-tech stereo equipment, with music being channeled into the swimming pool speakers. Delighting in parenthood, Bob created a game he called "Snipe Hunt." A Snipe was a fictitious creature that could be caught only at night. One young hunter held a burlap bag open while the other chased the imaginary creature until both agreed it had been caught in the snare. Often on Saturday mornings he would bundle the girls into his station wagon and drive out to an auction or yard sale. He would buy them a soda and a bag of Frito's Corn Chips and hunt around to find some item of outdoor equipment or playground toy, always keen to strike a deal. He would sometimes collect them from school in his red Porsche and drive them out for riding lessons, the girls struggling to change into their riding gear in the cramped confines of the back seat. He taught them to ride bicycles and occasionally took them gliding. Laurie recalls taking the controls while Bob told her to bank to the left or right, lift the nose, *feel* where the glider should be, and take it there.

In contrast to his domestic life, Bob's professional career continued to be hectic, so much so that barbiturates became a regular element in his diet. Monroe Productions metamorphosed into

Monroe Enterprises, with a wider range of interest, and in 1954 he was invited by RKO General, Mutual Broadcasting's parent company, to become vice president in charge of programming. The deal he struck involved Mutual buying four of his own shows. He was also made responsible for Mutual's radio stations situated in various cities throughout the United States, which gave him an insight into the rewards that might be obtained from ownership. For two years he commuted daily to RKO's offices on Broadway and in whatever time remained he busied himself with his other interests. The pressures mounted inexorably. At one time his corporation was producing a record number of nineteen programs weekly, with Monroe writing the scripts, directing, and composing the music for most of them himself. Then, midway through 1956, feeling he needed no more of this kind of life, he resigned from Mutual and threw the barbiturates away.

It was, he realized, time for a change. He was now a wealthy man with a family and with a number of ambitions that he had not yet fulfilled. He wanted to write books and plays and yearned to produce his own play on Broadway. He flirted with the idea of moving to Hollywood to enter the world of film production, but soon concluded that this would quickly exhaust his capital.

But before he came to a final decision, a totally unexpected prospect opened before him. A Westchester County neighbor offered him a partnership in an oil concession in Ecuador on which he held an option. He asked Bob if he would fund an expedition to examine the asphalt lake and oil seeps that formed the concession. The opportunity sounded too good to miss. Through his aviation interests Bob had a contact in Ecuador, Ernesto Estrada, always known as Chicho, who flew planes at the Air-Hoppers Club every summer. They arranged to meet in Guayaquil. Bob estimated that the expedition would cost about fifteen thousand dollars, which he hoped could be written off against tax, and with Mary and his proposed business partner took a commercial flight to Quito, planning to stay in Ecuador for about three weeks.

The 11,000-foot altitude of Quito presented Bob with a severe breathing problem. He was much relieved when after a few days they left, flying to Esmeraldas on the Pacific coast in an ancient Ford Trimotor with ducks, geese, chickens, and dogs as copassengers. The flight, for which the only navigational aids when crossing the Andes ridge in cloud were a compass and the steward's watch, was a lesson in itself. So was Esmeraldas, its main street a muddy track lined with single-story wooden stores, half of which were closed, and its only hotel consisting of four rooms set around a courtyard. The mayor invited them to a council meeting where one member, the council's only Communist, reviled them as filthy capitalist pigs who had come to seize the local people's land. After the meeting this Communist took Bob aside and offered him a half-share in his crystal mine for ten thousand dollars. (Years later he wondered if he had been right to refuse.)

Next day the party chartered a fishing trawler for the thirty-mile passage along the coast to the oil concession. They anchored off a cluster of thatched-roof huts built on poles that comprised the settlement of Cabo de San Francisco. They were paddled ashore in a couple of dugout canoes and were received by the young headman, Juan, who took them around the village and served them lunch. He led them three miles into the jungle to the oil seeps and the asphalt lake, where they took samples and attempted to take readings with a scintillator, a portable item of oil-prospecting equipment.

Returning to Quito, Bob called his friend Chicho and they arranged to meet in Guayaquil. When he attempted to pay the hotel bill, he was told it had already been settled. "Senor Estrada owns the hotel," said the clerk. It transpired that he owned a lot more, his father having been nicknamed "the Simon Bolivar of Ecuador." While Mary made friends with Chicho's sister, Bob learnt to scuba dive, searching for gold doubloons in the wreck of a Spanish galleon. He inspected a gold mine, and soared up to 16,000 feet over the Andes in one of Chicho's many oxygen-equipped sail-planes. One item Chicho lacked was a helicopter. Bob encouraged him to buy one to make it easier for him to visit and oversee his various concerns. As soon as it arrived, Chicho insisted on piloting the helicopter himself despite never having had a single lesson.

Chicho admired Bob's spirit and enjoyed his company. He offered him the sulphur concession for the Galapagos Islands and told him that if he wanted the oil concession as well he could have it. For a rent of a dollar a month he could also have a distillation plant to produce liqueur from the stems of millions of overripe bananas that would otherwise be thrown into the sea.

The temptation to carve out a new and immensely profitable life in Ecuador was hard to resist; perhaps if it had come a few years earlier Bob might have yielded to it. Ecuador could have provided him with uncountable wealth. But, he said later, he felt that something seemed to be pulling him back to the States. Moreover, attractive though the prospects were, they would not provide the sort of life that he considered right for Mary and their two young daughters. Despite Chicho's many appeals for him to return, he made up his mind that the Ecuador chapter would remain closed. Several weeks later than planned, the Monroes flew back home. As a mark of thanks to his friend he sent him by air four Siamese kittens, which nearly drove the pilot mad with their screaming. In later years Bob was intrigued by the thought that their descendants might be roaming the jungles and slopes of the Andes.

Toward the end of 1956 Monroe set up an office on Madison Avenue, New York, and moved into ownership. He bought two radio stations, one in Winston-Salem and the other in Durham, North Carolina. On his business visits to Winston-Salem, he came to know

Agnew Bahnson, an engineer by training, who ran a manufacturing company in the city. He had the sort of mind that appealed to Bob, being a flying enthusiast and the first person he had met who was investigating antigravity, a theory that appealed to his inquiring mind. Bahnson encouraged him to enter into the social life of the city and it was not long before Monroe felt himself quite at home there. Now that he was no longer involved full time with the production and direction of radio shows, he had time to look around for ideas and projects to investigate and possibly develop. He was attracted by a new process called Biorhythm, based on the idea that one's life is affected by rhythmic biological cycles, physical, emotional, and intellectual. Readings could be obtained and charts produced with the intention of helping you improve your life. Bob tried this out on himself, found that it had possibilities, and decided to market it. After six months, however, he dropped the idea, saying later that he failed to put enough energy into its promotion.

A second project was sleep-learning. Again, Bob decided to try it out on himself. He created his own research and development program and constructed a booth containing a waterbed and a stereo system with headphones. He developed a number of exercises that involved learning factual information, such as multiplication tables from twelve to twenty-four and phrases in Spanish and French, and recorded them on tape along with direct suggestions and various sound patterns, one of which was a simulation of ocean surf, designed to induce a state of relaxation leading the listener into sleep. He tested these tapes on himself, claiming that he could recall everything that was recorded. So far, so good, but the process had to be tested on others if it was to be found acceptable. He found eleven subjects, of whom his daughter Laurie was one, to try it out. Each subject was required to have the tapes playing during the night and on waking to use a physical-mental cue to recall the recorded information. With a reel-to-reel tape player beside her bed and speakers on either side,

Laurie would fall asleep to the sound of ocean surf and her father's voice reciting multiplication tables and phrases in different languages. Laurie's cue was to touch the center of her forehead with her right forefinger as soon as she woke up. The tapes also carried suggestions that all systems in the listener's body would be working normally and effectively on returning to full wakefulness. The results were carefully recorded, although they were not sufficiently conclusive to warrant further action. Nevertheless Laurie felt they had some value, as she discovered a facility for language and math in later years.[1]

Now that Bob Monroe had succeeded in making the career change from writer-director-producer of radio shows to ownership of broadcasting stations, with his knowledge, energy, and business skills there was no reason why he should not expand his business interests much further—and during the next few years this is what he did. Yet although he was not aware of it, a whole new world was about to open up before him, a world that so far had been beyond his wildest imaginings.

The out-of-body experiences that Monroe recorded in *Journeys Out of the Body* took place between 1958 and 1963. Laurie recalls sitting with her father in the log cabin in the grounds of their Westchester County house. Here Bob would tell her stories, some of them about the adventures he later described in his first book. When she was ten years old he told her that these experiences really happened to him. She thought for a moment. "Doesn't everyone do that?" she asked. This made him laugh, and years later he wrote an inscription to her on the flyleaf of his book. "To Laurie—Who lived through much of the chronicle herein—with great unconcern."

In April 1958 Bob had been subjected to the first of a number of physical seizures, accompanied by vibrations that seemed to sweep along his body. Before long the pain ceased although the vibrations, which lasted for no more than five minutes, continued. Then in the fall his out-of-body journeys began. "Gradually I became more accustomed to this strange condition in my life," he wrote later. "More and more I was slowly able to control its movements. In a few ways it had actually become helpful. I had become reluctant to part with it. The mystery of its very presence had aroused my curiosity."

Once he found himself able to accept what was happening to him, disturbing though some of the episodes were, Monroe began to search for others, present or past, who had reported something similar. "I was a conventional person, convinced of conventional reality," he said. "Whom could I talk to?" Failing to find anyone who could provide help or advice, he was compelled to accept that he would have to undertake his own research, with the only experimental subject being himself. After some thought he installed a small laboratory in his home, using his technical know-how to incorporate an isolation unit, consisting of a Faraday cage suspended on a rope and charged with a hundred thousand volts. He would shut himself in this from time to time, relaxing as best he could, and found that he was still susceptible to out-of-body experiences even when isolated by the powerful charge.

It is worth noting that this was happening nine years before Charles Tart began preparing his classic study *Altered States of Consciousness*. In his introduction to the second edition Tart outlines the attitude of orthodox science in the late 1950s to "the mystical states, psychedelic drug use, meditation, and other phenomena that involve altering one's ordinary state of consciousness to a radically new one, all with profound results on one's religion, philosophy and life style." These and similar subjects were not considered "respectable" for investigation. They were treated as relics of superstition or manifestations of mental illness, with no attempt made to examine or investigate them. The only references to the out-of-body experience, generally known as "astral projection," appeared in texts devoted to magic or the occult, as Dr. Hereward Carrington discovered when editing the accounts of Sylvan Muldoon's experiences. Robert Crookall's study of 160 accounts of OBEs, *The Study and Practice of Astral Projection* (1960), has a strongly spiritual slant, with its conclusion that "astral projection assures us of survival" and that "the information obtained accords with that revealed in our Scriptures." Such texts, like the phenomena listed by Charles Tart, did not attract the attention of orthodox science.

A few months after Bob's out-of-body experiences began he was booked to fly on a business trip from Newark to Winston-Salem. The previous night he had dreamt of a crash that he himself survived. This made him wonder whether he should cancel his journey. He decided to go through with it and boarded the plane. On arrival at Winston-Salem, he was taken ill with a heart attack and spent the next three weeks in the hospital. Meantime, Mary, deeply concerned about his well-being, made copies of notes he had made on his out-of-body experiences and gave them to a friend, Dr. Andrija Puharich, who she knew was interested in unusual types of experience.[2] She later explained that she had done this because Puharich might be able to tell whether the heart attack was related to these seemingly inexplicable happenings. Puharich made no comments at the time, and in the relief and excitement of Bob's return Mary forgot to tell him what she had done. Three years later, however, Bob came across Puharich's newly published book *Beyond Telepathy*. It contained a chapter that, to his amazement, dealt with his own OBEs. "Bob Rame," as Puharich refers to Monroe, is said to have been addicted to glue-sniffing and, according to Puharich, it was this that had stimulated his out-of-body escapades. It happened that Monroe knew about the effects of glue-sniffing, as he used to make model aircraft and ships with his daughter Laurie and was aware of the feelings that inhaling the fumes could bring about. In a previous book Puharich had focused largely on drug-related experiences and for this sequel he had shuffled Monroe's notes, making it appear that an accidental inhalation of fumes while repairing furniture, referred to in the notes, was responsible for what followed—despite the fact that a year separated the two occurrences. Monroe wanted to sue, but his attorney advised against it, on the grounds that a jury might feel his own sanity was in question rather than Puharich's libel. All this, which hung around Monroe's reputation for the next few years, led him to conclude that "the woolly world of Consciousness expansion does not necessarily include integrity, empathy, or honesty."

In the early days of his OBEs, Bob's mind was set at rest, to some extent at least, when he discovered that Edgar Cayce (1877–1945), whose writings he admired, had also experienced out-of-body travel. Cayce, known as "The Sleeping Prophet," whose work was being carried on by the Association for Research and Enlightenment (ARE) at Virginia Beach, was a trance-channeler renowned for his psychic and healing abilities, with whom Monroe felt a degree of affinity. This, however, was not sufficient verification for Monroe's inquiring mind and he was eager to discover what the contemporary academic world had to say on the subject. One of the few investigators of parapsychological phenomena at the time was Professor J. B. Rhine of Duke University. Visiting him, Monroe was disappointed to find that out-of-body exploration was not among the professor's concerns. Then, as he was leaving, one of Rhine's students who had been present during their conversation approached him and said quietly, "There's nothing to worry about, Mr. Monroe. I do it too." Further confirmation that his experiences were not unique came when he called to discuss them with the well-known medium Eileen Garrett. She told him she went out-of-body whenever she wanted to; it was very useful, she said, to be able to pop round behind herself to see if her slip was showing.

At first, Mary was supportive of Bob's ventures into this little-known world of psychic exploration. She had an open and inquiring mind and, although brought up as a strict Catholic, she had no problem in accepting, for example, that communication with those who had died was possible, and she admitted that on more than one occasion she had herself conversed with her deceased mother. However, there were now signs that the couple were beginning to grow apart. Bob, concerned with creating and developing business opportunities in Winston-Salem and then in Richmond, was often away from home. Mary missed her social life and shared few of his outdoor interests. She was also fully occupied with bringing up the two girls. At first she had taken an interest in her husband's out-of-body experiences, which he had been ready to discuss with her, especially his attempts to check out their validity. But as they continued, becoming more and more removed from "everyday life," he ceased to confide in her. She began to feel rejected and also became uncomfortable with the different sorts of people who now visited the house to talk with Bob about his other life in which she had no part. It may also be relevant that Bob discovered that during his frequent out-of-body experiences he needed to control his sex drive if he wished to venture more than a few feet from his bed.

In 1961 the Monroes moved to Richmond. It was not only business opportunities that attracted Bob to the city. Richmond was on the same latitude as his hometown of Lexington and he assumed its climate would be similar. Also, it was not far from the ocean, where he enjoyed sailing whenever he could. For the previous thirty years the city had been almost stagnant, with not a single office building erected within its boundaries. Suddenly, there was an explosion of commercial activity, with the downtown area rapidly transformed by an upsurge of skyscrapers. A new city hall together with a vast coliseum formed a civic center, and construction began on an ultramodern expressway system. It was an exciting place to be and for a while Mary seemed to flourish there. Her interest in acting was revived and she took leading roles in several plays staged at the Virginia Museum, becoming widely known in the locality for her beauty and her sociable nature. Meantime, Bob became the owner of two radio stations and a recording studio, Richmond Sound Stages, and moved into the forefront of local entertainment. One of his radio stations, WGOE, concentrated on popular music, while the other, WRGM, played mostly easy listening and classical and also broadcast what Monroe considered to be the "good" news. If there was any "bad" news that might disturb the optimism of this go-ahead area, it was carefully played down.

At the same time Monroe's out-of-body experiences continued. He had brought with him his laboratory equipment and the records he had compiled, and he continued to research these experiences when time permitted. Then he discovered a new dimension to the OBE when two of his closest friends died within a short time of each other. The lawyer Agnew Bahnson was killed when his aircraft crashed and caught fire. Three months later during an OBE Monroe expressed the desire to meet him. He was led to a level area and told to wait. As he described it, a cloud of what appeared to be something like gas emanated from a gap in the floor and formed itself into the appearance of Agnew. He spoke to Monroe about the hi-tech activities he was busy with, and then disappeared as he had come. He looked young and strong, as Monroe remembered him. Shortly afterwards Dr. Dick Gordon, whom he had first consulted about his OBEs, was found to be suffering from cancer and died. Monroe waited a while and then in the out-of-body state asked if he could see him. He was escorted, as he put it, to a place where he observed two men on what looked like a stage, as if they were performing in a theater. A younger man hurried in, stared at Monroe, and declared, "I see you." Later Monroe saw a photograph of Gordon as a young man, enabling him to confirm that this was indeed Gordon whom he had seen. These glimpses into the afterlife are recorded in *Journeys Out of the Body* as if they are nothing out of the ordinary.

As far as his business life was concerned, Monroe found Richmond less congenial than he had hoped. It was highly competitive and not everyone he had to deal with was trustworthy. Instead of a word or a handshake, contracts drawn up by notaries were essential, and even then bills were not always paid. But before disillusion could take over, a new prospect appeared. While on a flight from El Paso, where he had gone to investigate the purchase of another radio station, a media broker he was traveling with mentioned CATV—Cable-Antenna Television. Monroe, always on the lookout for innovation, became interested immediately. He investigated the possibilities but soon realized that to install this system in a city as large as Richmond would cost him far more than he could raise. Moreover, he felt that there was nothing to keep him in Richmond and a change in both direction and location would be welcome. His inquiries revealed that the CATV franchise was available for the nearby and rapidly developing city of Charlottesville, home of the University of Virginia. This was more like it. To raise funds for this new and exciting undertaking he sold his radio stations and obtained a four hundred thousand-dollar loan from a courageous life insurance company. Once negotiations were completed, the Monroes moved to Charlottesville.

Jefferson Cable Corporation was the name of Monroe's new company. The Charlottesville installation was only the second twelve-channel cable TV system in the whole of the United States. Before it was completed, Monroe also obtained the franchise for nearby Waynesboro. This meant selling the insurance company's interest and most of his own shares to a financial house, American Financial Systems. Both systems quickly proved successful and Monroe became deeply involved in developing these new businesses, buying a feature film package and instituting one of the first twenty-four-hour movie channels. Within a few years both cable systems were fully operational, eventually being extended to ten cities as far south as Lafayette, Louisiana.

What spare time Bob had was devoted to working on the book he had decided to write about his out-of-body experiences. He was intent on conducting research into OBEs but felt it essential to keep the funding for this separate from his cable interests. To raise these funds he turned to the property market and founded a company, Monroe Industries, to build prefabricated houses for students and cheap rural housing for farm-workers. In this he was following the example of his father, who also invested in property. To begin with, however, he was less successful. There was nothing wrong with his ideas, but he soon ran into difficulties with his suppliers and the local authorities. Eventually, he was compelled to close the construction business and Monroe Industries went into abeyance. The opportunity for research into the out-of-body state had not yet arrived.

Meanwhile the situation between Bob and Mary continued to worsen, so much so that they decided to consult a marriage counselor. Surprisingly, in view of the fact that the counselor was a Roman Catholic priest, he gave their marriage little prospect of continuing. They struggled on until, in 1967, after eighteen years together, they decided to separate. Their children were now spending much of their lives away from home. Maria, whom Bob later adopted, had moved on to college and Bob, sensing difficult times ahead, had arranged for Laurie, now sixteen years old, to attend boarding school in Pennsylvania. In the following year the Monroes divorced. A financial settlement was agreed upon and Mary moved back to Richmond, where she later remarried.

Among the friends they had made in Richmond was Nancy Penn Honeycutt, a member of an old Virginia family. Nancy's husband, Bud, was an officer in the Marine Corps. They had three daughters, Virginia Penn (Penny), Nancy Lea (usually known as Scooter), and Lucinda Beale (Cindy), and a son, Terry (known as A. J.).

46

Penny and Laurie soon became friends, often visiting each other to play together. It so happened that both families had left Richmond in 1965. Contact, however, was interrupted for the time being, as Bud Honeycutt was assigned to a three-year tour of duty in California. Nancy and their three younger children accompanied him, while Penny was sent to St. Anne's boarding school in Charlottesville.

After three years in Charlottesville, Bob came to the conclusion that cable television, although profitable in comparison with some of his previous business ventures, was not providing the fulfillment he now sought. There is no doubt that his frequent out-of-body experiences had unsettled him. He needed more time to investigate them, to consider what meaning they held and what they had to teach. He resigned from Jefferson Cable Corporation and turned once more to property development, in the belief that it would provide him with more free time to pursue his researches and to complete his book. However, instead of venturing into the construction business, he purchased two existing apartment complexes in Charlottesville, the Jeffersonian and Cavalier Court. Now all he needed was someone reliable to manage them for him.

About this time Nancy Honeycutt left California, returning to live in Charlottesville, where she was hoping that she and her husband would be able to obtain their graduate degrees. It might also, she thought, be a good place to settle when Bud retired from the Marine Corps. But despite these hopes her marriage was now failing, and before long the couple decided to separate. Bob and Nancy resumed their friendship and, while she was awaiting completion of divorce proceedings, he was sufficiently impressed by her ability to employ her to manage his apartments. Soon they became close. They discovered that they had many interests in common, most strikingly a deep interest in the paranormal. For Bob, this was an unexpected bonus. Nancy was a Christian mystic, well versed in the Bible but able to see beyond the expressed belief systems of the church and with a sympathetic attitude towards Bob's accounts of his OBEs. She was also a very practical person, having from time to time been a school-teacher, a music teacher, an interior decorator, and a real estate manager. In addition she had, in Bob's own words, "a bright, warm and joyful personality."

On February 6, 1971, they married and Bob found himself at the age of fifty-four stepfather of a considerable brood. Fortunately, the children soon took to him. Cindy remembers him sitting on the white couch telling them stories of his adventures in New York— they could never decide if they were true or he was making them up. She also recalls the excitement he brought into their lives. He would appear after work "in his blue-black Mustang with a souped-up engine and the fast-back window. Terry and I used to love to ride in the back seat and look at the dials and extra light-things which 'Mister Monroe' had installed around the dash. He had a horn that he switched a flipper-switch to blow and it sounded like a freight train." For the youngsters life with Bob Monroe as Dad might be unpre-dictable, but it was certainly fun.

Meanwhile, Dr. Puharich suggested to a young researcher, Charles Tart, with whom he shared an interest in OBEs, that he make contact with this Robert Monroe who had something to say about the subject. Tart, who was concerned with altered states of consciousness, had recently obtained his PhD, and was currently researching at the University of Virginia under Professor Ian Stevenson, widely known for his work on reincarnation theories, took this advice. He soon became intrigued by this middle-aged businessman with no back-ground in metaphysical studies but with plenty of practical intelligence and experience. Although the two of them functioned in totally distinct worlds, they found they had many interests in com-mon. Together they conducted a series of tests at the University Medical School to see if Monroe could produce an out-of-body experience while connected to various instruments measuring physiological functions. The requirement was for Monroe to leave his body and visit the control room, where certain digits were written on the wall. He was to read these and report at the end of the session. To begin with he found this impossible, until one night he managed, as he put it, "to roll out of his body" and enter the control room. It was empty. He looked along the hallway and saw the young technician who was supposed to monitor the experiment standing outside the control room talking to a friend. After trying unsuccessfully to attract her attention, he returned to his body and called out. The technician ran in and, to her amazement, he told her what he had seen. After he assured her she would not get into trouble for leaving the room, she confirmed the accuracy of his account.

Tart wrote up the series of experiments for the December 1967 issue of the *International Journal of Parapsychology*. He commented that the most important aspect of the investigation "is the demonstration that OBEs and similar 'exotic' phenomena are not mysterious happenings beyond the pale of scientific investigation," and expressed the hope that such experiences should no longer be regarded as "weird" but required proper scientific study. Soon afterwards Tart moved to the University of California at Davis, where Monroe visited him and took part in further tests in better conditions, this time producing two brief OBEs. Before he left, Monroe gave Tart a copy of his recently completed book, then unpublished, which Tart found wholly fascinating.

Shortly afterward, Monroe received a phone call from Bill Whitehead, who introduced himself as an editor at Doubleday. "We'd like to publish your book," he said. At first Monroe didn't know what he was talking about. He had sent a copy to a literary agent, but that had been more than a year earlier, and he had heard no word. Tart, discovering that Monroe had heard nothing from his agent, had mailed his copy to Whitehead, who was the editor for his own book,

Altered States of Consciousness. Doubleday is due much credit for accepting this unusual manuscript from a hitherto unpublished writer.

In the meantime Monroe's physical health was causing concern and, while *Journeys Out of the Body* was in press, he was advised that he urgently needed surgery on his carotid arteries. It was arranged for this to take place in Dallas, then the only city where this particular operation was performed. Nancy, Maria, and Laurie accompanied him to Dallas. While Bob was having his preparatory examinations in the hospital, they went into town, did some shopping, and—on the spur of the moment—asked a cab driver if he knew of any good psychics. To their surprise he said he knew of a very good one and drove them into the country to a small cottage at the end of a dirt road. Laurie, skeptical about professed psychics, made sure that no information about who they were would be revealed, only that a relative of theirs was about to undergo surgery. They were amazed when the woman told them that a lady named Georgia, who described herself as Laurie's grandmother and who, as they knew, had died three years previously at the age of eighty-four, was accompanying them, and that she would be present at the forthcoming operation along with several others in white coats. On their return to the hospital, they told Bob what the psychic had said. He was greatly heartened by the idea that his mother with her medical experience would be assisting at what was then regarded as a particularly risky procedure—which proved successful.

Later that year as word of Monroe's experiences began to circulate, he was invited to speak at the Harold Sherman Parapsychology Conference in Hot Springs, Arkansas, along with several of the better-known psychics and healers of the time.[3] In the audience was a psychologist, Dr. Ray Waldkoetter, whose inquiring mind had led him to attend. Monroe was scheduled to speak late in the afternoon, by which time the audience was in a cheerful, chatty mood, so much so that the chairman's introduction was barely audible. Monroe, no stranger to showmanship, waited until all were silent. From then on, he captivated the audience for over an hour, describing, to their surprise, not his OBE adventures but an interest that he had only recently acquired. This derived partly from his experience in radio and was concerned with developing means of using sound to modify behavior. Despite the nonparapsychological nature of the subject, he imbued his audience with what Waldkoetter described as "a taste of wonder." This also marked the beginning of a friendship between the two, with Ray Waldkoetter eventually becoming one of the first members of The Monroe Institute's advisory board.[4]

Monroe, as he once said himself, was a driven man. He had experienced the Depression years; he knew what it was like to be hungry and have nowhere to sleep. He delighted in living on the edge of danger, in gliding, sailing, flying rickety aircraft, and driving fast cars that he had built himself. His college education was a thing of shreds and patches, bits of this and bits of that; what he could do best was the result of observation, experiment, and self-teaching. He was certainly curious as to how things worked and was eager to test any new discovery upon himself. For humankind in general, however, at this time in his life he seemed to have little concern. Up to this point there is no evidence of vision, of altruism, of a sense of there being anything other than what is tangible, explicable, and subject to control. If Monroe ever looked forward, it is likely that what he envisaged was a growing business empire based on property ownership, enjoying his role as parent of a lively young family, and eventually years of active retirement, exploring the influence of sound, flying, sailing, and so on, although not taking quite so many risks as when he was younger. How wrong he would have been.

Notes

1. Elements of this procedure were later adapted and incorporated in The Monroe Institute's training programs.

2. Puharich, sometimes nicknamed "the mad scientist," was best known for his pursuit of the magic mushroom and his research on Uri Geller.

3. Harold Sherman (1898–1987), though an author and playwright, was best known as a leader in the field of psychic research, cooperating in experiments with various notables, including Dr. J. B. Rhine, Sir Hubert Wilkins, the famous Arctic explorer, and the astronaut Neil Armstrong. The conferences he organized brought together many of the most forward-looking thinkers of the time.

4. Waldkoetter came across Monroe again at another Parapsychology Conference, this time in St. Louis. They lunched together afterwards, and Monroe promised to support him in his own research. A few years later Waldkoetter experienced Hemi-Sync for himself and began to look for the opportunity to use the technology in his own practice.

CHAPTER 3

Out of the Body!

When Bob Monroe decided to sort out his notes on his out-of-body experiences for the book he intended to write, he had no idea of the impact this book would have. Nevertheless, his stated purposes for wanting to publish the record of his experiences were not especially modest. First, he expressed the hope that, by reading it, others who had traveled out-of-body would find comfort in knowing that their experiences were not unique and would have their fears assuaged by the knowledge that they did not need treatment and were not going mad. His second, more ambitious, purpose was to encourage science to expand its horizons, "to open wide the avenues and doorways intimated herein to the great enrichment of man's knowledge and understanding of himself and his complete environment." At the same time, he was concerned that, as president of a large and successful corporation, he could be criticized, and perhaps ostracized, by his board of directors, who might well think that such an apparently unstable person was ill-suited to run a multimillion-dollar business. As it turned out, his concern was unnecessary. Not only did his fellow directors make no comment, but soon after the book was published his chairman's wife asked him to autograph her copy. Then the chairman himself drew him aside, telling him that his own wife had psychic powers, adding that he always consulted her before making an important deal.

Journeys Out of the Body, first published in 1971, dealt with events that occurred between 1958 and 1963. But in his foreword to the 1977 edition, Monroe declared that nothing had to be altered in the light of later experience. He had always recorded his out-of-body journeys in note form when he felt himself securely back in his physical body and had written them up as soon as possible afterwards. He expressed the hope that his readers would accept his accounts as they stood—as accurate records of out-of-body experiences, no matter how bizarre they might seem. The reviews were mostly favorable, and although sales were slow to begin with they soon gained momentum. The book has been reprinted almost every year since its initial publication, with sales to date approaching a million copies, and it has been translated into several languages.

Not content simply to record his experiences, Monroe devoted one-third of the book to discussing and analyzing them. He also included two chapters of instruction for those who wished to experience the out-of-body state themselves. As an epilogue he reprinted a report on a psychological investigation to which he had submitted himself at the Topeka Veterans Administration Hospital, together with the results of a physical observation and brainwave analysis carried out in the hospital's psychophysiological laboratory while he put himself into the out-of-body state. The researchers, directed by Dr. Stuart Twemlow, chief of Research Service, were mainly interested in discovering what they could about the relationships between his personality and his out-of-body experiences. They found him to be "the almost traditional businessman and father who is not a freak, does not wear unusual clothes, and does not constantly put himself on-stage for examination of his special abilities." They added: "He pursues relentlessly his own research, makes his own contacts, and takes responsibility for his own life," and commented on "his high sense of purpose, and his need for and relentless desire for understanding." Their investigations revealed nothing untoward in his personality. The result of all this is that *Journeys Out of the Body* stands as a comprehensive account of the phenomenon as experienced by someone who, as Professor Tart says in his introduction, "is unique among the small number of people who have written about repeated OBEs, in that he recognizes the extent to which his mind tries to interpret his experiences, to force them into familiar patterns. Thus his accounts are particularly valuable, for he works very hard to try to 'tell it like it is.'"

A phrase that Monroe frequently used in response to questions about his experiences is "go find out for yourself." Such experiences are unique to the individual. Reality in the out-of-body state is likely to depend on, or be conditioned by, the individual's own belief system. Monroe, however, impresses as a methodical reporter and his accounts are not influenced by anything he had previously heard or read. One indication of this is his refusal to use the word *astral,* as in "astral travel" or "astral exploration," expressions frequently employed in previous, and many subsequent, accounts of out-of-body journeys. As he said, "the word 'astral' has dim origins in early mystical and occult events which involve witchcraft, sorcery, incantations," and he was always careful to avoid any such association.

As Monroe describes it, in the spring of 1958 he was experimenting with a technique to promote learning during sleep. For this purpose he had designed a tape carrying a combination of verbal instructions and sound signals intended to relax the listener and encourage retention and recall. He listened to the tape, had brunch with the family, and then about an hour later was seized with a cramping pain just under his rib cage. This lasted for about twelve hours, leaving him feeling sore but with no other after-effects. Three weeks later he was resting on a Sunday afternoon when he sensed that "a beam or ray" entered from outside and struck his body, causing it to shake or vibrate. This happened several times in the next six weeks. Not surprisingly, he found this worrying and arranged to have himself medically checked, but there was no sign of any illness or malign condition. These inexplicable vibrations continued to occur from time to time over the following months, always when he was lying down ready to go to sleep.

The first indication that something else was going on came when he was lying in bed on a Sunday night. The vibrations, which he was now finding rather tedious, began once more. His arm was draped over the side of the bed, with his fingers touching the rug. Idly, he moved his fingers, pushing them against the rug. They seemed to go right through the rug and touch the floor beneath. Then his fingers went through the floor and he could feel what he took to be the upper surface of the ceiling of the room below. He could feel a small chip of wood, a bent nail, and some sawdust. He pushed harder and his arm seemed to penetrate the ceiling and his hand felt water. Suddenly, he awoke, becoming aware of the moonlit landscape through the window and himself lying in bed next to his wife, while at the same time his arm was stuck through the floor, his fingers playing with water. The vibrations faded. He pulled his arm out of the floor, got up, and switched on the light. There was no hole in the rug or the floor and no water on his hand. It was, he thought, a hallucination.

About four weeks later, he was again aware of the vibrations while lying in bed with his wife asleep beside him. He was thinking about taking up a glider the next afternoon when he felt something pressing on his shoulder. He felt behind his shoulder and found a smooth wall. At first he thought he had gone to sleep—as he later realized he had—and fallen out of bed, landing propped up against the wall. But he could find no windows, furniture, or doors. Then he became aware that what he was touching was the bedroom ceiling. He was floating against the ceiling! He rolled over and looked down.

He could make out the bed with two figures lying in it. His wife was one—and he was the other!

At first he thought he was dying—that somehow the vibrations were killing him. He managed to dive down into his body and found himself again beside his wife in his bed. But what had happened brought him to the verge of panic and it was some time before he was able to overcome the fear that this experience evoked. Was he physically or mentally ill? Was there *any* meaning to what was happening to him?

A few days later he had himself fully medically examined, including an electroencephalograph (EEG) analysis. Nothing seemed to be amiss, so his doctor gave him tranquillizers and sent him home. He discussed what was happening to him with his friend, Dr. Foster Bradshaw, who told him to try to repeat the experience, casually remarking that some yoga practitioners and followers of Eastern religions claimed they could leave their bodies and travel whenever they wished. It took some time before Monroe overcame his natural resistance to experiment willfully. Eventually, he determined to try, going to bed and after some time willing himself to leave his body and float around the bedroom, returning to his body when he felt ready to do so.

His conversations with Dr. Bradshaw led Monroe to formulate an explanation as to what was happening to him. Dr. Bradshaw, he says, had given him the clue he needed—that he was performing "astral projection"—leaving his physical body for the time being and traveling around in a nonmaterial or "astral" body. Rejecting the word *astral*, Monroe adopted the term *Second Body* to describe the nonphysical body that he seemed to possess. The condition when he was no longer resident in his physical body he described as the *Second State*. At this time he knew of no one else who had reported similar experiences and therefore came to think of himself as unique.

To begin with Monroe was fearful of what might happen to him if the episodes continued. He was wary of being treated as a patient if he discussed the matter with the doctors whom he knew as friends, and of being regarded as a freak or psychotic if he mentioned what was happening to him to his business acquaintances or to people he knew in the local community. He embarked on a survey of religious writings to see if they contained any helpful information. This proved negative; he found, he said, the Bible too concerned with judgment and the Eastern religions mainly involved with lengthy processes of spiritual development. He was also disappointed with what he called "the underground," divided into the professionals, ranging from parapsychologists to fortune tellers, and the consumers, dedicated believers in the potential of man's inner self and preoccupied with matters psychic or spiritual. In reviewing the literature, he discovered that most of the reported out-of-body events were spontaneous and happened once only, often when the individual was in ill-health physically or emotionally. He found no useful research and no proper experimental work and the concrete data he was searching for did not exist. In much of the literature, the analytical and empirical approach he sought was submerged in what he called "the vast morass of theological thought and belief." The road ahead—the purposeful exploration of the Second State—was one he would have to travel alone.

Throughout Monroe's accounts of his early out-of body experiences we are aware of his efforts to make sense of what was happening. This is very apparent in his preoccupation with the reality of the Second Body. When he found himself able to induce the out-of-body state, he tended to confine his explorations first to his immediate environment and later to the surrounding neighborhood. It seemed to him that he could feel his physical body with his non-physical hands, that he sometimes met resistance when moving through a wall, and that on one occasion when he paid an out-of-body visit to a friend some eight miles away she appeared to be frightened. When he met his friend the following day, she told him that the evening before she had noticed something "hanging and waving in the air"—resembling "a filmy piece of grey chiffon"—on the far side of the room. She thought it might be him and asked if it was would he please go home and not trouble her. Then it vanished.

From these various experiences Monroe deduced that the Second Body had weight and a small degree of gravitational attraction. Under certain conditions it became visible. Its sense of touch was similar to that of the physical body. It was plastic, in that it could take whatever shape or form the individual desired. From some episodes he thought it possible that the Second Body was a direct reversal of the physical (left to right and toe to head). It was connected with the physical body by a cord that could convey messages from one body to the other and was capable of extreme elasticity. He also felt that the Second Body was affected by electricity and electromagnetic fields.

Monroe's concept of the Second Body arises from his attempts to rationalize his experiences. Reading his first book, one becomes aware of the tension between the experiences themselves and the author's attempts to explain them, to make them fit, bizarre though many of them are, into a frame or a pattern, something that the intellect can get hold of. He seems to be searching for some physical explanation, to associate the OBE with the cramping pain or the vibrations that occurred months before his first experience. The cord that he describes connecting the two "bodies" is another example of this. Mention of a cord appears frequently in the pre-Monroe literature, often being related to the silver cord in the biblical book of Ecclesiastes, and sometimes accompanied by the assumption that if it is broken both "bodies" will die. As the years pass, however, references to this cord become rarer and eventually disappear altogether, as they do in Monroe's later books. One explanation is that the cord is a mental construct: that the mind, seeking to make sense of what is happening, creates this tangible link between the body and the out-of-body as a sort of safety mechanism.

Once he was convinced that his experiences were not indicators of illness or insanity, Monroe felt able to discuss them with various friends and acquaintances. That these individuals were aware of what was going on in his life may help to explain their reports declaring they sensed he was around their houses from time to time. The odd-est report comes from an episode in 1963, when one Saturday Monroe decided to travel out-of-body to visit a close friend, a busi-nesswoman he identifies as R. W., who was on vacation somewhere, although he did not know exactly where, on the New Jersey coast. He found her, together with two teenage girls, sitting in a kitchen. Monroe spoke to her and she replied; then he said he had to be sure that she would remember his visit. He pinched her just below her rib cage. "Ow!" she exclaimed. He then returned to his physical body. A few days later, when R. W. was back home, Monroe asked her what she had been doing the previous Saturday. She said she had been in the kitchen in her holiday house, talking with her eighteen-year-old niece and her friend of similar age. She could not recall anything of Monroe's visit until he mentioned the pinch. "Was that you?" she asked, astonished. She lifted the edge of her sweater and pointed out "two brown and blue marks at exactly the spot where I had pinched her."

Monroe's earliest explorations were confined to what he calls Locale I, the material world, its people and places, especially those in the surrounding neighborhood. He would fly over the area, choose a house whose occupiers he knew, and call in to see what was going on—and, he says, sometimes engage in a kind of conversation. To prove the validity of the experience, he often tried to collect what he called evidential data. Still at this period convinced of the existence of a real Second Body, he felt the need to prove beyond doubt that his observations were accurate and that the conversations he reported actually took place. Whether he succeeded in his objective has to be left to the judgment of his readers.

While Locale I was familiar and nonthreatening, Locale II, where Monroe's experiences soon began to take him, was quite different. He describes it as "a non-material environment with laws of motion and matter only remotely related to the physical world. It is an immensity whose bounds are unknown (to this experimenter), and has depth and dimension incomprehensible to the finite, conscious mind. In this vastness lie all the aspects we attribute to Heaven and Hell, which are but part of Locale II. It is inhabited, if that is the word, by entities with various degrees of intelligence with whom communication is possible." In this world, linear time does not exist and measurement and the laws of physics do not apply. Thought is action, and reality is composed of "deepest desires and most frantic fears." In many respects Monroe might be describing the world of dreams and he does suspect, he says, that many, perhaps all, humans visit Locale II at some time during sleep. On occasion he seems to be uncertain whether a particular experience was a dream rather than an exploration out-of-body, and sometimes he finds it difficult to distinguish between the two.

In later years, when Monroe describes the experiences of himself and others in *Far Journeys* (1985), the line between the dream and the out-of-body experience becomes much clearer. At this early stage, before he, with others, had developed the technology that enabled such a distinction to be made, he tends to gloss over the problem. But whatever the definition of the experience in Locale II may be, he is able to reach certain conclusions. His first visits to Locale II brought out various repressed emotional patterns, of which fear was dominant. In order to cope in this Locale these emotional patterns had to be controlled. He deduced that in that area nearest to the physical world are beings who are insane, or nearly so, drugged, "alive but asleep," or physically dead but still dominated by the need for sexual release. In another part of Locale II Monroe found a park with lawns, trees, flower-beds, paths, and benches, where those who had recently died were resting and waiting to be taken on the next stage of their journey.[1] Elsewhere he came across cities, armies, scenes of activity of different kinds but without any context—such as you might find idly flicking through television channels, pausing for a few seconds and then moving on. At times on these journeys helpers appeared to him, who seemed to understand what he needed but whom he could not identify. He also reports periodic visitations by a mysterious authority figure, at whose passing everything comes to a standstill and each living thing lies down in an attitude of submission. As this figure proceeds, "there is a roaring musical sound and a feeling of radiant, irresistible living force of ultimate power that peaks overhead and fades in the distance." Monroe adds, "I remember wondering once what would happen to me if He discovered my presence, as a temporary visitor. I wasn't sure I wanted to find out."

One particular problem, which he described as "a tricky matter" that disturbed Monroe in the earlier days of his OBEs, had to do with sexuality. Almost all of his experiences at the time took place when he was in bed with his wife Mary. On one occasion in his out-of-body state he tried to awake her to make love—but fortunately for her peace of mind she did not respond. His desire kept recurring and he began to feel disgusted with himself for being unable to shut it off. He found a solution when a recollection of what was known as the "Gene Autry love scene," familiar to adherents of the popular Western films of the time, came into his mind. After the cowboy hero had saved the girl from the villains, they would wander across to the corral fence, gaze into each other's eyes, and, just as the audience expected the couple to join in a long and loving kiss, Gene would pull out his guitar and say, "First I want to sing you a little song," which was usually about horses. After the song the kiss never took place because the picture ended. For Monroe this proved a model—delay rather than deny. It worked.

However, Monroe certainly found that sexuality was sometimes present in the out-of-body state. He describes its fulfillment as "not an act at all but an immobile, rigid state of shock where the two truly intermingle . . . in full dimension, atom for atom." It is, he adds, as if there takes place a short, sustained electric or electronic flow from one to another. "The moment reaches unbearable ecstasy, and then tranquility, equalization, and it is over." Both participants are out-of-body when this occurs. Monroe, who was in some respects very much the old-fashioned Southern gentleman, did not pursue the topic into further detail, declaring that most of the material in his notes was "too personal" for him to relate.

The experiences that were of special importance to Monroe were those when he appeared to find himself at the farthest distance from the everyday world. There were three occasions in September 1960 when he reports being penetrated by what he describes as an "intelligence force" to which he feels he is inextricably bound by loyalty—that he always had been so bound, and that he had "a job to perform here on earth." This intelligence force was far beyond his understanding; it was cold and impersonal, unemotional and omnipotent. "This may be the omnipotence we call God," he says. Then on awakening in the early morning he found himself crying, "great deep sobs as I have never cried before." He continues: "I knew without any qualification or future hope of change that the God of my childhood, of the churches, of religion throughout the world was not as we worshiped him to be—that for the rest of my life, I would 'suffer' the loss of this illusion."

Yet there were contrasting experiences also in those earlier days. On three occasions in the out-of-body state Monroe found "a place of pure peace, yet exquisite emotion," that he equated with Heaven or Nirvana. This was a place where ultimately you belong, where there is music, beauty, and love, where you are in perfect balance with others—in short, where you are Home. From here he was reluctant to return, feeling lonely, nostalgic, and even homesick when he reentered the physical world. Both the intelligence force and Home reappear in Monroe's later experiences, yet at the time he described them he would have had no idea of how things would develop.

While Locale II has certain similarities to the dream state, Monroe's Locale III, which he came across early in his explorations, is quite different. He describes a series of experiences that took place between May 1958 and February 1959 that introduced him to this "alternative world," altogether unlike anything he met with in Locale II and quite closely related in many respects to Locale I and the everyday physical world of his waking hours. In analyzing the nature of his experiences, Monroe records that only 8.9 percent of his journeys took him into Locale III, compared with 59.5 percent in Locale II and just over 31 percent in Locale I.

Monroe discovered Locale III quite involuntarily. One afternoon in May 1958 he sensed the vibrations that seemed to preface an out-of-body excursion, but found himself unable to lift out of the physical. He rotated his Second Body through 180 degrees and became aware of an endless wall with a hole that appeared to be the shape of his physical body. The hole also appeared to be endless so that he felt he was looking into the blackness of infinite space. He moved into the hole but found nothing but this blackness. Disturbed, he withdrew, returned to his physical body, and sat up. Checking the time, he found he had been "out" for over an hour although it felt as though only a very few minutes had elapsed.

In the following weeks Monroe explored the hole further. Reaching through it, he felt his hand taken in a friendly clasp by what seemed like a warm human hand. On one occasion he was given a card with an address on it; on another it was a hook, not a hand, that he encountered. Once when he put both his hands into the hole they were grasped by two other hands and a female voice called his name: "Bob! Bob!" He resolved to explore further, traveled right through the hole, and found himself in a landscape with a building nearby that resembled a barn and near it a tower about ten feet tall. He ascended the tower, jumped off, and instead of finding himself flying, as he felt would happen, simply fell to the ground. Exploring further, he saw a man and a woman sitting by the building. The woman seemed to know he was there but did not communicate.

Further experiments in visiting Locale III enabled Monroe to produce a coherent picture of what he took to be "a physical-matter world almost identical to our own." He observed "trees, houses, cities, people, artifacts . . . homes, families, businesses . . . roads, rail-roads and trains." Yet this world in many respects was very different from the world in which we live. There was no electricity, no internal combustion, gasoline, or oil. The locomotives were steam-driven but the steam, so he understood, was created by some form of radiation. He could not make out how the motive power for the large, slow-moving automobiles was provided, but noted that they lacked tires and were steered by a single horizontal bar.

At first the people in Locale III were unaware of Monroe's existence. But then, quite without intention, he found himself on these visits merging with a person living in this different universe. This was a rather lonely architect-contractor who lived in a rooming house, worked in a city that he did not know well, had few friends, and traveled to work by bus—a wide vehicle seating eight abreast with the seats rising in tiers behind the driver. No fares were charged, as Monroe discovered when once he tried to pay. In these experiences Monroe took on this man's activities, memories, and emotional patterns, although all the time he was aware that he was not him.

In subsequent visits, Monroe (or "I There," as he describes himself in this other life) met a wealthy woman called Lea, mother of two young children, whom he made friends with. She was a sad and withdrawn person who had recently suffered some tragedy, although he never knew the details. Eventually Monroe "I There" and Lea married and moved into a large house, where he had a workroom. On occasions he found himself in awkward circumstances, usually when he was ignorant of something he ought to have known. To escape from embarrassing Lea or himself, and to avoid suspicion (presumably of "I There" being thought to be insane) he would move back immediately to his own physical body, allowing Lea's "real husband" to return.

When he was resident in his physical body, Monroe had no way of telling what was going on in his life in Locale III. There were times when he moved in to Locale III at a difficult moment, as on one occasion when Lea and the children were riding in a self-propelled vehicle on a mountain road. He took over the driving but, unaccustomed to the vehicle, he rolled it off the road into a pile of dirt. On a later visit he found that Lea and "I There" had separated. He was greatly saddened and strongly desired to visit her. She gave him her new address, but he lost or forgot it. On the last visit he describes, he found "I There" lonely and unhappy, searching for Lea and the children but failing to find them.

This life as "I There" was not an enviable one—not a life Monroe would in any sense have chosen to live. Among the many questions his narrative raises is what happened to the "I" of the architect-contractor when Monroe took him over. Did these intrusions cause him embarrassment or distress? Did he perhaps think he was subject to moments of forgetfulness, or even insanity? How was it that no one seems to have called him by his name? Another interesting point is that Locale III, which Monroe describes in much detail, does not appear to fit into any period of the Earth's history and in no way does it seem to be attached to Locale II. In trying to establish its reality, Monroe wonders if it might be "a memory, racial or otherwise, of a physical earth civilization that predates known history." Other possibilities he mentions are "another earth-type world located in another part of the universe which is somehow accessible through mental manipulation," or "an antimatter duplicate of this physical earth-world where we are the same but different, bonded together unit for unit by a force beyond our present comprehension."

Strange though it may seem, however, Monroe's experience of an "I There" is not unique. Professor J. H. M. Whiteman, a mathematics professor at Cape Town University and author of *The Meaning of Life: An Introduction to Scientific Mysticism* (1986), suggested the term *mediate identification* to define a situation "in which one finds oneself in a tangibly real three-dimensional scene, with a human form and disposition quite unlike what other people would take us to be physically, and with memories appropriate to the situation in which one finds oneself." Whiteman claimed to have experienced between sixty and seventy such instances himself, when he moved into what he calls "secondary separation," which seems to be no different from an out-of-body state. To give just one example: he found himself as the recently married wife of a captain of a ship, sailing on a kind of delayed honeymoon trip and feeling extremely contented. Then as he joined the company for breakfast at the captain's table, he—the wife—became disturbed by the facial expression of a man sitting at the table who seemed to be resentful of the presence of a woman on board but at the same time to be personally interested. Shaken by this, he returned to his physical body.

In his analysis of this and other comparable experiences, Whiteman distinguishes four different kinds of entry into another person's life: physical (entering the life of a person in today's world); nonphysical (entering the life of someone not physically alive); fictional (entering a fictional scene, as if in a novel or play); and retrocognitively (entering a scene in a nonphysical world based on individuals' or cosmic memories but so effective as to appear to be a "present living reality"). In Monroe's books instances of all of these occurrences may be found.

However, whereas Whiteman's experiences appear to be singular in that he does not visit a particular location more than once, Monroe's are repeated. Once he is through the hole, the world he inhabits is consistent no matter how often he visits, and the life story he leads there is continuous and coherent. His experiences can be contrasted with those of two instances of other individuals who have reported dual lives. One of them, a female social worker, for several months would lie down in the evenings after work and find herself living a parallel life as a male medical student residing in a strange town and traveling each day to lectures and classes, returning in the evening to continue studying or occasionally going out to try to develop a social life. The other, a teacher's wife, would withdraw for hours or sometimes days at a time to live a contrasting life of excitement and challenge with a wealthy gangster somewhere in Europe. Both these women, like Monroe and Whiteman, were able to induce out-of-body experiences to continue with their alternative lives.

Monroe's experiences in Locale III seem to have ended after 1960. He gives no sign of wanting to continue with them; it is as if that particular chapter was closed and the story, as far as it went, was over. Yet in the light of theories and ideas about the existence of parallel universes—see, for example, physicist Fred Alan Wolf's *Parallel Universes*—Monroe's documentation of Locale III may in time come to have a relevance he could never have imagined.[2]

Not all of Monroe's out-of-body journeys fitted neatly into one of the three Locales. He quotes a few instances of what appear to be precognition, some of which turned out to be accurate. One included a description of the interior of a house where, years later, he and his wife came to live. There were also disconnected scenes of happenings—some in recognizable environments and some not—in which he played a part. These might be interpreted as snapshots of past-life experiences, although he does not define them as such. Often he was glad to return to his physical body after such experiences, most of which did not fit into any recognizable context.

In the closing chapters of *Journeys Out of the Body* Monroe provides advice and instructions for those who wish to experiment for themselves. He is convinced that most individuals, if not all, leave their physical bodies during sleep, although what he calls the "conscious, willful practice of separation from the physical" is not in accordance with a natural sleep pattern. He warns his readers that once they have opened the doorway to this experience it cannot be closed, and that what they will discover will be "quite incompatible with the science, religion and mores of the society in which we live." Nevertheless "something extremely vital" will be missed if this exploration does not take place.

Fear, Monroe maintains, is the only major barrier to out-of-body exploration. There are several reasons for this. Separating from the physical body is what is usually expected to occur at death. Hence, it is natural to feel the necessity of getting back into the body lest you die before you can reenter it. Associated with this is the fear that you may not be able to return to the physical; that once out you may never get back in and will be fated to roam around in the unknown for all eternity.[3] There is also the fear of the unknown itself; nothing that you have learned or experienced in ordinary life will help you find your way in this totally different environment where the rules do not apply and the map does not exist. Lastly, there is the fear of the effects of the experience on the physical body and the conscious mind. Is there something wrong with you? Are you going mad? It was some time before Monroe came across anyone else—a "normal" person— who had experienced out of-body travel. When eventually he did so he was greatly relieved.[4]

After October 1962 the frequency of Monroe's out-of-body excursions diminished. He felt that this was because he was more involved with material affairs and also with evaluating the experiences of the previous four years. He found that the vibrations that in earlier years preceded separation from the physical ceased to occur. He was no longer troubled by fear in the journeys he undertook to Locales I and II. Then, towards the end of the period, he began experimenting with the process under observation in laboratory conditions. Reflecting on his experiences to date, he recorded two conclusions. First, while in the Second Body it was possible "to create a physical effect on a physically living human entity while the latter is awake." Second, "there are unfolding areas of knowledge and concepts completely beyond the comprehension of the conscious mind of this experimenter."

Despite this second conclusion, Monroe presents a statistical analysis of the 589 out-of-body experiences he recorded over the twelve years between his first OBE and the completion of the text of his book. Here he is striving to organize the material he has recorded in his notes, to fit it into categories, to provide evidence, and to make it scientifically acceptable. He also describes a couple of unusual incidents that happened in his childhood and youth and speculates as to whether dental work he had undergone, anesthesia and other inhalants, and the use of the auto-hypnotic tapes he created to experiment with sleep-learning might have been relevant to instigating his first out-of-body experiences. He details the physical symptoms—the feeling of constriction, the vibrations, the awareness of a kind of hissing sound—that in the early days prefigured an out-of-body episode, but which became less obvious and eventually ceased as the episodes continued.

Monroe also seeks to distinguish the Second State from dreaming, declaring that in dreaming "consciousness as the term is understood is not operative," while in the Second State "recognition of 'I am' consciousness is present." However, this distinction does not hold up in the light of subsequent work on lucid dreaming, which purports to show that the lucid dreamer is aware that he is dreaming and is able to exert conscious control of the dream. This leaves the question open as to whether at least some of Monroe's Locale II experiences might have been lucid dreams. He does himself go so far as to say that if any experience did not contain a majority of the conditions he lists as defining a Second State category, then he would consider it as a dream.

Monroe's own ideas and beliefs during the second half of his life were strongly influenced by his out-of-body experiences. Perhaps the most significant of these influences is his acceptance of some kind of immortality. While he does not propose that everyone who dies automatically moves into Locale II, or that one's afterlife presence in Locale II continues forever, he is convinced that this is the destination of most of us after our physical death. Although Locale II is not centered on the Earth, he suggests that there is some form of contact with our physical world that provides a means of entry. It is through this portal that we proceed after we die.

This belief in some form of afterlife derived from a series of encounters that he describes in a chapter he entitles "Post Mortem." The first was with his close friend Dr. Richard Gordon. He had been lunching with him in the spring of 1961 and noticed that Gordon was looking ill. Gordon admitted he was feeling below par but said that he was about to leave with his wife on a European holiday and would seek advice when he returned. Six weeks later Mrs. Gordon called Monroe to say that the doctor had been taken sick and they had returned home. Soon afterwards he was diagnosed with abdominal cancer. Monroe wanted to see him but was told he was too ill and under deep sedation. His wife suggested that he write to him and she would read him the letter when he was conscious.

In this letter Monroe outlined his own out-of-body experience and suggested that Dr. Gordon might accept the possibility that he could "act, think and exist without the restriction of a physical body," and that while he was in the hospital he might consider the implications of this and see if he himself could develop this ability. Some weeks later, Dr. Gordon died. Monroe waited for several months and then decided to try to contact his friend, despite the possibility that the experiment might be dangerous. He moved himself into the out-of-body state with the intention of somehow finding Dr. Gordon. He felt he was being guided into a room where three or four men were listening to a younger man with a big shock of hair who was excitedly relating something to them. A voice said, "The doctor will see you in a minute." Monroe began to feel uncomfortably warm and decided he could not wait. Then the young man stopped talking and turned to look intently at him before continuing his discussion.

Monroe moved away and returned to the "in-body" state, feeling he had failed. The following week he decided to try again and was surprised to hear a voice saying, "Why do you want to see him again? You saw him last Saturday." On checking the notes he had made on his earlier attempt, he realized that the man who had looked intently at him was indeed Dr. Gordon in his early twenties, a realization that was confirmed when he later saw an old photograph of Gordon at the age of twenty-two, and when Mrs. Gordon said that when she had first met her husband he often talked excitedly and was proud of his big shock of hair.

In this same chapter Monroe relates two further encounters with individuals who were physically dead, concluding with an episode with his father, who died in 1963 at the age of eighty following a stroke that left him paralyzed and deprived of speech. Months later Monroe woke up about 3 A.M. and felt he should try to visit his father. He found him in a room in what might have been a hospital or convalescent home. His father, now a younger man, turned to him, seized him under his arms, and swung him over his head, just as he used to do when Monroe was a child. Then he moved away, as if he had forgotten his son was there. Monroe left the room and soon returned to his physical body.

These and similar experiences led Monroe to the conclusion the Second Body—or whatever it is that can leave the physical body and return again—can survive "what we call death" and that personality and character "continue to exist in the new-old form." His three visits to the "place or state of being" that he called Home, "where you truly belong," relieved him from any fear of what might happen after the cessation of physical life. He adds also that he was aware in many of his OBEs of someone or something who helped, but whoever or whatever his helpers were he could not tell. Subsequent experiences, as detailed in his later books, illuminate these discoveries, but the light comes in from a rather different angle.

Having worked with Monroe and others and examined a large number of accounts and reports from a variety of sources, Professor Charles Tart emphasizes the significance of the out-of-body experience, pointing out that "because of the immense effect on the individual's belief system—namely, convincing him that he will survive death—the OBE is one of the most important psychological experiences, even though it occurs rarely." He continues: " I am convinced that most of our great religious traditions are based on this sort of experience. We will not be able to understand our religious heritage or our philosophies of life until we come to an understanding of OBEs. OBEs are one of the world's most important and most neglected phenomena. Even psychic researchers generally do not pay attention to them. But their importance in understanding man cannot be overestimated."5

Commenting on *Journeys Out of the Body,* Joseph Chilton Pearce wrote that "Robert Monroe made the most systematic and intelligent exploration and reportage of this state ever recorded (so far as I know)." He added that Monroe has "an exceedingly strong, active, well-developed system of imagery transference. He had the capacity to transfer imagery over a wide spectrum, which means the capacity to perceive where ordinary, weak perceptual systems cannot. Monroe could enter a field of experience alien to our ordinary one because he has a strong and flexible imagination, images capable of transferring alien imagery into meaningful perception . . . I am sure that some of his reportage was only an approximation of what the states might have been to someone within those states. And he came across situations where no approximation of any sort was possible, where there were insufficient points of correspondence to make any transfer."[6]

By 1976 Monroe had received more than 15,000 letters from readers of *Journeys Out of the Body* describing their own out-of-body experiences, with most of them adding how relieved they were not to be psychotic. In his foreword to the 1977 edition, Monroe says that having reviewed the text he was content that nothing had to be altered in the light of later experience. "From the point of my exper-imental level at that time," he adds, "it is still accurate." But his own subsequent experiences and the experiences of others that he records in detail in *Far Journeys* (1985) open more perspectives on the nature of the out-of-body experience. In one quite important respect, his preoccupation with the physical reality of the Second Body has almost vanished and his understanding of the nature of consciousness has deepened considerably. Nevertheless, *Journeys Out of the Body* remains a classic in its field and has both comforted and inspired countless numbers of readers who have endured experiences, some-times disturbing or frightening, that without Monroe's help they could in no way understand.

Some copies of *Journeys Out of the Body* seem to have acquired a life of their own. People have reported finding it on the floor of the bookstore, or falling off a high shelf and hitting them on the head. One purchaser discovered it lurking in the cookery section and more than one came across it under "Travel." In an interview in 1982,

Monroe remarked that the book's publication gave him the opportunity to meet very many new people, which he found rewarding in itself. It also gave him the chance to come, as he said, "out of the closet, instead of being a closeted, out-of-body hidden-away person." He continued: "It was funny the way I began to be looked upon . . . people would stare and look at me and say 'Is that who he is? That's the person who goes out of his body?' Or these strange looks, like 'He's a weirdo' or freak or something.' But it was a lot of fun to see this change. And, of course, one of the most rewarding things that has taken place is the mail—the mail of people from all over the world . . . and the most important were the ones that said 'Thank God, I know I'm sane!'"

In the same interview Monroe commented on the immense changes that had taken place in public attitudes over the last ten years or so. "Now it's OK to talk about out-of-body experiences as a reality. And from that point of view, we participated in the presentation last year of three papers before the American Psychiatric Association on out-of-body experiences, which ten years ago would have been unheard of. It was beyond my wildest imagination that the APA would seriously listen to a phenomenon known as the out-of-body experience."[7]

Notes

1. Monroe revisited these two areas several years later, as recorded in his other two books. They also appear as Focus 22 and Focus 27 in the *Lifeline* program.

2. In his book, subtitled *The Search for Other Worlds* (Simon & Schuster, 1988), Wolf says that his reasoning leads him to the following conclusions: (1) there is an infinite number of parallel

universes; (2) quantum waves carry information moving from past to present and from future to present; (3) we should be able to "talk" to the future as clearly as we "talk" to the past; (4) existence as we know it is a subset of reality that is unknowable. Think on!

3. Many times Monroe was questioned about this particular fear. His reply was always the same: "No need to worry about that. Your bladder always calls you back!"

4. Monroe visited Professor J. B. Rhine, well known for his work on extrasensory perception, to see if he could advise him with regard to his OBEs. Rhine was not helpful, but as he was leaving a young intern, who had been sitting in on the discussion, came up to him and said, "Don't worry, Mr. Monroe. I do it too."

5. *Psychic Exploration,* edited by J. White (Putnam, 1974).

6. *From Magical Child to Magical Teen,* by Joseph Chilton Pearce (Park Street Press, 2003 [1985]).

7. A fully referenced study of the out-of-body experience, by Carlos Alvorado, may be found in the American Psychological Association's (APA) publication *Varieties of Anomalous Experience* (APA, 2000). The final sentence reads: "It is my hope that this chapter will inspire further research and that future discussions on OBEs will not have to be conducted solely in the context of a psychology of the exotic or the unusual, but in the wider context of the study of the totality of human experience." Such further research, particularly in the field of consciousness studies, is taking place. Professor Charles Tart proposes a definition of the OBE as "an altered state of consciousness in which the subject feels that his mind or self-awareness is separated from his

physical body and this self-awareness has a vivid and real sense about it, quite different from a dream." Physicist Amit Goswami suggests that "the nonlocality of our consciousness" is the key to the understanding of the OBE.

Author's Note: As a point of interest, if you asked Monroe to sign a copy of *Journeys Out of the Body,* instead of a "standard" message, he would often inscribe an equation. Here is an example:

$$\frac{6N + L\,(R^2 + 5)}{T + 2P} = STC$$

Each one is unique. As far as I know, none has ever been solved or explained.

CHAPTER 4

The Whistlefield Years

The year 1971 marked a major turning point in the journey of Bob Monroe. Now deeply in love with his elegant Southern lady, he aimed to acquire a Southern home that Nancy would be proud of. He sold the apartment blocks and bought a country estate of 430 acres, most of it forest and pasture, at Whistlefield, some twenty-five miles from Charlottesville. With six bedrooms and five bathrooms the house, together with a studio house used by Bob as an office, could comfortably accommodate all of the Monroes' extended family. In February of that year Bob and Nancy were married, the civil ceremony followed by a spiritual blessing by Father Michael, a Catholic priest with whom Bob was friendly. The same year saw the publication of *Journeys Out of the Body*. All this he later described as repatterning his entire way of life.

Shortly after the book appeared, Monroe was invited to give a presentation at the Menninger Foundation Conference in Council Grove, Kansas. This was an annual event organized by Elmer and Alyce Green, the founders of Biofeedback. Attendance at these conferences was limited to ninety-six individuals, all invited by the Greens and all involved in investigating aspects of altered states of consciousness. This was probably the first time that the CEO of a flourishing television cable company had taken part in such a gathering. Monroe described his out-of-body experiences and the problems that arose with the various professionals he consulted while he tried to reach an understanding of what was happening to him. In the audience was a psychologist, Dr. Fowler Jones, assistant professor of psychology at the University of Kansas Medical Center, whose interest was immediately aroused. He was impressed by Monroe, who seemed to him to be a down-to-earth sort of person whose accounts of his experiences sounded entirely credible. It was essential, he considered, to do whatever possible to validate Monroe's out-of-body skills and also to inform the professional world that the out-of-body experience was a distinct psychological state and should not be dismissed as merely a hallucination.

To further this, Fowler Jones attracted the interest of a psychoanalyst, Dr. Stuart Twemlow, chief of Research Services at Topeka Veterans Administration Medical Center. Together with another analyst, Dr. Glen Gabbard, they organized a questionnaire study. Some 1,500 individuals responded to an item in a national periodical asking for letters from anyone who thought they might have had an out-of-body experience. Almost half of the respondents claimed to recall occasions when they felt that their consciousness was separated from their physical body. Questionnaires were issued to all of these and 420 valid forms were received in return. Of these, 339 reported out-of-body experiences, detailing the preexisting conditions, the nature of the experience, its impact, and its after-effects, while the remainder were interested in learning more although they had not had such experiences themselves. The results of this questionnaire led to the publication of several papers in leading psychiatric journals.[1] A few years later the authors gave a presentation at the APA's annual meeting in San Francisco. They were scheduled to speak early on the last morning of the conference and were dismayed to find that the room they would be using was vast. Anticipating an audience of twenty-five at most, they were amazed to be confronted by a full house, mostly supportive of their work. Fowler Jones continued to keep in contact with Monroe and eventually became a part-time trainer at the Institute and a member of the advisory board.[2]

Once the Monroes were settled in their new home, Bob would occasionally drive out for a meal at the Howard Johnson on Skyline Drive, a few miles away. One evening he had a word with a young kitchen worker, George Durrette, who lived with his wife, child, and father-in-law on land adjoining Whistlefield. Something about George appealed to Monroe, and he invited him to come over to his house the next Saturday. "That's the day I drink a lot of iced tea and maybe you'd want a glass of it," he said. This was the sort of invitation that George, very much a down-to-earth character, was willing to accept.

That Saturday, after an hour or so of random conversation, Monroe changed the subject, broaching the idea that he needed someone to look after some of his land. George made no comment, but he did agree to bring his family over the following weekend. During that visit, Monroe asked him formally if he would come and work for him. "I don't know about that," said George. "I just met you and you just met me." Monroe smiled. "That's a good way to meet somebody," he said.

On his next visit to the restaurant Monroe encouraged George to fix his hamburger the way he liked it, rare with sautéed onions, together with a glass of sweet milk. He asked him back to Whistlefield the next weekend, this time to accompany him to an auction some twenty miles out of Richmond where he persuaded George to act as the third bidder to fight off a competitor for a lot that he wanted. The ploy worked and they drove back with a truckload. "He called 'em goodies," George recalled, "but in my mind it was all just junk." This auction visit was repeated almost every month.

George agreed to work part time for Monroe, usually going over to Whistlefield between two and five every afternoon but occasionally responding to emergencies out of hours, such as when Monroe called him at one in the morning to change a tire on his Cadillac, punctured when he and his step-daughter Scooter were returning from a concert. Then one day Monroe told him that he really wanted him to work full time. He drove him around the area, pointing out some of his various business enterprises and explaining how he had designed the television cable network in Charlottesville. As they passed Cavalier Court he turned to George. "By the way," he said, "I have something for you to do today." George looked at him inquiringly. "I've got a hundred sofas to get rid of. I need you to carry them out to Whistlefield and stack them up in an outhouse there. Then I want you to go out and find someone to buy them." George asked no questions. "OK," was his only response. Within a couple of days he had moved the sofas and found the owner of a used furniture store, who drove out, inspected the sofas, and said he'd take them all.

So began George's full-time employment with Robert Monroe. Thenceforth whatever there was to do at Whistlefield—build fences, raise calves, keep an eye on young A. J., transport equipment, attend auctions, repair this, dispose of that—George did it. He soon became an essential part of the Whistlefield establishment and a friend and companion to Monroe for the next thirty-four years.

Life at Whistlefield was both stylish and fun. The house and grounds were modeled on the notion of an English country estate— an impressive house on a hillside, approached by a long driveway, extensive grounds with houses intended for the farm manager and greenhouse manager, two lakes, large greenhouses, barns and stables, with children of various ages running about, and several horses, dogs, and cats, all presided over by a mildly eccentric lord of the manor, usually dressed in a shabby tweed jacket and with a more than mildly eccentric hobby, together with a gracious lady who was patient, hospitable, and a wonderful hostess. Of the many well-proportioned rooms, the family's favorite was the den, formally known as the Quail Room on account of the pictures of hunting and quail scenes on the paneled walls. This was the most comfortable room in the house, with bookshelves, a fireplace, the television set, and several large, overstuffed chairs. Here the family spent most of their time together, all of them making the effort to be at home, if possible, for Thanksgiving. Outside scattered around the estate were seven cars and trucks in various states of disrepair. As Monroe remarked to his nephew Robert, he would trade them all for one that worked. The eccentricity was also manifested inside, with an organ installed in Monroe's office and one room displaying a collection of Monroe tartans.

There were now six children in Bob's new family. Maria and Laurie, in their early twenties, were completing their university studies and visited the farm during vacations, enjoying riding the horses and painting fences. Following graduation the two settled in Richmond, where Maria embarked on a career in real estate, while Laurie became a horse trainer and a teacher of riding to some 150 students a week. They both visited Whistlefield whenever they could. Looking back, Maria described her times there as idyllic and life-changing, recalling her talks with Bob on the possibilities of human potential and, in contrast, sharing with Nancy her interest in interior design. Meantime, Penny was "being a hippy in Charlottesville," as she described it, moving on to become a bartender for a while. She called in at Whistlefield occasionally, especially when she heard that interesting visitors were to be staying for dinner. Monroe appreciated her sense of humor, at one time suggesting she might become a stand-up comedienne or a broadcaster on late-night radio. Scooter was at college, returning to the farm for vacations and, after the research laboratory was built, spending time there listening to the new sound frequencies that Monroe was experimenting with and discussing the effects these sounds had upon her. He appreciated her quickness of thought and adaptability, while she came to regard her stepfather as both friend and mentor.

While Penny, Scooter, and Cindy had grown up "in the Marine Corps," with plenty of love but not much money, A. J., who was nine years old at the time of the move, had a very different upbringing. He greatly enjoyed his childhood on the farm, especially being able to drive the lawn mower over the acres of grass. He had plenty of freedom, and Monroe, perhaps sometimes relieved to have a boy to talk to among so many girls, provided him, as A. J. recalls, with sound advice, intellectual stimulation, and an initial education in the study of consciousness. However, Monroe did not always find it easy to fill the paternal role for the third of Nancy's strong-minded daughters. Cindy, now a teenager, he found especially challenging. She did not fit smoothly into the totally different life into which she was pitched and sometimes, despite her affection for him, she found herself at odds with her stepfather over issues such as boyfriends and experimentation with drugs. His attempts to lay down the law were not always kindly received.

The move to Whistlefield, along with the love, support, and confidence deriving from his marriage to Nancy, enabled Bob to make a major step forward in his investigation into the out-of-body experience. During the series of experiments that he had conducted on the possibility of sleep-learning, he had come up with the idea that a radio network could act as a nighttime teacher by broadcasting material, such as advanced multiplication tables, with a backing of soft musical sounds. With the radio on, the listener would absorb the material while asleep and hopefully be able to recall it next day. That was the theory, and he was now inspired to return to this idea and see if it could be adapted to more interesting purposes—perhaps even to creating the circumstances in which an out-of-body experience might occur. Then he realized that a radio network would not be necessary.

The sounds could be recorded on tape and played to the listener through headphones, as he had previously tried with Laurie as one of the subjects. Taking the idea further, if sound could send you to sleep it followed that sound could alter your state of consciousness. Now he intended that the process would be carried out in as scientific a way as possible.

The interest shown earlier by Charles Tart had inspired Monroe to create a simple laboratory in the basement of his office building in Charlottesville. The move to Whistlefield provided the opportunity for him to construct a larger and far better-equipped research facility, using materials from his modular housing project that was shortly to be closed down. This laboratory incorporated a control room, a debriefing room, and three isolation chambers, one with electromagnetic shielding to protect against interference during experiments. Another room in which five people wearing headphones could listen simultaneously was also added. Using more of the modular materials he built a guest house—the Owl House—where participants in the experimental work in what he named the Whistlefield Research Laboratories could stay overnight. All that was now needed was help from scientifically trained individuals who would sort out the technical problems and work with him to further his investigations.

One of the first of these individuals to appear was Jim Beal, a researcher into electromagnetic field effects on living systems. Monroe invited him to visit and give a presentation on his work. Jim was impressed by the extraordinary beauty of the place. Close to the entrance was the laboratory building with the Owl House nearby. The drive was lined with white board fences: on the left was a green meadow with horses grazing and a red barn beyond. In a valley to the right was a lake with a dock and canoe. The spacious single-story white-painted house nestled on a hillside with a large garden close by where tomatoes were cultivated. To his surprise, the first item Jim noticed as he entered the house was a framed genealogy of the Beale family. Beale was a family name of Nancy's and this was also the middle name of her youngest daughter Lucinda. Although Jim's specialty was not immediately relevant to Monroe's research, his visit was the beginning of an enduring friendship.

Among the earlier readers of *Journeys Out of the Body* was a twenty-six-year-old physics graduate, Tom Campbell. He was working in a government organization in Charlottesville with some five hundred employees. His particular task was to apply classical physics and mathematics to electromechanical and electromagnetic systems. One day an electrical/electronics engineer, Bill Yost, who was in charge of Campbell's department, tossed a copy of Monroe's book towards him and told him to read it. Having done so, Campbell found himself both intrigued and nonplussed. Was it for real? Or just a wild concept intended to deceive the gullible? He said as much to Yost, who admitted he felt likewise.[3]

A few weeks later Yost told Campbell that a group from work had arranged to visit Monroe. Campbell agreed to join them and that Friday evening a party of twelve in three cars drove the twenty-five miles to Whistlefield. As they approached the house they were greeted by the canine establishment, two large Dalmatians and a German Shepherd. For some minutes everyone stood around wondering what to do until the heavy white-painted door swung open. All were silent, expectant. "The one, the only, the Amazing Out-Of-Body-Man was about to turn to flesh and blood before our eyes," Campbell wrote later. "We would all soon know if this guy was nuts, or what." He went on to describe what followed.

> Out stepped Mr. Monroe into the doorway. For a second or two he seemed the slightest bit tentative—like a man who clearly knew he was about to be examined and evaluated like a captive alien or a strange animal at the zoo. He gazed out at the crowd of nameless

heads staring silently back at him. After the briefest of pauses, he stepped onto the elegant open stone porch with confidence and a solid presence. He was not wearing a white suit with matching hat and string tie like Col. Sanders (the only Southern gentleman I could bring to mind). Instead he looked comfortable, informal and friendly—more like the dogs than the house.

Monroe greeted the group individually, making jokes and quips as he shook hands. He reminded Campbell of Santa Claus, "a jolly old elf, passing the summer sipping mint juleps on the veranda of his country estate." As conversation developed, Campbell became impressed by Monroe's genuine interest in science and his rational approach, and deduced that what he was after was legitimacy rather than financial reward or public recognition. He found him "more straightforward and intellectually precise—less emotionally driven—than most of the technical professionals who were now pelting him with questions."

The group was taken to see the laboratory, at the time still unfinished. There Monroe issued his challenge. He was seeking, he told them, some professionally qualified hard-core science and engineering types who could help him do proper research that would be acceptable to other scientists. Campbell, who had a keen interest in altered states of consciousness and also meditated regularly, was first to volunteer, followed by a young electrical engineer, Dennis Mennerich. Monroe waited, but no other hands were raised. He invited his two new associates to call him in a few days' time.

Some three weeks later the two young scientists drove over to Whistlefield on Campbell's powerful Honda motorcycle. They arranged with Monroe that they would visit the laboratory two or three times a week and occasionally on weekends. Their first task was to complete the connections between the control room and the isolation chambers and to install various measurement devices. Included in the equipment that Monroe and his new team installed were an EEG setup for recording the electrical impulses produced by the brain, a professional standard audio mixer, electrostatic sensing equipment, an especially sensitive high input-impedance voltmeter (provided by Bill Yost), and a device for tracking galvanic skin response (measuring the voltage passing through the body) that Campbell and Mennerich themselves designed. Once all this was in place and operational, the investigation into the effects of sound on altered states of consciousness could begin.[4]

In intervals between the work on equipping and perfecting the research facility, Monroe took time to train his two associates in exploring nonphysical states by linking them up to his audio equipment and leading them into deep relaxation, guiding them to release their minds from their physical bodies and from the surrounding environment. He was particularly interested in the sleep state, as many of the reported OBEs, including his own, occurred when the subject was physically asleep. A small group of local volunteers, including a few doctors, social workers, friends, and family members, would call in after dinner to help in the research, but by the time they were wired up to the equipment with all the electrodes in place Monroe found them either too tired or too restless to be able to stay awake and sufficiently alert to report on their responses. A method was needed to enable them to stay awake and then move into a borderland sleep state—the hypnagogic state as it is known. As we shall see, the method that proved effective involved the use of sound.

All this took, as Monroe says, hundreds of hours of experiment. Many of the volunteer participants were able to report verbally on any changes in their mental or physical condition, finding that they could speak and perceive when the normal pattern would be to lose consciousness or fall asleep. Out of this research emerged a point of identification that was given a label that carried no connotations:

Focus 10. This was a state defined as "mind awake, body asleep." While the physiological responses are those of sleep, the brainwave patterns are different, showing a mix of waves ordinarily associated with sleep, light and deep, with overlying beta signals indicating wakefulness.

On occasion Bill Yost joined the research team, although he was not concerned with taking part in consciousness exploration himself. He was about the same age as Monroe; Campbell regarded him as "a very bright man searching for truth wherever he could find it . . . curious, professionally sharp and open-minded." He saw himself as the support person in the investigations and experiments that Bob and his younger associates were undertaking. In a way Bill Yost acted as the elder statesman, observing, advising, and, as an experienced technical professional, legitimizing Monroe and his research. This was exactly what was required. Monroe greatly needed this kind of support from one of his peers whose opinion he respected, support that his much younger associates were unable to provide. Above all, he wanted to be taken seriously by credentialed scientists and technical experts, and Bill took him, and what he was doing, very seriously indeed.

While Monroe and his small group of scientists tucked away in their corner of rural Virginia worked quietly away, elsewhere in the United States, and especially in California, the late twentieth-century version of the New Age was in full flourish. "Human consciousness is crossing a threshold as mighty as the one from the Middle Ages to the Renaissance," wrote M. C. Richards in *The Crossing Point* (1973). "Distinguished thinkers from many disciplines were describing an imminent transformation," asserted Marilyn Ferguson in her comprehensive study *The Aquarian Conspiracy*. She quoted Willis Harman, then director of policy research at Stanford Research Institute, who maintained that spirituality might well become the philosophical basis for the New Left, "a matrix of linked beliefs—that we are invisibly joined to one another, that there are dimensions transcending time and space, that individual lives are meaningful, that grace and illumination are real, that it is possible to evolve to ever higher levels of understanding." Along with this came a growing belief that before long we would see "a worldwide expansion of consciousness," and an increasing number of consciousness-expanding techniques and practices. As far as the "growing belief" is concerned, subsequent history so far does not provide much encouragement that this is in process of being justified. But the last three decades of the twentieth century certainly witnessed an increasing number of consciousness-expanding techniques and practices, many of which were founded, in contradistinction to Monroe's efforts, more on the prospects of profit than on intensive science-based research.[5]

Many visitors now came to Whistlefield, most of them "middle-aged, serious professionals looking for serious answers to serious questions," as Campbell described them, drawn there by Monroe's growing reputation in the field of consciousness research. All were welcomed, except for those such as guitar-playing hippies who wanted to describe their personal drug-induced experiences and associate themselves with Monroe's work, who were soon sent on their way. There was also the occasional eccentric, including a man claiming to be the physical incarnation of both Alexander the Great and Thomas Jefferson, and a PhD aspirant writing a thesis on "The Tone of the Universe." A different sort of visitor was a Swiss doctor, Frank Lang, who had forsaken medicine for filmmaking, who arrived with a small team to make a documentary on Monroe. His smooth, urbane manner made him popular with the local ladies, who were quite upset, to put it mildly, when he departed.

Nancy delighted in entertaining guests. She loved cooking, even though it drove Bob almost out of his mind to see his elegant Southern lady hard at work in the kitchen. The gracious hostess was a role she seemed born to play. Her dinner parties included many of those who attended meetings of the American Parapsychological Association at Charlottesville, although as a nonacademic Monroe was not able to attend those meetings himself. Among the more frequent guests were the physicists Hal Puthoff and Russell Targ, both researchers into psychokinesis and designers of the U.S. Army's Remote Viewing program at Stanford; Elmer and Alyce Green; Stanley Krippner, professor of psychology and a leading figure in parapsychological research; John Lilly, researcher into dolphin behavior; and the transpersonal psychiatrist Stanislav Grof. Penny, as she said, would "blow in and out" and make a special effort to stay for dinner when some "visiting dignitary" was present. She recalled that her favorite dinner was when Edgar Mitchell came shortly after his voyage to the Moon. She was enthralled by his account of the return journey, seeing our planet as our home and our host, with no boundaries, an experience that transformed his life.

No matter who was present, dinner was always followed by lively discussions around the big dining room table. Would humankind survive into the next century? What did we really know about UFOs and aliens? Monroe, who was less than enthusiastic about dinner parties, would ask a question and then sit back to see where the discussion would go. Sometimes, when he remembered that *Star Trek* was on TV, he would slip out of the room to watch it in the den.

The attention that his work was attracting gave Monroe the confidence in its value that he hitherto had lacked. This confidence was enhanced by the content of the reports received from several of those undergoing sessions in the Whistlefield laboratory. It was becoming clear that he was on to something, but what that "something" actually was he was not yet able to define. So the research continued, although he could always find time to travel elsewhere, curious to find out what was going on in the area of consciousness exploration. One such experience was a visit with Nancy to John Lilly on the West Coast, where they tried out his flotation tank, designed to encourage deep relaxation and exploration of the inner self, which they found enjoyable if not revelatory. Then in April 1973 they drove to Elmira, New York, to meet Jane Roberts, whose books containing transcripts of her channeling of an entity known as Seth were becoming widely known. On the night of Sunday, April 1, Jane recorded that "Seth came through . . . in a long recorded discussion with the Monroes." The following evening, Jane used her personal abilities to tune in on a diagram of a machine that Monroe had seen on an out-of-body journey. She drew her own version of this and gave it to Bob together with her notes. This meeting is referred to in her book *The Nature of Personal Reality* (1974).

Progress in the laboratory, however, was slow, despite the enthusiasm of Monroe's team and their willingness to try anything that looked as if it might show the way to a breakthrough of some kind. But, as so often happens in scientific discovery, when that breakthrough occurred it was, or so it seemed, almost by accident.

In October 1973 Dennis Mennerich came across an article in the current issue of *Scientific American* by Gerald Oster, a researcher at the Mount Sinai School of Medicine. The article was entitled "Auditory Beats in the Brain." Oster began with a clear explanation:

> If two tuning forks of slightly different pitch are struck simultaneously, the resulting sound waxes and wanes periodically. The modulations are referred to as beats; their frequency is equal to the difference between the frequencies of the original tones. For example, a tuning fork with a characteristic pitch of 440 hertz, or cycles per second (A above middle C on the piano), and another of 434 hertz, if struck at the same time, will produce beats with a frequency of six hertz.

Oster went on to explain what happens when stereo headphones are used and the signals are applied separately to each ear:

> Under the right circumstances beats can be perceived but they are of an entirely different character. They are called binaural beats, and in many ways they are more interesting than ordinary beats, which in this discussion will be called monaural . . . Binaural beats require the combined action of both ears. They exist as a consequence of the interaction of perceptions within the brain, and they can be used to investigate some of the brain's processes.

Farther into his article, Oster poses the question, "What is the neurological basis of binaural beats? The simplest explanation," he continues, "is that the number of nerve impulses from each ear and the route they travel to the brain are determined by the frequency of the incident sound, and that the two nerve signals interact somewhere in the brain." It took more than two decades before that "somewhere" was identified in the laboratory of The Monroe Institute.

Mennerich had known about the binaural beat phenomenon for some months (it had in fact been discovered by a German experimenter, H. W. Dove, in 1839, but had been thought to be of little significance) and this article immediately captured his attention. He handed his copy of the journal to Campbell, who read it with growing interest. They agreed to try working with binaural beats in the lab. They soon found that listening to binaural beats in certain frequencies significantly affected the state of consciousness of the listener and concluded that it would be possible using this method to put anyone into a specific state of consciousness whenever required. Observing this, Bill Yost realized at once the importance of this discovery. Working with Monroe the team proceeded to create audiotapes, using binaural beats to activate in the brain the very low frequencies, not discernible by the human ear, which appeared to correspond to particular altered states of consciousness. At certain frequencies the left and right cortical hemispheres of the brain appeared to move into synchronization. This effect they described as a frequency-following response. The effect of these audiotapes, they hoped, would be to take the listener into a state that Monroe called "Non-Physical Matter Reality." For several months Campbell and Mennerich tried out the tapes on themselves but one question kept occurring to both of them—"Is this stuff real?" Was what they were experiencing "inside"—was it simply imagination?—or was it "outside," with its own independent existence?

Eventually the time came when Monroe considered that his associates were sufficiently versed in the material to begin collecting evidence. He settled them in separate soundproof units, each with headphones and a microphone suspended above so that they could record their experiences; applied electrodes to their fingers to obtain readings on temperature, skin potential voltage, and skin galvanic response; and began to feed the same audio signals to both of them. "Dennis and I met in the nonphysical as planned," said Campbell. "We went places, saw things, had conversations with each other and with several nonphysical beings we happened to run into along the way."

When the session ended they reported their experiences to Monroe. He looked quizzically at them. "So you think you were together?" he asked. They looked at each other. "Maybe," said Dennis tentatively. "At least we perceived meeting each other."

Bob rewound the tapes that each had recorded during the session. "Listen to this," he said.

"The correlation was astonishing," Campbell reported. "For almost two hours we sat there with our mouths open, hooting and exclaiming, filling in the details for each other. Bob was now grinning. 'Now that tells you something, doesn't it?' he exclaimed beaming. He was every bit as excited as we were. I was dumbfounded . . . The undeniable fact was: we had seen the same visuals, heard the same telepathic conversations, and experienced the same clarity . . . There was only one good explanation: This stuff was real!"

The experiment was repeated with similar results. Campbell and Mennerich found they could read numbers written on a blackboard outside the control room, make out-of-body trips around the neighborhood, and diagnose illnesses in other people. They learned to discriminate between those altered states of consciousness where things appeared to work well and those states where their findings were negative. Over the next two years they refined their processes and improved their efficiency, with trial and error the only methodology. However, it dawned upon them that the data alone, no matter how carefully it was collected and analyzed, would not be sufficient to provide conviction to the outside world. You simply had to experience it yourself. There was only one way of doing this: by designing programs using purpose-made audiotapes carrying the appropriate sound signals for groups of individuals with no prior knowledge of the process and who had no or very little idea of what they were letting themselves in for.

Toward the end of 1973 Monroe received an invitation from Michael Murphy, co-founder of Esalen (described by Charles Tart, who may well have suggested that Murphy issue this invitation, as "*the* prestige entry to the humanistic psychology movement of the time"), to present two weekend programs, one at Big Sur and the second in San Francisco. The opportunity to test out the new technology was too good to miss, even though it meant transporting all the equipment three thousand miles across the United States. Monroe and Bill Yost conducted the programs that continued around the clock, with food available when required and occasional short breaks for sleep. There were twenty-four participants in each program who had no idea of what they were about to experience, except for those who had come across Monroe's book and thought that it might have something to do with the out-of-body state. That, however, was not the object of the sessions; this was to introduce the idea of what Monroe called "Focus 10," the state of "mind awake, body asleep," and to show some of the potentials of this state. Because the participants in these programs were unknown to Bob, as a kind of precautionary measure he devised an affirmation, beginning with the words, "I am more than my physical body . . ." that they were to memorize before starting the session. This affirmation remains an integral part of Monroe Institute programs today.

Bob, Nancy, and Scooter at Whistefield

These workshops were generally accounted a success and requests for more programs began to arrive. It was becoming clear that what was needed was a full-time workshop trainer. It so happened that about this time Scooter, who had been studying in France and Japan and in 1974 had graduated cum laude from Wittenberg University, Ohio, joined the family at Whistlefield. She soon became deeply involved with what was going on. She agreed to act both as Monroe's secretary and as a program trainer. Being a fast learner, before long she was conducting a number of weekend programs in hotels in Charlottesville and the surrounding area, hauling along bundles of headsets, harnesses, and tapes. She also traveled to Richmond, where workshops were held in the Episcopal Diocesan Center. With George Durrette driving, Scooter would load a truck piled high with up to twenty mattresses, bought by Monroe at one of his auction visits, as well as all the rest of the necessary equipment. It was, she recalled, an amazing, but also an exhausting, experience.

Elegance at Whistlefield

Eventually, it occurred to Monroe that they should ask a nearby hotel if they could obtain permission to wire up several rooms for their programs. He approached the Tuckahoe Motel, a few miles from Whistlefield, and the management agreed. All the equipment needed, including that for measuring individual responses to the sound signals, had to be designed and created during evenings and weekends. Together with Yost, Campbell, and Mennerich, Monroe set to work. Each of the rooms allotted to them was wired for sound and connected to a control center, known as Mission Control. Bill Yost's engineering skills were especially helpful, as were Scooter's organizing talents. When all was complete, some twenty or so individuals who had previously shown keen interest were invited to attend.

Tom Campbell sums up the weekend:

> During Friday night, all day Saturday and half of Sunday, the attendees had the time of their life. There were so many paranormal happenings that weekend that we had a difficult time getting them all recorded. These naïve subjects were reading numbers in sealed envelopes, remote viewing, manifesting lights in the sky, visiting their relatives, reading next week's newspaper headlines, and much more, It was a circus! Things were never the same after that.

It was not long before word got out about the effectiveness of this program. Monroe was swamped with requests from people of all sorts wanting to participate. He began to realize that there were far more possibilities than he had foreseen. Not only did he have something with the potential of great value to those who wished to share in it, but also his own life was moving into a completely new direction. He decided to sever one more link from his past by selling Jefferson Cable, in order, as he said, "to devote all my time to our present activities." This marked the end of a long and successful career in public entertainment, as well as the end of a substantial income.

Courses continued to be held at Tuckahoe according to demand. Joseph Chilton Pearce, author of *The Crack in the Cosmic Egg*, who had just sold his next book, *Magical Child*, to E. P. Dutton, had been intrigued by *Journeys Out of the Body* and, on a visit to Lexington to see his sister, decided to call on Monroe "to check in with him." Bob invited him to join a workshop at the hotel. Pearce found it fascinating. He went out-of-body easily and enjoyed himself "doing barrel-rolls in space." Knowledgeable in research into hypnotism, he found Monroe's voice possessed an almost hypnotic quality that brought about in the listener a willingness to suspend the ordinary way of creating reality and a willingness also to take a risk. Monroe, he thought, was creating a system, but at the same time he was doing no more than playing his tapes to people to see what would happen. He told him later that he had "a tiger by the tail"—a phrase that stuck in Bob's mind.

Jim Beal also attended one of these programs, recalling his experience after the workshop ended. Monroe had learned to warn participants not to rush off immediately but to allow a few hours for cooling down before returning to everyday reality. Jim, however, was booked to attend a conference at the University of Maryland on the farther side of Washington, D.C. He asked for a lift with a fellow participant who was heading that way. She worked for *Psychic Magazine* and wanted to interview and photograph Monroe, but he proved reluctant. Jim agreed to persuade Bob to give a brief interview in exchange for her giving him a lift. She asked a few questions and took several photographs, and immediately afterwards left with Jim. However, time and time again they mistook their route—an experience shared by many others who took to the road too soon after the end of a course—and by the time they eventually arrived at the university only the night watchman was awake. Not one of the photographs she had taken revealed an image.

Meantime, experimentation continued in the Whistlefield laboratory with Campbell, Mennerich, and Scooter testing out the signals that could produce identical experiences for the listeners. As word of what was happening at Whistlefield began to spread, more and more people called in, most of them hoping to investigate and try for themselves these new scientifically designed audiotapes that were apparently effective in moving the listener into certain altered states of consciousness. With the increasing demand for programs, Campbell and Mennerich, their confidence in the process now fully established, joined Scooter as program trainers.

Elisabeth Kübler-Ross

Among those who visited to take a weekend program were the psychologists Stuart Twemlow and Fowler Jones, both of whom in subsequent years were to become involved in examining Bob Monroe both physically and psychologically. Another visitor was Dr. Elisabeth Kübler-Ross, already internationally famous as the author of the ground-breaking book, *On Death and Dying,* and for her courses on "Life, Death and Transition" that she conducted in several countries across the world. In her work with seriously ill and dying patients she claimed to have listened to hundreds of reports of near-death experiences. Early in her career she had been moved to consider the possibility of reincarnation, and she had become increasingly interested in what she described as "the mysteries of the mind, the psyche, the spirit that cannot be probed by microscopes or chemical reactions." Jim Beal, who first met Elisabeth at Whistlefield, commented perceptively, "I remember that she was a delightful person of small stature; however, the more she spoke, the bigger she became!"

It had happened that, one morning after leading a workshop in Santa Barbara, this dynamic, practical, argumentative little woman had what she felt was a spontaneous out-of-body experience. This led her to seek out and read *Journeys Out of the Body* and then to make her way to Whistlefield. She was immediately impressed by the well-equipped laboratory, as hitherto the only information she had come across with regard to mind experiments involved the use of drugs. She was also impressed by Bob Monroe, who was to become a dear friend and with whom she later collaborated in designing the *Going Home* program. Because of its significant effect on her subsequent life and work, Elisabeth's experience at Whistlefield deserves recounting in some detail.

Her first session in the soundproof booth was a failure in that she felt she had nothing to report, but the second one gave her what she hoped to find. She asked Scooter, who was her monitor, to accelerate the process. The sounds, she said, cleared her mind of all thoughts and took her inward, "like the disappearing mass of a black hole." She continues:

> I heard an incredible whoosh, similar to the sound of a strong wind blowing. Suddenly I felt as if I was swept up by a tornado. At that point I was taken out of my body and I just blasted away. To where? Where did I go? That is the question that everyone asks. Although my body was motionless, my brain took me to another dimension of existence, like another universe. The physical part of being was no longer relevant. Like the spirit that leaves the body after death, similar to the butterfly leaving the cocoon, my awareness was defined by psychic energy, not my physical body. I was simply *out there*.[6]

Elisabeth was angry at being brought out of this experience, which had lasted far longer than was usually permitted. Questioned by her monitor, she was in no mood at the time to say much about what had happened, except that two physical problems she had were no longer troubling her. Later that day she returned to the Owl House, where she was staying, and sensed, as she says, "a strange energy which convinced me that I was not alone." She went to bed and fell fast asleep—and a succession of nightmares began. It was as if she was reliving the deaths of all the patients she had attended, "re-experiencing their anguish, grief, fear, suffering, sadness, loss, blood, tears." She asked for three reprieves—a shoulder to lean on, a hand to hold, and lastly a fingertip to touch. Each time she was refused. Then it came to her that to survive this ordeal, to survive life itself, it was a matter of faith—faith in God and faith in herself. With this, the agony ceased.

The nightmares were followed by a dramatic out-of-body experience during which Elisabeth found herself moving through an enormous lotus blossom towards a light—the same light, she believed, that her patients reported seeing during their near-death experiences. Merging with that light she felt an indescribable sensation of love, warmth, and welcome. Then she heard two voices. The first was her own, saying, "I am acceptable to Him." The second came from somewhere else, with the mysterious words, "Shanti Nilaya."

Early the following morning, she donned a hand-woven robe (it looked like a nightshirt, she said) and a pair of sandals and ran down the driveway from the Owl House to tell Monroe what had happened. As she did so, she said, she continued to see "every leaf, butterfly and stone vibrating in its molecular structure. It was the greatest feeling of ecstasy a human being can experience." Bob, Nancy, and Scooter were sitting on the porch as she approached. "She looked gorgeous," Scooter remembered. "I don't know what it was but she absolutely glowed!"

The experience gave Elisabeth a sense of grace that took many days to diminish. Then some months later, during a lecture she was giving to several hundred people at Berkeley, she described her out-of-body experience at the Owl House. Afterwards a monk in an orange robe stood up to clarify some of the points she had made. "Shanti Nilaya," he said. "It is Sanskrit and means 'the final home of peace.' It's where we go at the end of our earthly journey when we return to God." Some years later when Elisabeth founded her Center in California, Shanti Nilaya was the name she gave it. When she moved to Virginia to live at Healing Waters Farm, she transferred the name to her new Center close by.[7]

Elisabeth returned to Whistlefield at various times and became very close to Bob and Nancy. The family loved her visits. She brought boxes of delicious Swiss chocolates, made bouquets of four-leaf clovers—which she could find anywhere—laughed a lot (or cackled, as Penny recalls), and told stories of her childhood as the least favored of a set of triplets and of her struggles with the medical profession over her work with death and dying. Elisabeth maintained her contact with the family until shortly before her death in 2004.

Although the majority of those who visited Whistlefield were serious investigators into human consciousness, many of them being leading figures in their own specialties, there was the occasional exception. One was journalist David Black, who published a skeptical, if not libelous, article in *Penthouse* in 1976, claiming, among other accusations, that Monroe practiced astral sex. This article was picked up by the investigative writer Scott Rogo, who repeated some of the material in *Fate* magazine. In face of a threatened lawsuit, Rogo was compelled to issue a retraction. Some years later, in his book *Leaving the Body,* he expressed further doubts about Monroe's credibility, although he was unable to deny that his OBEs actually took place. Nevertheless, considering the significance and the implications of Monroe's discoveries, the amount of hostile criticism is surprisingly small.

A new phase of life was now opening for Bob Monroe. He was in demand as a speaker, mostly as a consequence of the increasing sales of *Journeys Out of the Body.* He continued to attend some of the Council Grove conferences, where he became interested in Elmer and Alyce Green's Biofeedback process. Always ready to take on anything that attracted his interest, he later adapted some of the

Biofeedback techniques for use in his own programs. In conversation with others he became convinced that the name Whistlefield Research Laboratories was not sufficiently specific to indicate the direction of his work. After some thought he renamed his undertaking—The Monroe Institute for Applied Sciences. In 1975 he applied for and received a patent for the frequency-following response, under the name of Mentronics, the first name he chose for the new technology.

Although for the most part the results of the workshops at Whistlefield were, in Bob's words, "not spectacular" they provided a much broader base for experimental testing. As requests for more workshops came in, he decided to extend their scope. With his associates he designed what he entitled the *M-5000* program. The *M* stood for Mentronics and the 5000 was a signal that Monroe's ambition at that time was to train five thousand people in the exploration of states of consciousness. For the benefit of program participants he developed a simple terminology to identify certain states. Focus 1 was the starting point, "ordinary everyday consciousness." Moving on from there, the sound signals led you to Focus 10, the state of "mind awake, body asleep," and thence to Focus 12, "a state of expanded awareness." He was also creating frequencies to take the listener into two further states: Focus 15, "a state of no time," and Focus 21, "the edge of here-now." These terms continue to be used in Monroe Institute courses today.

It soon became clear that five thousand participants was an overambitious target at the time and the name of the program should be reconsidered. After some consideration Monroe came to recognize that, as he wrote in *Far Journeys,* "we were creating for the participant a doorway, a window through which he could achieve other states of consciousness." Mentronics was dropped, the technology was titled Hemispheric Synchronization[8] (Hemi-Sync for short), and the program became known as the *Gateway Voyage.* The instructional text accompanying the subtly engineered sound signals has been described as "the best play Bob ever wrote." His recorded voice, gentle, encouraging, and authoritative, conducts the listeners through a sequence of states of consciousness as far as the very edge of our time-space continuum. As the program proceeds, the participants themselves are able to record on tape what they are experiencing. It is estimated that by 2006 more than twenty thousand individuals had taken this six-day residential program.

The first program under the *Gateway* title was held in 1977 with forty participants at Feathered Pipe Ranch, near Helena, Montana, a center for leading-edge workshops at the time. This was very much of a trial run. For this program Monroe designed a set of taped exercises that he called the Elation series, most of which carried frequencies to take participants into Focus 10 and Focus 12. Chris Lenz, who had followed PhD courses in history, philosophy, and psychology at the California Institute of Asian Studies and who first met Monroe at Council Grove in 1975, trained the program under Monroe's supervision. His experience was limited to training weekend courses in the previous year, having been inducted by Scooter and Tom Campbell. Lenz invited the young Karen Malik, who had been involved in spiritual practice for several years and had just completed a year of silence, to assist in the training. Karen's only previous contact with the Monroe material had been acting as cook for a program in California.

Monroe himself took no active part in the training. He was curious as to what was going on but as yet, despite the glowing reports, he had no real trust in the process. Then midway through the program he handed the trainers a new tape they had never heard before, with the instruction, "Just play this." It took the participants into "the state of no time"—Focus 15. Fortunately, the sound signals that led the listeners into "the state of no time" were also effective in bringing them back. Many of them reported having mystical and kundalini-type experiences, and one claimed to have been in a state of utter bliss for three days.

Despite the success of these programs, this was a difficult period for Monroe. He had given up a highly profitable career and moved into an area where he was uncertain of his way. Whistlefield provided no source of income and was eating up his capital. He often felt both lonely and depressed; he looked unhealthy and, according to Karen Malik, whom he found to be a sympathetic listener, he thought he might be dead within six months. What was he going to do with this process—so powerful, so effective—that he had discovered? He recalled the phrase that Joe Pearce had used. "I have a tiger by the tail," he told her, "and I don't know what to do with it." But he realized that there was no turning back.

However, reports on the Feathered Pipe course were so encouraging that it was not long before Chris Lenz found himself training programs for Monroe Institute West, a rudimentary organization based in a handsome building in Mill Valley, north of San Francisco. Monroe then summoned Lenz to Whistlefield to train a ten-day program. This had quite dramatic effects on the participants, some of whom found themselves hyperventilating, much to the surprise of the trainer, who had no experience in dealing with this. As yet there was no philosophy or organized method of helping participants to handle their experiences. It was very much a matter of learning on the hoof.

Monroe then invited Chris to become director of training at Whistlefield. By this time what came to be known as the Explorer team was coming into being. This was composed of a number of individuals who visited the laboratory from time to time for sessions, usually conducted by Monroe himself, enabling them to explore what was becoming understood by those involved as "the realms beyond physical reality." Joining this team was what Chris would have preferred, but Monroe's response was that he had plenty of Explorers but only one regular full-time trainer.

After Chris's move to Whistlefield, the Monroe operations on the West Coast were taken on by Karen Malik. Over the next two years she organized and presented workshops wherever required, as long as the venue was west of the Mississippi, continually improving her training skills. In 1979 Chris and Karen combined to train workshops on a "Holistic Life" cruise on the Eastern Mediterranean. Elmer Green, also on the cruise, declared he would only recommend Monroe workshops if Chris or Karen were the trainers, as they brought what he described as "a spiritual dimension" to what they were doing. Karen Malik remained dedicated to Monroe's work throughout the following decades and continued training courses for the Institute into the twenty-first century.[9]

Despite the promise of its title, the post of director of training at Whistlefield was not one to be envied. The early programs had no set pattern and in some instances Chris heard new taped exercises only a few minutes before a course was due to begin. He stayed with Monroe and helped to prepare for the move to Faber, but in 1980, feeling altogether exhausted, he resigned. However, he never lost his interest or enthusiasm and twenty-three years later, now working with the Institute of Noetic Sciences (IONS), he returned to the Monroe fold to present *Gateway* courses at IONS headquarters in Petulama, California.

Among the many visitors who continued to flock to Whistlefield was one who in later years was to play an important part in the development and understanding of the Hemi-Sync process. Lieutenant F. Holmes Atwater was a young army officer working in military intelligence. Early in 1977 Atwater joined the army's secret counterintelligence operation at Fort Meade, Maryland. This very small and select unit was investigating the possibilities of remote-viewing and Atwater was searching for information on organizations and techniques that might be relevant. Having read *Journeys Out of the Body,* which brought back to him memories of out-of-body episodes he had himself experienced as a child, he was attracted to the newly formed Monroe Institute of Applied Sciences to see if its techniques might be useful. He concealed the purpose of his visit, saying merely that he had read Monroe's book and wanted to know if others could be taught his methods.

Impressed by the handsome house with its outbuildings, huge greenhouse, and fields scattered with a medley of horses and tractors, Atwater was even more impressed by Nancy Monroe's "gracious, ladylike manner" and her way of speaking "with a gentle southern accent, a leisurely segue from word to word that mysteriously focused one's attention and stirred the fires of the soul." She led him through a succession of finely furnished rooms to a patio, where a figure quite out of accord with the elegance of his surroundings was sitting on a divan. "Mr. Monroe," records Lieutenant Atwater, "wore sweatpants, suspenders, slippers and a partially unbuttoned, coffee-stained shirt . . . As he brushed cigarette ashes off his shirt, he looked up and calmly said, 'Well, hello.' No southern accent here. No pretentious social niceties either. I thought—as a first impression—that perhaps he was more interested in who he was 'out-of-body' rather than what I might think of him or how I might perceive him in the physical."[10]

After Atwater had described his childhood out-of-body journeys, Monroe took him across to the laboratory and made him comfortable in one of the soundproof booths. As he listened to the music and sound signals, he had the strong impression that the bed he was lying on was moving up towards the ceiling. He tried to work out how this was done—and suddenly became aware that he was traveling, in his own words, "through a white tube or tunnel, its walls lined with crystalline forms." He then found himself in a boundless white space watching himself emerging from the tube—which he later described as a giant "Flavor Straw," a confection he recalled from childhood consisting of a straw with sugar crystals inside that flavored whatever drink he fancied. Then he heard Monroe's voice, the sound patterns changed, the bed slowly descended, or so he thought, and the light came on. The first thing he did was to look under the bed to see how it was raised and lowered, but to his surprise there was nothing there except the floor. Monroe appeared and invited him out to lunch at a nearby restaurant, where he explained the workings of his new technology. Atwater then realized that the sound signals had lifted him out of his body. His interest fully aroused, he signed up for a program in Richmond in the following year. Although his visit made little or no contribution to the military operations he was then involved with, Atwater stayed in occasional contact with Monroe. There were hints and suggestions that he might be interested in a job at the Institute at some time, but no formal offer was made.

In the closing years of the decade things began to change. News of the Esalen program had resulted in inquiries and requests from all over the United States. The programs on the road, ranging from one day in Focus 10 to ten-day Explorations, made enormous demands on Monroe and his small number of helpers, particularly so on Scooter, who was in charge of this Outreach program, organizing and presenting workshops wherever they were requested. A program might be attended by as many as forty people with all their mattresses, blankets, and pillows, so there was a strong physical element to accompany the psychic adventures.

To meet the increasing demand for programs, Monroe accepted that it was essential to train more presenters and to recruit staff for purposes of administration. Various individuals were hired to act as directors or administrators, but none of them lasted for long. Monroe, who was very wary of anyone else taking authority and accustomed in his previous career to running his own show, would outline their duties and then perform them himself, with the result that, with nothing much to do, they quit. While he dealt—or failed to deal—with the administrative side, Scooter, who in addition to being a full-time trainer was also, as she says, "fan mail answerer, national program coordinator, secretary, monitor, Explorer, driver and public relations person," was responsible for selecting and training new staff to run the programs, a task that often proved thankless, as most of those who offered themselves as would-be trainers fell far short of what was required. By the end of 1978, now twenty-six years old, she decided that enough was enough. She felt that she herself had something to say, but had no chance to be heard. Monroe, she said later, "was one brilliant man, and a tough one to work for!" and the family relationship did not make it any easier. Feeling frustrated, she resigned from the Institute and turned to the publishing world to make a living.

Tom Campbell and Dennis Mennerich began to find that the increased activity at the Institute was making more demands on their time than they could handle. Moreover, the research in which they had played so large a part was ceasing to be Monroe's chief priority. Financing the laboratory work was a strain on his resources; his venture into property development had collapsed years before and the time was approaching when he would need a new source of income. The Institute would soon have to be put on a sustainable footing if it were to survive. This meant that a residential center for courses was essential, together with accommodations for administrative support, a purpose-built laboratory, and eventually a conference facility also. Research would have to go on hold until all this was accomplished. Aware of the situation, Campbell and Mennerich realized it was time for them to pull out. Bill Yost also withdrew from the team after a disagreement with Monroe. Sadly, he died from lung cancer the following year.

Towards the end of the 1970s Monroe agreed to submit himself to the Research Department of the Topeka Veterans Administration

Hospital for an in-depth psychological evaluation, conducted by Drs. Twemlow and Gabbard, to see if anything could be learned about how his personality and his out-of-body experiences, which were still continuing from time to time, related to each other. In their report they noticed his interest in flying and his preoccupation with movement, his creativity, and his mechanical ability. They commented on his leadership abilities, adding that he demonstrated a characteristic common to people exploring states of consciousness in that "he listened to and acted on his own subjective experience." They continued: "Monroe has been able to take some experiences, which most people would try to deny and avoid, and place them in a highly creative context . . . People such as Monroe are thus able to utilize their internal mental experiences for guidance in their lives." Later in their report they asked the question: "How can Monroe accept these highly esoteric journeys described in his book, and at the same time be the almost traditional businessman and father who is not a freak, does not wear unusual clothes, and does not put himself constantly on-stage for examination of his special abilities?" The question, however, remained unanswered. They summed up by saying, "He pursues relentlessly his own research, makes his own contacts, and takes responsibility for his own life."[11]

The years at Whistlefield had seen one man's personal experience transformed into a scientifically based program, tried and tested by hundreds of individuals, with rich possibilities for further development. What had begun as something intensely personal had been transmuted into a set of experiences that was proving to be of value to all who participated in it. While many of his New Age contemporaries had lost no time in launching their projects or discoveries on the market, Monroe had, at his own expense, devoted almost a decade to investigating, developing, and refining the audio technology that, he came to believe, would prove of benefit to humankind. Reflecting later on his years of experience at Whistlefield, Tom Campbell felt that the course Bob Monroe had followed was the right one. He wrote:

> He captained his ship flawlessly from the initial tentative launch, through tricky undercurrents of closed-minded rejection by the larger society, while at the same time skillfully avoiding the shallows of easy, safe, generally acceptable answers. With Bob at the helm, high standards of proof drove off pirate charlatans who wanted to co-opt his success and commandeer his hard won credibility. Through dedication to honest science, personal integrity, and an intuitive knowing that was steady and reliable, Bob optimized his gifts for the greater good.

Notes

1. This survey is reprinted in Monroe's book, *Far Journeys.*

2. Without drawing any conclusions, it is interesting to note that out of 151 references to the OBE state listed in Carlos Alvorado's article in *Varieties of Anomalous Experience* (APA, 2000) only fifteen were published before *Journeys Out of the Body,* and of those three were by Charles Tart commenting on Monroe's experiences before this book appeared. Both Fowler Jones and Stuart Twemlow later became occasional trainers at The Monroe Institute.

3. See *My Big Toe,* Book 1, by Thomas Campbell (Lightning Strike Books, 2003).

4. It is likely that Monroe's interest in the possibility of using sound to drive brainwaves derived from a conversation with Charles Tart, who had told him about the research by Andrew Neher, described in studies issued in 1961 and 1962, investigating how EEG responses could be driven by periodic acoustic stimuli, such as drumming. Neher used electrodes attached to the scalp to assess the effects. This study was replicated at Stanford in 2006.

5. *The Fringes of Reason,* edited by Ted Schultz (Harmony Books, 1989), provides a comprehensive survey of the New Age. The chapter on "Brain Boosters," contributed by Joshua Hammer, describes some of the devices being advertised. Among them were the Synchro-Energizer (cost approximately $6,500 each), the Digital Audio-Visual Integration Device (or David 1) ($3,000), a "brain chair" called the Cerebrex, and the Modified Graham Potentializer. John-David, who claimed to have spent many years studying with Tibetan lamas, founded his own Learning Institute and ran several "brain fitness centers," where he conducted seminars, as well as organizing Total Immersion Intensive Seminars in the San Francisco area. Another popular organization was the Universe of You, founded by Randy Adamadama (originally Mr. R. Stevens who, having found his mission, christened himself with what he declared was an adopted planetary name). Randy claimed to take a thousand dollars a day running Synchro-Energizer sessions at only ten dollars a throw.

6. See *The Wheel of Life,* by Elisabeth Kübler-Ross (Scribner, 1997), from which these quotations are taken.

7. Healing Waters Farm was destroyed by arsonists from the locality in 1994. A man from Monterey was later overheard saying that he had "gotten rid of the AIDS lady." (Elisabeth had been working with AIDS sufferers and was seeking to rescue babies of AIDS parents from hospital and place them with families who had lost their own young children.) She moved to Scottsdale, Arizona, not far from her son Kenneth, to a house on the edge of the desert identified by a tepee and a totem pole. After suffering a series of strokes, she died in a hospice in August 2004.

8. The following is adapted from a talk by David Mulvey, director of training, 1988–90:

> In the early sixties four basic brainwave states were recognized, distinguished by letters from the Greek alphabet, measured in cycles per second, known as hertz (Hz). Beta is generally associated with waking consciousness—awake, alert, focused, attentive—and ranges between 12 and 24 Hz (or so it was thought at that time, when many scientists believed that brainwaves stopped at 24 Hz). Alpha, associated with relaxation, light meditation, and creativity, is approximately from 8 to 12 Hz. It is a state of relaxation leading into the early stages of sleep. Theta, from about 4 to 8 Hz, is associated with deep relaxation, deep meditation, and various states of sleep, as well as what may be described as inventive creativity. Delta ranges from just above zero to 4 Hz and is associated with sleep. Zero brainwaves means that you are dead.
>
> Brainwaves, measured in the neocortex, are a reflection of consciousness—not consciousness itself. There are very strong correlations between brainwave

patterns and consciousness but we should not confuse the two.

However, the human ear is only capable of hearing sounds down to 40 Hz or thereabouts. By using the concept of binaural beats, meaning that you simultaneously play two tones of slightly different frequency, the ear detects the difference between the tones. So if one tone is 100 Hz frequency and the other 104 Hz, creating a vibrato effect, the ear and the brainwaves respond to the difference, 4 Hz. As the frequencies shift, the brain follows them. Monroe called this the Frequency Following Response. By using stereo, playing one frequency into one ear, and the second into the other ear, the brain produces the difference between the two with both hemispheres responding to the same frequency and amplitude at the same time. This is Hemispheric Synchronization, or Hemi-Sync for short. This synchronization may occur without this type of stimulation, but only for a very short time.

The CDs and tapes used by the Institute may have sixteen or more sound tracks recorded on them—layers of sound designed to produce specific responses. The sounds may be embedded in pink noise, in musical compositions, or accompanied by verbal descriptions or instructions.

For a full technical explanation of the Hemi-Sync process, see the appendix.

9. A lively and positive individual with many interests and abilities, Karen was elected president of the International Society for the Study of Subtle Energies and Energy Medicine (ISEEM) for 2003–4.

10. Quotations are from *Captain of My Ship, Master of My Soul,* by
    F. Holmes Atwater (Hampton Roads, 2001).

11. This report was later published in Gabbard and Twemlow's book
    With the Eyes of the Mind (Praeger, 1984), together with an
    account of an earlier experiment conducted by Twemlow and
    Fowler Jones in the psycho-physiological laboratory at the hospi-
    tal. Monroe was asked to put himself into what he considered to
    be an out-of-body state while various measurements were made,
    including tracings of his brain waves. Computer analysis of these
    tracings showed that "most of his brain energy was in the four to
    five (Theta) frequency range with nothing at all above ten cycles
    per second." See *Journeys Out of the Body,* pp. 275–80, for a full
    report. This was the frequency that Monroe and his coresearchers
    discovered that, when produced by binaural beat technology
    recorded on tape, provided the gateway through which a whole
    new universe could be observed and entered.

CHAPTER 5

Exploring Within and Without

In the early 1970s an increasing number of people appeared at the Whistlefield Research Laboratory curious to see what was going on there. Monroe would satisfy their interest, as well as further his research, by inviting them to a session in one of the three isolation units, which he named Controlled Holistic Environmental Chambers, better known as CHEC units (Monroe loved acronyms), monitoring them himself and questioning them as to how they were affected by the Hemi-Sync signals being fed to the headphones they were wearing. Each unit was equipped with a warm waterbed. Electrodes were attached to the user so that various readings could be measured throughout the duration of the session. This enabled Monroe to observe the physical state of the subject and to make minute adjustments to the frequencies to assist, for example, the maintaining of the appropriate degree of relaxation. A microphone was suspended in the booth so that two-way communication was always open and the complete dialogue was recorded on tape.

Some visitors just came, had one or two sessions, and left, but others, their interest awakened, returned whenever they could. Before long Monroe began to gather an informal group of the more regular, and more fluent, visitors that became known as the Explorer team. These were people who not only showed interest in what was going on at Whistlefield but were also prepared to give up many hours of their time to assist in the research. Monroe described them as "a very special group, a total of some eight subjects completely familiar with the Focus 10 state. Verbal communication in Focus 10 through the microphone/headphone system became as normal as if we were sitting across from one another in a conference room."

One of the earlier Explorers was a cheerful, lively minded, young married woman, Rosalind McKnight. Rosalind had traveled widely, held a master's degree in divinity, and had been working as a counselor at a YMCA facility in New York. In 1971 she and her husband rented a farmhouse in rural Virginia. Soon after they moved in, a friend from New York arrived on a visit and offered to take them to meet two long-standing friends of hers, Robert and Nancy Monroe who, they discovered, lived about an hour's drive from the McKnights' farmhouse. Arriving at Whistlefield, Rosalind's first impression of Monroe was of a man who, despite his wrinkled clothes, "had a rare mystique that completely set him off from other people." In conversation they discovered that the friend who introduced Rosalind and her husband to the Monroes had once been visited by Bob in the out-of-body state, an incident that he recorded in *Journeys Out of the Body*.

The McKnights were fascinated by the discussion that took place on out-of-body experiences and made a second visit to Whistlefield a few months later. On this occasion Monroe asked Rosalind if she would like to try a session herself in one of the isolation units. She readily agreed, was wired up, and, as the sound signals were played into her headphones, gradually fell asleep. At first she thought she had flunked her first experiment, but Monroe was impressed by her inquiring mind and interest in what was going on and invited her to return to try again.

Rosalind returned in April the following year, determined this time to stay awake. Soon after the session began she found herself in what she described as a blackout period, which she later interpreted as her consciousness "changing gears." Emerging from this she felt somehow detached from her physical body. "I suddenly experienced my consciousness as existing *outside* my body," she said. She felt as if she was "pure energy," able to move anywhere instantly "just by the mere thought of being there."

Then, so she said, she became aware of "two forms of light" who began communicating wordlessly with her, helping her out of her physical body and gently instructing her in techniques that would enable her to move out of body by herself. They told her how to create an "energy balloon" around herself to facilitate this. As she followed their instructions she became aware that her conscious awareness shifted from outside herself to inside what she described as her "light body." The two "forms of light" let her know that their intention was to take her into different levels, although she had no idea then what that meant. It seemed only a matter of minutes before they told her it was time to return. To her surprise she discovered that the session had lasted for nearly two hours.

Fascinated by Rosalind's report of her experience, Monroe invited her to join the Explorer team. She was, however, to meet very few of this group, as the policy was to keep them apart as far as possible to prevent them from comparing notes with each other. Rosalind was to become one of the longest-serving members, taking sessions with Monroe on many occasions over the next eleven years.

Some of Rosalind's explorations are recounted in her book *Cosmic Journeys.*[1] These range from accounts of greater energies and energy systems to a meeting with extraterrestrials on a spaceship, advice on healing, and a lecture on food and physical fitness. On most of these explorations she was instructed and aided by her "Invisible Helpers," as she calls them. The members of this "amazing team" were obviously familiar with human psychology, "having decided to assign just two light beings to work with me during the first session and then to bring in others when I was more familiar with the process." Sometimes one of the Helpers would speak through her, or would speak directly to Monroe. Looking back over her eleven years of sessions, she says that her Invisible Helpers "were always there guiding, directing and evidently planning the sessions ahead of time, even though there is no 'time' as we know it in their dimension."

On one occasion Rosalind had to cancel a session at short notice. The next time she saw Monroe he seemed to be in especially good humor. Something odd had happened on the day she missed her session, he told her. A visitor had arrived from Washington, a female psychologist, who wanted to learn more about what he was doing. After some discussion, during which she expressed much skepticism, he felt she ought to experience Hemi-Sync for herself. She agreed, and he placed her in the booth that Rosalind normally used. Some five minutes later her voice came through the intercom. "There is someone else in the booth with me," she said. "More than one . . . there are four of them . . . There are two at my feet and two at my head."

"What are they doing?" asked Monroe.

"They are trying to lift me out of my body, if you can believe that."

Monroe made a note of the time. It was ten past five, the precise time of Rosalind's regular session.

"What are they doing now?" he asked.

"They have stopped trying to lift me out of my body. And they are arguing . . . The four want to lift me out. And now there is a fifth that is arguing with them that they should not."

Soon afterwards the psychologist reported that they had stopped arguing and left. She relaxed into sleep until Monroe awoke her and released her from the booth. She was totally bewildered. He then played her a recording of one of Rosalind's sessions where this "lifting out" had been reported. She left "very puzzled and preoccupied," and never returned.

To begin with, Monroe took a keen interest in the Explorer sessions. He was persistent in his questioning and sought to elicit as much information as he could. Rosalind considered him to be very left-brained and scientifically oriented, in contrast to herself. She said, "I was so non-scientifically oriented that I had no idea what the tapes were all about until my husband explained the Hemi-Sync process to me after about six months of being an Explorer." She added, "I was able to relax into the tapes and have the experiences whereupon Bob could question my guiding energies about how they did what they did." These sessions sometimes lasted nearly three hours and were often followed by dinner together at the restaurant on the top of Afton Mountain.

Rosalind's Invisible Helpers provided her with information and advice on a host of different topics from recommending eating green leaf vegetables to the ability of domestic pets to read each others' minds, to tracking spaceships, the nature of gods (or God), the death of planets, the birth and nature of souls, and so on. Sometimes the subject was in answer to a question posed by Monroe, sometimes it arose seemingly spontaneously. Many of the sessions resembled lectures dealing with topics such as greater energies and energy systems or the hierarchy of Nature. In one intense experience Rosalind observed herself and the Earth "in both time and timelessness." She continued: "The balancing of my energies is related to my earth existence. We come into the time zone of earth at certain levels for special lessons in balance. Our souls choose these time-zone lessons, and we go to specific areas where the energies are right for our personal growth." She saw some of her past-life incarnations, in Scotland, in a Germanic country, in the Golden Age of Greece, and in an Indian nation in Central America. She viewed "the very highly evolved cultures called Mu and Atlantis" and commented that these and other similar cultures collapsed because of the misuse of energy and their imbalance in relation to the rest of the world. She moved on to sense "the overall presence of all the souls who have ever lived on earth" which, because there is no time, "actually exist in all levels at once." It was revealed to her that the highest energy is love energy, which Jesus came to Earth to demonstrate. Then she looked into the future of the planet, when "the highest and lowest vibratory souls will be back on earth at the same time." There will be shifts in the Earth's physical structure as it moves into a higher energy; new continents will appear "and many types of energy beings from other dimensions will be coming into the earth's atmosphere." Man's physical nature will change and our bodies will become less dense.

This session ended with positive messages. "Life is how you perceive it. Live every day on the tiptoes of excitement . . . Go with the flow of life and do not resist your lessons. Give everything away that you receive. You will find that what you receive in return is a greater understanding of your oneness with all. All is one, and one is all."

Some of the details from Rosalind's out-of-body explorations so intrigued Monroe that he later incorporated them into his *Gateway* program. One of these was what she described as a balloon of energy that she formed around her physical body as a kind of protection. Another was a bar of energy that she was told to create to cleanse her physical body. Both these concepts appear in *Gateway* exercises, although put to rather different uses. Rosalind also saw consciousness as a form of energy, a definition or explanation that appealed to Monroe, and in her explorations she was guided by her Invisible Helpers, who reappear in the *Guidelines* program—the follow-up to *Gateway*—as Inner Self Helpers, working with the program participants. Although Monroe was insistent that whatever an Explorer session revealed its validity was restricted to the individual explorer, he had no hesitation in adapting ideas or concepts emerging from a session that he felt would be of value to others.

Invisible Helpers, Guides, Energy Beings—these are the apparent sources of the information that the Explorers reported. Some have names, some have personalities; others are voices audible only to the Explorers, who record what they are hearing. The term *channeling* is generally used to describe this process. This has been defined by Jon Klimo, in his substantial study of the phenomenon, as "the communication of information to or through a physically embodied human being from a source that is said to exist on some other level or dimension of reality than the physical as we know it, and that is not from the normal mind (or self) of the channel."[2] Writing some ten years later, Michael Brown provides a slightly different explanation: "the use of altered states of consciousness to contact spirits—or, as many of its practitioners say, to experience spiritual energy captured from other times and dimensions."[3] One point that needs to be made about Monroe's Explorers is that they were delivering their information before the publication of Shirley MacLaine's *Out on a Limb,* the book and subsequent TV movie that were largely responsible for the promotion of the channeling phenomenon.

In his survey, Klimo discovered that, for the most part, there was nothing particularly distinctive or special about those who claimed to channel. "A pattern emerges of typical relationships, family settings, money worries, usual life problems and challenges being met." Many of them were private individuals, some of whom were willing to demonstrate their gift before others. "Channeling sessions," said Ted Schultz in his fascinating survey, *The Fringes of Reason,* "filtered into the middle class like a 1980s metaphysical version of the Tupperware party." There were also a number of "commercial channelers" such as

J. Z. Knight and Kevin Ryerson, whose public performances gained them both wealth and notoriety.

As well as visiting Jane Roberts,[4] Monroe showed some interest in some of the other well-known channelers. Out of curiosity he attended sessions by J. Z. Knight, whose channeled entity, Ramtha, the Enlightened One, claimed to have incarnated some thirty-five thousand years ago in Lemuria, and by Penny Torres, a young house-wife from Southern California, channeler of Mafu, who declared that he was at one time a Greek living in the first century A.D., yet who somehow seemed to have adopted several of Ramtha's turns of phrase. Although he was hugged by both Ramtha and Mafu, Monroe did not feel that either of them had especially enlightened him.

There is a marked distinction, however, between Monroe's Explorers and the New Age channelers, whether commercial or pri-vate. The Explorers worked in strictly controlled conditions and with a monitor who could observe and modify those conditions if neces-sary and stayed in communication throughout the session, asking questions and commenting from time to time, so that the session was a dialogue rather than a monologue. They were essentially private individuals with no followers and no financial rewards. Shut away in the soundproof booth they were freed from the constraints and con-ditions of daily life and could allow their consciousness to move away from the limitations of time and space.

While Monroe, speaking both for himself and for the Institute, was careful not to endorse information gained from the Explorers' sessions, he was alert to anything that appealed directly to his own interest in consciousness. One concept that particularly impressed him emerged from the experiences of an Explorer, Shay St. John, a social worker by profession, referred to by her initials SHE. What emerged from Shay's sessions Monroe described as "one of the most interesting descriptions of total reality we have yet encountered."

During several sessions this Explorer made contact with a guide, a male energy who gave his name as Miranon. We have seen that Monroe had already devised a kind of code for referring to certain states or levels of consciousness. Focus 1 was "ordinary, everyday consciousness"; Focus 10 was a state where the mind was awake and alert and the body to all intents and purposes asleep; Focus 12 was a state of expanded awareness. In conversation with Monroe, SHE describes her experience of moving through levels 15 to 22, which Miranon had previously referred to as the levels of human life on Earth. Miranon (who refers to SHE as "Leana" and keeps careful watch over her physical condition) then enters the discussion, promising to help Monroe explore the various levels in a future session.

Before the commencement of the next session, SHE produced a complex diagram of the twenty-one levels of physical existence on Earth that, she said, "just came" to her. During the session Miranon referred to this diagram and then proceeded to deliver what amounted to a lecture on the seven planes that, according to him, express the entire spectrum of consciousness. Each plane contains seven levels that comprise various stages of existence, physical and nonphysical. The first three planes contain the whole of physical life on Earth. In summary: levels 1–7 are the region where plants exist; levels 8–14 are where animals exist; levels 15–21 are the realm of human life on Earth. At level 21 the individual has the choice of staying in human form or moving higher into the fourth plane—if one wishes to do this, then physical form must be abandoned. On physical death you enter levels 22 to 28, described as the bridge. Once the bridge is crossed, said Miranon, "for consciousness to evolve higher it would not again assume human form of any kind." The upper three planes comprise the spiritual realm. Here, says Miranon, is "where much of the work is done" and where the guides who choose to help those still in human form may be found.

This spectrum of consciousness described by Miranon is both coherent and comprehensive. Each level from 1 to 49 has its appropriate color and the whole concept can be clearly depicted in diagrammatic form. Miranon explained that he was on level 46. When he reaches level 49, which he says he eventually will, he is destined to leave "all of this realm of existence." He continued: "It does not mean I have reached the highest point by any means. It simply means that I have left this group of seven . . . Imagine, if you will, the seven circles enclosed in an even larger circle upon which seven more circles are stacked. Which is in turn enclosed in an even greater circle. And then you can have some idea of what infinity is. It does not ever stop."

Throughout these sessions Monroe came to regard Miranon as a dear friend and also as a teacher. He was so impressed by the quality and consistency of the information he was given that he later made use of the levels 22 to 27 in the *Lifeline* program, the last residential program he completed, and in the Outreach workshop *Going Home.* He also authorized the use of Focus 34 and Focus 35 in *Exploration 27,* the final program he devised although he never lived to complete it.[5] As a tribute to the inspiration he had received, he gave the name of Miranon to the picturesque lake within sight of the Institute buildings after the move from Whistlefield.

There is a particular detail in the account of the Miranon sessions that is of special interest. At one time when Miranon and Monroe were in discussion, the Explorer herself was occupied with other deeply personal matters. She established connection with her deceased godfather, whom she found in what she described as a beautiful garden where he awaited her. So profound was the connection that she was unaware that the Miranon session was finished, and she failed to respond to the recall signal that Monroe sent to indicate that it was time for her to return. As the time passed—more than two hours—he became increasingly anxious and it was not until, as she reported, her godfather reminded her that she had children and loved ones who needed her that she rejoined her physical body in the laboratory. Miranon explained to Monroe that she was too strongly connected to her godfather to continue to work in this way and she needed at least a year before she resumed. SHE later commented that this was the closest Monroe came to losing one of his Explorers.

The program continued after the Institute moved to Roberts Mountain, where a purpose-built system for exploration was constructed. A control area was installed in the laboratory linked to an adjacent room containing a double bed for the Explorer. Later this room was replaced by a specially constructed shielded unit, familiarly known as the "black box." By this time most of the earlier team had moved on to other things, but there was no shortage of new Explorers eager to try out the equipment and record their experiences.

Rosalind McKnight was one of the Explorers who continued to work with Monroe after the move. There was one particular session, known as "The Patrick Event," that impressed him so deeply that subsequently he often included a recording of it in the *Gateway* program. It took place soon after the Institute was relocated but before the laboratory was ready for use, so the session was held in one of the units in the Residential Center. At the time it appeared that a group of "entities" were accustomed to speaking through Rosalind McKnight. As the session proceeded, they began to talk about "earthbound spirits" or "ghosts." "There are many millions of souls that are in the earth vibration with the feeling that they are still in their physical bodies," they declared. "They are locked into a time zone. It is necessary to penetrate their time zones, to talk to them individually and bring them into the awareness that they are no longer in physical form." Such souls, Rosalind was told, need an especially sensitive approach, as they feel they are still in their Earth bodies and it requires someone from the Earth to make them aware of their situation. Once they realize they are, in Earth terms, dead, then helpers from the spirit dimension can take over and "help them adjust to their new vibrations and new reality."

The entities added that they were going to send one such soul, "lost in the earth-time zone," who needed help. Monroe intervened to question whether there was any risk to the Explorer herself. He was assured that she was quite safe, adding that the only souls who would be sent were those "on the threshold of enlightenment." Those who were in "great darkness" had to be worked with in a different way, they added. They went on to clarify the situation:

> There are many delightful souls who are locked into the physical universe of reality because they are imprisoned by their own thought-forms. Often it is fear that confines them, brought on by the trauma of the event of death. It is such souls that we bring through in a crying need of help, and on the verge of breakthrough.
>
> All souls have surrounding them many helpers . . . That is why no soul is really lost in the universe. The term "lost soul"—a concept that a soul can be lost for eternity in "hell"—is not a reality in our dimension, because there is no time. Time is a creation of the earth-consciousness. Hell is actually a level of consciousness—in which a soul can exist whether in the body or out . . . We work in a timeless level, and souls exist in a timeless level. It is a continuous process to help souls become aware of the true nature of their reality.

The soul who needed help then spoke through Rosalind, identifying himself as Patrick O'Shaunessy. He said he was born in Oban, Scotland, in 1821. In answer to Monroe's questions he said he was floating in the sea, holding on to a log. He was a cook on board a small vessel, the *Laura Belle,* transporting lumber to various countries.

There had been an explosion and as far as he knew no one else had survived. He thought he had been in the water for something like twelve hours. He was freezing cold, he said, and had almost given up hope of rescue. He told Monroe that both his parents were dead.

"Well, one of the things you have to consider is that you are like your mother and father now," said Monroe. "You have graduated. You have grown; and you are ready to move to another place." As Monroe continued to talk to him, Patrick began to accept that he was in fact dead—and yet he was still alive! "Naturally, you're still alive," said Monroe. "You do not die when your physical body dies. Let go of the log and see what happens."

Patrick released his hold on the log. "I feel so light," he said. "I've been clinging to my log, and to my life . . ." He found himself floating above the water, feeling light and free. He saw his parents reaching down for him and grasped their hands.

Rosalind's "Invisible Helpers" commented that this soul had transformed into a new level of energy and would be able to continue on from there. It had been locked in by fear. "Often it is the emotional level that locks the soul into the earth plane. Because of a very strong emotional earth attachment, it still vibrates on the slower earth level. Therefore the complete transition cannot take place until the soul mentally and emotionally releases the earth vibrations."

The complete recording of "The Patrick Event" invariably makes a deep impression on its hearers. The whole episode has a coherence that is sometimes lacking in the Explorer materials. The sailor's voice as it emanates from the Explorer in an altered state of consciousness has an urgency and plangency that stir the hearts and minds of listeners, while Monroe's total commitment to the task in hand is unquestionable.

The episode is unusual as it deals with an event that appears to have occurred in what we know as earthly or everyday reality. Patrick O'Shaunessy, born in Oban in 1821, whose parents died from influenza and who had four brothers and sisters, who became a sailor on the *Laura Belle,* a vessel carrying lumber to Ireland and other countries, that sank following an explosion in 1879—there is so much detail that one would think it possible to discover whether Patrick really existed and whether the shipwreck really happened. However, certain questions do arise. Patrick O'Shaunessy is an Irish, not a Scottish, name. Oban, where Patrick says he was born, is on the west coast of Scotland (not the north, as Patrick says—but the name O'Shaunessy does occur in the Oban registers), and the family, like many others over the years, could well have migrated from Ireland. Patrick said he worked in the kitchen of the vessel, not the galley—the usual term; but it has been claimed that kitchen was an acceptable alternative during the nineteenth century. Even if there may be a few lurking doubts, to the vast majority of those who have heard it, the information in the episode has a kind of solidity very difficult to ignore.

Soon after the move, Monroe, who hitherto had monitored the Explorers himself, withdrew from active participation in the program and invited two of the residents of the New Land, Rita and Martin Warren, to take it over. Rita had been a participant in two of the early *Gateway* programs on the New Land and the Warrens, along with their friend Nan Wilson, were among the first to buy a plot there. They lodged nearby while their house was being built and were look-ing forward to an easygoing retirement. Rita, with a PhD in psychology, had recently completed a distinguished career during which she researched and published her findings concerning the causes of juvenile crime and the treatment of offenders. She also taught psychology at the State University of New York. Martin spent much of his career in youth welfare, holding positions in the Departments of Health and of Social Welfare in California. Their interest was aroused by Monroe's offer and ideas of retirement went out of the window. They ran the *Explorer* program as unpaid volunteers for four years, often working for seven days a week. It transpired that this work, as Rita later said, "was among the most exciting and personally rewarding of their careers."

Well over a thousand recordings of channeling sessions are stored in the Institute archives or in the personal collections of the Explorers themselves. Occasionally, some brave individual will express interest in working through this material but faced with the immensity of the task soon thinks better of it. From the samples that are available—recordings of thirty-two sessions were made available for purchase in 1991—it appears that much of the content could be broadly described as spiritual. Jon Klimo comments that this type of personal, as opposed to public, channeling "involves receiving knowledge or understanding, ineffable though it may be, which includes the sense of revelation and the uplifting of one's spirit, and feelings of oneness with the Universe and all that is." The messages, information, and insights received may be of great significance to the channeler, and are often of interest to the monitor also. Looking back on the *Explorer* program, Monroe commented that "without exception, each 'entity' has as an original purpose the well-being and growth of the living human individual through whom the contact was made. If others benefited from such counseling, this was incidental and relatively unimportant. None had as an avowed purpose or intent the delivery of a vital message for humankind in general."[6]

As for the channeling process itself, Monroe pointed out that "it has always been a part of history under various guises, reaching back into antiquity and pre-Biblical eras." He adds that "prophecy, meditation, hypnosis, and certain dream states all bear a remarkable resemblance to the basic phenomenon." In all these phenomena, as with Monroe's Explorers, movement into an altered state of consciousness, no matter how achieved, is an essential part of the process.

In their sessions Monroe's Explorers are transported from the world of physical reality that is subjected to the time-space continuum to regions where physical reality, time, and space no longer exist. Their consciousness is not controlled by mood-altering drugs, medication, or any stimulus apart from certain subtle sound frequencies. They are able to understand and respond to the voice of the monitor and to describe the experience that they are undergoing. As an Explorer you may make contact with nonphysical beings who provide information that may or may not be relevant to your earthly life. You may move into the distant past or into the future; you may participate in conversations on consciousness or meet the inhabitants of Mars. There are no restrictions—and whatever your experience may be, you are always brought safely back to "normal, everyday consciousness" when your time is up.

The monitors themselves were careful not to frontload issues about beliefs or discuss expectations, although one Explorer, with the initials HBW, appeared to question this approach. HBW was in the booth discussing with the monitor, Rita Warren, the process of this kind of exploration and said that it was important to warn Explorers that what they might discover was likely to be in accordance with their belief system and expectations but this did not mean that their beliefs were true. It simply means that the information they do discover is in accordance with their expectations and beliefs. To gain a higher level of knowledge Explorers should move their belief structures and their expectations out of the way so that they obtain the freedom to get in touch with uncolored knowledge—meaning knowledge not colored by one's expectations and beliefs. For the majority of those who took part in the program, this was asking too much.

It is not surprising, therefore, that much of the content of the Explorers' channeling, especially in the 1970s and 1980s, reflects the ideas and aspirations of the New Age. There are many references to "energy" and "energy-beings," to "vibratory patterns" and "entities," although there are few, if any, attempts at explanation or definition. There are warnings of Earth-changes in the near future and an unquestioning acceptance of the concept of reincarnation. Yet there are also occasions when the Explorer seems to be taken over by something other, and is used as a mouthpiece for messages, ideas, and concepts that the Explorer was previously unaware of, although he or she would probably not disagree with them. After monitoring countless sessions, Monroe himself came to compare the Explorer sessions to gold-mining. Most of what you unearthed was dross, but every now and then you might hit upon something that was of significant value. So you persisted, in hope rather than expectation that reward would come.

An example of such reward resulted from the experience of an Explorer known as Winter. For a time Winter was an Institute trainer working with the *Guidelines* program. As a participant in that program she slept through the whole six days. During that period, she said, she made a number of decisions at an unconscious level. Sometime later she was in a group of Explorers, guided by Rita Warren, practicing remote viewing in the laboratory. She was given a target but instead of continuing with the exercise she made sudden and unexpected contact with a cartoon character—Yosemite Sam—who proceeded to scrutinize Rita's body and produced, through Winter, an accurate medical diagnosis. Soon afterwards Winter met the professor of biochemistry at Brown University, who was a member of the Institute's board of advisors, and shared this experience with him. He invited her to work with him and was impressed by her (or Sam's) diagnostic accuracy as they toured the hospital wards, so much so that he persuaded the National Institutes of Health to finance two medical students to study what she did and hopefully to learn from her.

On another occasion Winter found that she was channeling an energy by the name of Kryndon, who claimed to be "anything you want me to be." The Kryndon energy, she said, was extremely direct and was always ready to bring out anything you didn't want discussed. Monroe was fascinated by this energy and asked Winter if she was prepared to channel in public before an audience that would include Charles Tart and two leading proponents of J. Z. Knight's Ramtha. Winter agreed, although she had little idea of what it was all about, and a sizeable group assembled to witness the event. Winter sat behind a table with Rita and Martin Warren on either side of her. In his introduction, Monroe declared that no one to date had ever opened their eyes during a channeling session. "All I remember," said Winter, "was that after Bob introduced me I was sitting in the middle of the table. I had swept all the papers onto the floor and asked that they turned down the lights. I remember watching from a distance, thinking, 'So this is what they call channeling.'" Everything that happened, including Winter's open eyes during the process, was contrary to what Monroe expected, but subsequently he had several conversations with Kryndon. Winter believed he was trying to find out just what Kryndon was, but neither she nor Monroe ever came up with an answer.

Another Explorer, Ria, developed a remarkable ability to perform body scans. In so doing, she was able to visualize and detect any impairments or obstacles that were detracting from the physical, mental, or spiritual health of a given subject. That subject would normally be present in the laboratory at the time, although Ria was also able on request to perform a scan at a distance. On one occasion Monroe and Martin Warren were in the lab with Ria when Martin asked if the entity or channel that she worked with had a name. "It doesn't matter," was the reply. "Are you part of this earth plane?" asked Monroe. "No, I am not," came the response. "Well, if you're not Here then you must be There," said Monroe—and the name stuck.[7]

Many of Monroe's Explorers were professional people with some interest in spiritual concerns. There were, however, a few exceptions. Once the Institute was established on its present site, it created a certain amount of suspicion among the neighboring rural community. "That's where they do brain transplants" was one of the rumors floating around. To allay these suspicions, open house sessions for the local people were arranged from time to time. On one such day, after completing the tour of the Center and the laboratory, Marie, a young woman living in the locality, asked for a particular taped exercise and told Monroe that she would work with it and come back in a year's time to request a job at the Institute. And so she did. Every day of that year, she said, she listened to that tape, one of the introductory exercises in the *Gateway* course, and discovered in herself such a capacity to channel that she was asked to join the Explorer program. She became, in the words of Rita Warren, who was then coordinator of the program, "one of our most prolific Explorers," adding that "the energy that speaks through her always has a great deal of useful information to share with us."

In several of her sessions, IMEC, as this Explorer was known, discussed what she described as "the countless Aspects that make up the individual's personality and emotional characteristics." She allowed some of these Aspects—they included several young children, a nun, a doctor of philosophy, two older children, and a psychopath who sometimes tried to kill them all—to speak through her, each in its own voice and in its own way, and all under the charge of a "protector" identified only by initials. Commenting on the various messages, one of those monitoring her sessions said that the information "provides fascinating insights for us into questions of multiple personalities and the seeming phenomenon of possession." According to IMEC's guides, "such appearances occur when the central consciousness abandons its leadership role and allows various of the Aspective energies to gain control of emotions and behavior. It illustrates what an ordinary individual can do through conscious awareness of his own Aspects to facilitate his growth towards freedom for the central self to choose more consciously the reality that one desires to experience."

Early one morning, Rita Warren was awakened by a telephone call from IMEC, who said that she had been up since 4 A.M., waiting until the time was right to phone. She told Rita there was a man in Richmond, diagnosed with multiple personality disorder, who was being treated by a psychologist that she and Rita knew. She was afraid because one of the personalities of this patient was trying to kill both himself and his other Aspects by drowning them. She asked Rita to call the psychologist and warn him. Rita did so and was told that the patient was at that moment in the waiting room.

A couple of days later the psychologist called to see Rita and asked for any more information about what had happened. She told him about IMEC's abilities, whereupon he produced a tape from his pocket—a record of the session with the patient talking about his various personalities and explaining that one of them was trying to kill the others by drowning them. Rita commented that all these interactions were occurring in the ether, with no contact between the participants.

IMEC herself monitored a few Explorer sessions and also addressed course participants from time to time, revealing a degree of knowledge and perception remarkable in one from a comparatively limited background. She admitted that these talks sometimes presented difficulties as everything she said was actually channeled—she and her guides, whom she called Friends, had become as one and could no longer speak separately. So when, after her introductory remarks, the participants asked her to channel she feared they would be disappointed, as that is what she was already doing.

All this gives rise to a vital question. Is information received in an altered state of consciousness of any greater significance than information received in the normal course of events? To the individual receiving the information the answer may well be yes. In this regard, however, two sentences quoted by Jon Klimo from a letter to the editor of *Common Boundary* are highly relevant. "Each of us has the ability to get information specific to our life situation from our personal inner source. It is dangerous to rely upon the inner voice of someone else, as it is to accept our own without careful evaluation."[8] Most, if not all, of Monroe's explorers, who never sought publicity in any shape or form and never attempted to force acceptance of their experiences upon others, would agree.

In 1987 Monroe felt it necessary to clarify the Institute's attitude towards the channeling phenomenon. He pointed out that since 1975 the Institute had conducted more than 800 experimental sessions in the laboratory with a total of 156 volunteer subjects, adding that throughout all these sessions the Institute acted only as a reporter, making no judgment on the validity, source, or intent of the material. Reviewing the program, he concluded cautiously: "there may be many profound benefits from the wide and growing interest in the channeling process. More and more individuals are discovering that they, too, can 'channel'; in so doing, each can become his own authority with his own source."

It was about this time that the *Explorer* program, which was entirely free of charge for its participants, was terminated. Rita and Martin Warren felt that they were no longer able to continue with the program as it stood, and there were no suitable volunteers to take on the tasks of organizing and monitoring the sessions. Monroe's own interest in the program had waned, although he still felt that it might be able to produce information of value. Rita then proposed that it would be possible to continue under a different protocol. She suggested that Dr. Darlene Miller who had recently become a trainer and, like Rita Warren, had a PhD in psychology, be appointed to administer what became known as the *Personal Resource Exploration* program (PREP). This provided a session in the isolation chamber for all participants in the Institute's *Guidelines* course. In addition, anyone who wished could pay for a personal monitored session in the isolation booth. Each session was recorded on tape, one copy for the participant and the other for the Institute records.

It is, of course, not necessary to undergo a session listening to phased sound signals, whether in a laboratory or in your own home, to contact your personal inner source. The transcendent or mystical experience, those "astonishing moments of insight," as Alan Watts described them, or that "awareness that transcends the individual and discloses to a person something that passes far beyond himself," to use Ken Wilber's words, can come to anyone at any time. An altered state of consciousness may also be induced by fasting, dreaming, substance-ingesting, over-breathing, or flashing lights, although the result may be hallucinatory rather than insightful. But the advantage of the laboratory session is that the subject is held in an altered state for a considerable time—an hour or more. The presence of a monitor, able to check on the condition of the Explorer and to prompt when required with questions or comments, helps to add direction to the session, and the recording of what is being said enables discussion and development when the session is over.

Whether the Explorer is an adept, having experienced forty or fifty sessions, a participant in a regular Monroe Institute program that includes a session as a matter of course, or a person who is ready to pay in dollars for the experience, what happens during the event may sometimes prove of great personal significance. Then again, it may be a fun trip—a visit to a playful planet, for instance—or it might deliver an answer to a question or solution to a problem. An advantage of considering questions or problems in an altered state is that perspectives are changed, complications can be resolved, the crooked becomes straight and the rough places plain—and all this with or without the help of "entities." But what Monroe and his scientific colleagues could not have foreseen is that a project originally designed to investigate the effects of certain sound frequencies on human consciousness would become a means of acquiring insights, information, ideas, even entertainment, that has proved of interest and sometimes of value to thousands of people who have allowed themselves to be installed on a waterbed in a sensory-deprivation isolation unit, wired up to various recording instruments, equipped with headphones and a microphone, and given permission to explore.

Notes

1. Rosalind McKnight, *Cosmic Journeys* (Hampton Roads, 1999).

2. Jon Klimo, *Channeling* (Tarcher, 1987).

3. M. F. Brown, *The Channeling Zone* (Harvard University Press, 1997).

4. See Brown, *The Channeling Zone,* p. 194.

5. The *Starlines* program, devised by the Monroe trainer Franceen King and first offered in 2003, takes participants even farther into hitherto unknown territory.

6. Not quite so. There are references to Earth Changes and various natural disasters, topics much discussed in certain New Age circles, in some of the transcripts.

7. On one occasion I submitted myself to a body scan by Ria in the Institute laboratory. She (or "There") indicated a block located at a point on my right shoulder that she said had been there for many years and was a consequence of intensive study in my late teens. As this block caused no pain I paid little attention to it at the time. Then a few years later I was being examined by a leading osteopath specializing in craniosacral work. At the end of the treatment I asked what if anything he had found. "Just one thing," he replied. "There was some sort of block on your right shoulder. It must have been caused by something you were doing many years ago— working too hard perhaps. Anyway, I've released it."

8. The writer of this letter was James B. DeKome, of El Rito, New Mexico.

CHAPTER 6

On Roberts Mountain

By 1976 Bob Monroe was convinced that the time was approaching when they would have to move from Whistlefield. He was sixty-one years old, secure in his marriage and with his extended family now off his hands. He was not always in the best of health, yet his energy and enthusiasm for his new enterprise continued to grow. With the increasing interest in his work it was becoming clear that what was needed was something quite different from a handsome manor house on extensive grounds with a collection of ancillary buildings. To fulfill its promise the new Institute required a residential center with ample space for seminars, an administrative building, and a purpose-built laboratory with up-to-date facilities for research. The Albemarle County authorities were altogether unlikely to grant permission for this kind of development as, being commercial, it would be detrimental to the upmarket image of the locality that they wished to preserve. That was not all. Now that the novelty had worn off, Monroe himself was no longer comfortable with the role of lord of the manor. He was not impressed, he said, to be seen as "the rich guy on the hill in the neat white house," and the estate itself, grand enough to be featured in "Estates of Virginia," was very expensive to maintain. It cost $250 a month simply to cut the lawns. He now talked of Whistlefield as "a huge white elephant." All the same, it was Nancy's house, her "Up Home," and he found it hard to imagine leaving.

Nancy was at first deeply distressed when Bob told her that Whistlefield had to be sold. For her, after so many years of making-do in Marine Corps accommodations, the house was a dream come true. Here, for the first time in her life, she was able to shine. What chance was there of finding anything that could compare with its spacious elegance in such a beautiful setting? But her basic common sense and her understanding that if her husband's work was to progress—and it was work that she not only believed in but was also a part of, as she had taken her own turn as an Explorer—then a purpose-built center was essential.

So the Monroes started to search the newspapers for a tract of land in the vicinity that they could develop. Next to Albemarle is the much less affluent and wholly rural Nelson County. Here, the authorities let it be known that a commercial undertaking would be warmly welcomed. Monroe contacted a realtor who drove them to Nelson County to view some eight hundred acres of tree-clad countryside, including a farm, on Roberts Mountain in the foothills of the Blue Ridge. They both loved it but the price the realtor quoted was out of their reach.

For the time being the matter was put on hold. Then a few months later a friend who claimed to have psychic abilities offered to do a reading for them. Monroe told him that they were seeking a place to move to. "You've already seen it," said the friend, "but you haven't considered it." They agreed this could only mean that Roberts Mountain was the land in question. They visited it again, made further inquiries, and discovered that it belonged to a real estate developer in Florida. Then Nancy spotted an advertisement in the local newspaper for Roberts Mountain Farm. Clearly they needed to act before someone else stepped in. By-passing the realtor, Monroe contacted the owner—his name, he was amused to see, was Warren Harding—who was delighted to find that the prospective buyer was the author of *Journeys Out of the Body*. "I've been looking for you for the past four years!" he declared.

Monroe invited Harding to Whistlefield, where he discovered that they shared a wide range of interests in a variety of metaphysical matters. They talked with barely an interruption, except for meals, for a whole week. When at last they took time out for business, the sale was quickly agreed for a cash payment of some six hundred thousand dollars plus a slice of the Whistlefield estate. To raise the funds Monroe needed to sell the rest of the estate, the apartments that he still owned in Charlottesville, and most of his remaining interest in Jefferson Cable Corporation. In so doing, he demonstrated his faith in the process that he and his scientist colleagues had worked so intensively to develop and which, he hoped, would also secure his and Nancy's future.

While Monroe was still in the process of financial negotiations, Joseph Pearce stopped by to spend a few days with him. Eager to share his enthusiasm for future possibilities, Monroe took him to see the land where the new Institute would be built. Nancy and he had begun to refer to this as the New Land, not for any spiritual reason but to distinguish it from another stretch of land that they had briefly considered earlier. He talked to Joe about wanting to found what he called a "Survival Community" of some half a dozen farmers, in case some of the widely circulating New Age prophecies of impending disasters happened to come true. The beauty of the area appealed to Pearce immediately, survival community or not. He found a site in woodland in the northeast corner and realized that this was where he wanted to live. Over the next few months he built a wooden house there, becoming the first member of the New Land community despite the fact that the purchase of the land had not then been completed.[1]

The purchase of the New Land was finalized in 1977. Then, as they were planning their move, Nancy's old home on the James River near Roanoke came up for sale. She dearly wanted to buy the property, but Bob, with his finances now fully committed, had to tell her this was impossible. Having to disappoint Nancy, he said later, made this one of the most difficult decisions he had ever faced.

It was two years before the Monroes were able to relocate. In that time Bob had to sell off the rest of the Whistlefield estate, sort out his financial obligations, and get things moving on Roberts Mountain. While the Center was under construction he sought to form what he described as a Partnership "to own and operate a new training and conference center" and offered "limited partnership" for $15,000 a unit, hoping to attract up to twenty investors who would be granted one free program a year and an estimated 12.5 percent return on their capital. It was an ambitious scheme that failed to attract enough interest and never came to fruition.

The changes in his own life seemed to Monroe to be symptomatic of the major changes that were being prophesied and anticipated by large numbers of adherents of the New Age way of thinking. Although he had been attracted by the writings of Edgar Cayce and Jane Roberts, he was wary of this new enthusiasm and of the "love and light" type of expressions now often bandied around. At the same time he thought there was something to be learned from those, including some of his Explorers, who, like Cayce—or, possibly, influenced by him and by others with apparent prophetic gifts—forecast imminent Earth changes and the subsequent challenges that would have to be faced. But while the New Age bandwagon carried certain items that caught his interest, he was not tempted to jump onto it.

The New Land, for all its promise, presented a host of problems. There was no power, no drainage, and only one rough road on the property, winding up from the entrance to the top of the mountain.

As well as the requirements for the Institute that Monroe envisaged, there also had to be a house for the Monroes themselves. Such a house would at the very least have to compensate Nancy for the loss of Whistlefield, but it would have to wait until the new Institute was up and running. Monroe himself drew up plans for the Residential Center, but before matters were finalized an offer arrived from an anonymous donor willing to pay for the building on condition that the plans were altered to his own requirements. With his own finances now seriously stretched, Monroe agreed. Then, partway through construction, the donor withdrew, claiming that his investments had failed. This left Monroe with a bill for more than seventy thousand dollars, a building more like a bunkhouse for VIPs instead of the spacious and comfortable center he had himself envisaged, and a very sour taste in his mouth.[2]

As eventually completed, the Residential Center could accommodate twenty-two participants, although there was a marked shortage of toilets and washing facilities. The upside of this, as many *Gateway* participants remarked, was that the long queues for the toilets provided a good opportunity for them to get to know each other. A research laboratory incorporating a sound studio was built close by. Near the entrance to the New Land was a partly completed structure that was transformed into a three-story building known as the Gate House. Here on the main floor was the administrative center with office spaces and storage facilities. Below there was further office space and an apartment at one time occupied by Cindy and her young daughter Tiffany. The upper floor was to be Bob and Nancy's home while their own house was planned and built. Bob could accept this, but for Nancy it was not a happy time. The idea of living "over the shop" was wholly unattractive—and so very different from the style of Whistlefield. Moreover, the area of her new staging-post (which was perhaps the best way of regarding it) was less than a third of her previous home. There was, however, promise of better things. At one time Nancy had visualized her ideal of a home, to be sited on the very top of Roberts Mountain. So they could begin to draw up plans for the Gift House, as it later became called. But it took seven years before the Gift House was ready for occupation.

Now the owner of a large tract of undeveloped land, Monroe saw the opportunity to put into practice a concept of a kind that resembled certain aspects of the "new thinking" of the time. The land was not only to be the home of his Institute; it was also to become a model of community living, self-sufficient and productive, providing a whole way of life. Farming was to continue, with George Durrette, who had proved at Whistlefield that he could turn his hand to anything, as farm manager. Plans were drawn of the remainder of the land not occupied by the Institute and seventy-nine parcels, each between three and six acres, were offered for sale. Purchasers were to be responsible for building their own houses and digging their own wells for water supply, and were free to earn their living in whatever way they wished. A New Land Association was to be formed to take responsibility for various communal areas, and additional land could be rented from Monroe for vegetable gardens, greenhouses, pasture for horses, chicken runs, and similar purposes. A compulsory payment would be levied on householders for the construction and maintenance of the roads. Membership in the Association included permission to make use of the fourteen-acre Lake Miranon that was formed when he discovered a spring in the valley feeding a stream running through the fields, and so named by Monroe after the channeled entity who had greatly influenced his thinking. The stream was dammed until, as a kind of celebration on Nancy's birthday, the dam was opened and the lake began to fill. The New Land Association stocked the lake with fish and provided all the materials for recreation, including the float that soon became highly popular with *Gateway* participants.

In 1981, as inquiries about the purchase of lots on the New Land began to arrive, Monroe drew up a document headed "Charter of New Community of Virginia." This was to be signed by "the Founders and First Elders to establish and form in the service of our Creator the fellowship to be known as New Community." The original document ran to over 180 pages but a condensed version was made available. The language is a sort of seventeenth-century pastiche; the content is an amalgam of New Age spiritual theory and elements of Monroe's philosophical reflections derived from his out-of-body experiences and also from information and ideas conveyed by some of the Explorers. The document incorporates a set of Beliefs, which could be "translated into Knowledge and Truth by both communal and direct personal experience on the part of the individual." These Beliefs were to be implemented by certain Purposes, one of which was "to establish, operate, maintain, extend and expand a Pathway into all realities and energy systems, along which human Consciousness may proceed at an accelerating rate to greater wisdom and understanding of that which is perceived."

To these somewhat magniloquent sentences a list of twelve Basics was appended. Most of these were of an admonitory nature, warning New Landers about profiteering and speculation, informing them not to expect to derive income from either the New Land or the Institute, and instructing them to "conform to the laws of the external culture." New Landers were told to "respect the space and property of one another, without extreme focus on material possessions, yet with sure recognition that materiality at present is essential to physical survival." There was, New Landers were advised, one rule: "grow, adapt, evolve—or die."

It seems that Monroe originally saw the Institute as the lodestar for the New Land. In 1981 he offered a free *Gateway Voyage* to the residents and repeated the offer in the following year. He hoped that when the laboratory was completed the New Landers would become "the first of a new breed of Explorers." But while the presence of the Institute and of Monroe himself attracted some of the early purchasers, to those coming later these factors had less relevance. They were drawn by the beauty of the area, the wide choice of location, the reasonable price of each parcel of land, the freedom to design their own houses, and, for some, the prospect of self-sufficiency. To them, Bob Monroe was primarily the developer, to be held responsible for whatever was unsatisfactory or needed attention.

The move to Roberts Mountain marked a shift in both the inner and outer worlds of Monroe himself. At Whistlefield he was the practical investigator, using his knowledge of electrical engineering and audio technology, coupled with his experience in the out-of-body state, to develop a system that would, as it were, intertwine these two very different strands. He lived in a grand house with a gracious wife and several children, entertained frequently, and was in contact with a large number of people who were interested in his research, some of whom were eager to participate in it. At Roberts Mountain he was restricted to quarters on the top floor of the office building. The Institute's Residential Center, laboratory, and lecture hall had to be completed, furnished, and equipped, there were staff members and trainers to be appointed, financial problems to be solved, the *Gateway* program to be revised and standardized, new programs to be designed, and his second book, *Far Journeys,* to be finished. In the distant future—or so it must have seemed—was the promise of the house on the mountaintop, together with Monroe's private retreat close by, the log cabin where he would be able to write, compose music, and create new programs for the Institute.

As well as all this activity, there were also physical problems for Monroe himself. Looking after his own health was not a priority; he smoked quite heavily and his diet was horrific. In earlier days he had enjoyed scuba-diving, sailing, and piloting gliders and light aircraft. Now it was his out-of-body adventures that possessed him and the poor old physical body had to cope as best it could. In 1981 he had to undergo an operation on the subclavial artery, followed a year later by surgery to deal with an aortic aneurism. In both these instances he recovered consciousness while still on the operating table. After the second occasion he described the pain as "exquisite." He added, "That kind of pain only programs you for the same kind of pressure you feel in other realities." This episode made him reconsider his priorities, leading to a decision to withdraw from day-to-day responsibilities as soon as it was practicable. It was not a decision that he was always able to hold to.

So much for the outer world, but the New Land Charter and accompanying documents are evidence of a transformation in Monroe's mindset. The words and concepts are those of a visionary. They express an idealistic view of human nature. It was almost as if the New Land was to be the New Jerusalem, supervised by a benevolent deity. At Whistlefield, Monroe was very close to the Explorers and monitored the great majority of the sessions. The prophetic nature of some of the information that the Explorers transmitted seems to have influenced his thinking and led him into believing that it was time for a new vision of community living. The purchase of the New Land, with its forests, meadows, and streams, distant from the bustling, competitive life of the late twentieth century and presumably safe from the Earth changes and other calamities predicted by, among others, Edgar Cayce and the interpreters of Nostrodamus, gave him the opportunity of translating this vision into action.[3] On paper, dignified by the archaic language of the Charter, it looked fine. But, as with an earlier idealistic vision, it was not long before the serpent appeared. In this case the serpent was simply human nature.

A letter that Monroe circulated to New Land residents in March 1983 included these sentences: "All of us have made this our home and our future lives, for reasons beyond the beauty of the locale. We might all put it in different words, but basically it would come down to wanting to be a part of the philosophy and future work of the Institute and the Community." That was no more than an assumption. As one resident remarked: "We moved to the New Land primarily because of the location. I confess that we were somewhat attracted by the idea of community, but this ideal quickly disappeared after attending a few New Land meetings." Regardless of Monroe's hopes, summed up in *Gateway Unity,* the name he gave to the Institute programs he offered them, the New Landers failed to fulfill his aspirations that they would become "the first of a new breed of Explorers."

Unless the vision is strong, shared by all, and reinforced by a unified belief system and the certainty of mutual trust, community living to the satisfaction of all participants is unlikely to endure for long. On all these points the New Land venture fell short of the expectations of its founder. Monroe himself was regarded with suspicion by a number of the residents who felt that in his role as developer some of his transactions were open to question and that his judgments were not always sound. One episode showed that there was some justification for this. A somewhat eccentric scientist from Texas convinced him to buy a large quantity of an algae fertilizer, which he stored in gallon containers in one of his barns. Assured of its value, he bought the rights to its production, entering into partnership with an individual who later turned out to be a swindler. The fertilizer proved useless. A court case ensued, but in the event the whole episode cost him well into six figures.

A particular cause for dissatisfaction was that in issues to be dealt with by the New Land Association, Monroe held two votes for the lots he owned while everyone else had only one. On his part, Monroe complained that some residents were slow to repay loans he had made and showed no gratitude for help he gave them. He was also annoyed that protests were made about *Gateway* participants walking along the roads or swimming in the lake, when his hope had been that at the end of every course New Landers and course participants would meet and socialize to their mutual benefit.

As long as Monroe took an active role in New Land affairs, he bore the brunt of criticism and complaint, including a petition "to have the cows removed because of their poop," presumably because the smell permeated the petitioners' cars or houses. The residents also had reasons to feel slighted. A group got together to produce a set of designs for greenhouses for the use of the community, to be serviced by hydroelectric power generated from the lake. Monroe scrutinized the plans and seemed at first to approve, but then summarily rejected them on the grounds that they did not represent the structures he himself had in mind. Whether that was so or not is irrelevant, because for Monroe it was ultimately a question of control. In his earlier career as producer and director, and later as sole owner, firm control was essential for success, and this was carried over into his new life, very different though it was. To put it bluntly, if it wasn't his idea and was not going to be as he wanted it to be, then it wasn't going to be at all.

For six years Monroe struggled on until it all became too much. In a memo circulated in July 1987, he referred to "indirect allegations and innuendoes . . . regarding my development and administration of our New Land Subdivision, resentment of me by New Land residents, and most important, the obvious deterioration and fragmentation of what unifying spirit and purpose did exist on New Land." In view of all this, he declared that it was "vital to all of our welfare and growth" that he should change to a new direction. He would withdraw to his home on the top of the mountain and take no further part in the affairs of the New Land Association. Although his original intention to create a place of peace had been shuffled aside, he still hoped that at least some of what he wanted had been distilled into the area. But now, he said, as far as he was concerned he'd rather be playing cards.

Today there is still a New Land Association. It operates independently of the Institute, and its annual meetings are largely concerned with the state of the roads. As well as the residents' own vehicles there are, as there were from the very beginning, delivery vans, construction lorries, logging trucks, tractors—in short, all the varieties of traffic to be expected in an area undergoing continuous development together with a farm and extensive tracts of woodland. The roads are rough-surfaced and almost every passing vehicle raises clouds of dust. But the old arguments and resentments are long forgotten. New Landers live their own independent lives and are fortunate in enjoying a most beautiful environment which, over the years, has attracted several outstanding personalities, including a leading New York literary agent, a best-selling novelist, an influential philosopher, an internationally recognized speech-language pathologist, the U.S. Military's number one psychic spy, and a businessman who bred llamas. Some of the residents are associated with the Institute, but its presence and activities are far less dominant than in the earlier days.

For Monroe himself the New Land venture, at least in part, was a failure in that it did not come up to his aspirations. The help he hoped for to realize his vision never materialized. He named just one person, David Francis, owner of a coal mining operation in West Virginia, who had attended one of the early *Gateway* programs and became a close friend, as the only individual who understood his vision and was prepared to give practical help. Francis empathized with Monroe, made no demands upon him, and provided donations at critical times. He died from diabetes in 1985. In recognition of his generous financial support and his friendship, Monroe gave the name of David Francis to the fine new lecture hall that completed his plans for the Institute buildings.

Programs at The Monroe Institute of Applied Sciences were suspended from the winter of 1978 until July 1979, when the first

Gateway was held at the new Center, with Chris Lenz and Karen Malik as trainers. It was only a few days previously that Monroe had obtained permission from the county authorities in Lovingston to run such programs. "They didn't understand what the new educational institution was all about," said Nancy, "but Bob was persuasive and we got the go-ahead." Work on the building was still in progress when the participants arrived, with carpets being laid and wiring being installed. They had to wait around for two days before the course could begin. For technical reasons it was not an unqualified success, and those who complained were offered their money back.

The early programs each lasted for ten days and only four were held in the first year. In 1980 the program was reduced to eight days but again only four took place. Then things began to accelerate. Two years earlier, Melissa Jager, a Stanford graduate in philosophy with an MEd from the University of Arizona, who among a variety of rich experiences had been a program consultant for Silva Mind Control and worked with Ned Herrman's Brain Dominance Instrument, had come across a magazine article referring to a certain Robert Monroe, said to be "testing the out-of-body experience." Her attention captured, she discovered that this same Monroe had some association with the highly reputable Menninger Foundation. Her mother, whose interest was also aroused, suggested that Melissa and her son accompany her to a weekend program in Richmond, to be conducted by Monroe himself—possibly the first time that three generations of a family attended a program together. During the weekend Melissa experienced what she described as a very profound OBE. She signed up for two more weekend sessions and was then invited by Monroe to become a trainer for the *M-5000* program. Impressed by her ability, in 1981 he appointed her to succeed Chris Lenz as director of training. In the same year, the first six tapes of the *Gateway* program were made available to the public at large, under the title of *Discovery*. Melissa compiled almost all the manual that accompanied the album of tapes, and her informal and informative style set the tone for future publications. Some single taped exercises were also issued. One of those that still finds a place in the current catalogue is the memory exercise "Retain-Recall-Release," followed two years later by the popular "Catnapper," designed to provide thirty minutes of refreshing sleep whenever required.

In 1982 a couple arrived who were to have important roles in the development of the Institute. Dave Wallis had served in the U.S. Air Force followed by twenty years in senior posts at Lockheed. He and his wife Jean had attended one of the early *Gateway* programs in California. This had given them much to think about. They had already been feeling it was time to make a move into a different way of life. They began to investigate various communities around the United States, eventually settling on the New Land in 1981. Eager to make use of his skills, Dave volunteered to work in the planned laboratory, where he helped to design the building and much of the equipment and also installed the electronics. Monroe, appreciating his abilities, then appointed him technical consultant to the Institute.

Nancy Monroe and Dave Wallis

To earn enough to live on, Dave took time out for consultancy work on various communications systems overseas.

At the same time, a Professional Division was being established, consisting of individuals who had attended *Gateway* and who used Hemi-Sync tapes with their clients, patients, or students. Jean Wallis, also seeking to become involved, offered to serve as its director. To cope with the increasing interest in the Institute's activities more staff members were recruited and new taped exercises were developed. The *Gateway* program was trimmed further to fit into six days and settled into a format that has changed little since. Helen Warring, who joined the Institute in 1981 as secretary and later became program registrar, did much to encourage intending participants, some of whom were doubtful as to what they might be letting themselves in for. Helen was ever generous with her time and advice. From her office on the lower floor of the Gate House, hers for the next decade was the voice of the Institute for the outside world.

Of the new taped exercises issued at this time perhaps the most significant was the Emergency series. This consisted of six tapes to be listened to through headphones, before, during, and after an operation. The series was produced in collaboration with a distinguished psychiatrist from Oakland, California, Dr. Art Gladman, who had used some of the *Gateway* tapes with his own patients who were suffering from stress-related disorders. Gladman himself had undergone surgery for spinal stenosis that had failed to solve the problem and left him in considerable pain. Needing further surgery, he explained to Dr. Bob Roalfe, who was to be his anesthesiologist, how the Emergency series tapes might be helpful and Roalfe agreed that he could use them. This second operation was successful; more than that, Gladman needed far less anesthesia than usual and was able to leave hospital in five days rather than the ten he required after the previous surgery.

Impressed by this, Dr. Roalfe continued to use the Emergency series with his patients, and ran a trial with eighty-one individuals undergoing lumbar laminectomies and total hysterectomies. The results, based on his own observations and the responses of the patients, showed that sixty-three of the eighty-one received positive benefits from the use of these tapes.[4]

In 1983 further reports on the Emergency series were published in *Breakthrough,* the Institute's newsletter. One was from David Edgar, who underwent two days of operations for facial skin cancer followed by reconstructive surgery, all under local anesthetic. Unable to use headphones, he attached the tape player to his belt and was able to maintain continuity by simply turning it over. He commented that "the tapes were so supportive that I would not consider being without them." Reporting on the effect of the "Intra-Op" exercise, he remarked that "the most meaningful part of the tape was Bob's comment that I was not alone."

Later that year Gari Carter wrote a first-person account of her use of the Emergency series. In February the previous year she was driving to Baltimore with Tom, her eleven-year-old son, to buy items for her gift shop. It was snowing and the road was covered with ice. They were wondering whether to turn back when a station wagon appeared round a bend, lost control, and hit them head-on. Tom was miraculously uninjured, but Gari's face was crushed by the steering wheel and her legs shattered by the engine driven into them by the impact. Realizing that she had stopped breathing, her son, using training he had received in the Boy Scouts, managed to revive her. A woman living nearby phoned for help, a passing motorist extinguished flames issuing from under the hood, and the rescue squad arrived and freed her.

Gari underwent two long and painful operations at the Plastic Surgery Department of the University of Virginia Hospital and was due for the next operation when a friend told her of some surgery pain-control tapes and insisted that she try them. She listened to them before the operation and decided to trust them. This attracted the interest of the doctors and nursing staff, who were fully cooperative and fascinated by the difference that Gari's use of the tapes over a series of reconstructive operations made both to her degree of relaxation and to the speed of her post-op recovery when, she said, she had no need of pain medication.

Gari's final surgery to complete the reconstruction of her face, that the accident eight years earlier left, she said, as "one big gory hole," took place in October 1990. By this time the H-Plus series of exercises was available and she used several of these as extra support to the Emergency series. The last healing, she later wrote, was the best of all. Using the Hemi-Sync exercises together with neuromuscular and craniosacral therapies enabled her to feel "strengthened and invigorated by so much healing help from which to choose." In her book *Healing Myself,* in which she vividly describes the accident, the surgical procedures, and her life before and after the whole traumatic experience, she writes: "My tragedy evolved from the worst to the best event in my life. My recovery shows that the mind, body and soul can be transformed."

Among many others who made use of the Emergency series was Mary Lou Ballweg, who had been diagnosed with endometriosis in 1978. She underwent four operations for this condition and had co-founded the Endometriosis Association, which promoted research into the condition and offered support to those affected. She had come across various reports on the use of relaxation tapes during surgery, in particular one in which the Emergency series had been used in laparoscopy with meaningful results. Facing a fifth operation, Mary Lou decided to use these tapes, finding them helpful in diminishing anxiety, managing pain, and bringing about a feeling of peace and relaxation in the recovery period, so much so that her experience resulted in the Endometriosis Association purchasing a hundred sets for the benefit of their members.[5]

It is not only the Hemi-Sync sound signals that help the listener to cope before, during, and after a surgical procedure. Listening to Monroe's "calm, trustworthy voice" saying "You are not alone" over and over again, Gari Carter said, "made me feel totally supported by the surgical team and the entire world." Many others have made similar comments on the heartening effect of this remarkable voice and the absolute rightness of the timing. In addition to the hundreds of individual testimonies, there have been several favorable research articles published on the use of the Surgical Support series, as the Emergency series has been retitled. Among these is a report on a "Double Blind Randomized Trial" published in *Anesthesia* (54, no. 8 [1999]: 769-73) indicating that patients using the tapes during surgery required only one-quarter of the pain medications needed by the control group.

In the fall of 1982 came a new departure for the Institute. This was the first contact with the military, when three officers from a small army department established to look into new theories of consciousness met at the Institute Center with Monroe and about twenty-five New Land residents. The senior officer, a colonel with a PhD degree, introduced the subject and prepared the group for an experiment in nonordinary phenomena. Joe Pearce, who was among those present, describes what happened:

> Each of us had brought a piece of stainless-steel cutlery, and within about twenty minutes, simply by stroking them, twenty-three of us present had bent those pieces of tableware into every conceivable shape. The first to succeed was an eight-year-old girl who neatly creased the bowl of her spoon across its middle and folded the end portion of the bowl back over the shank, giving a double-thick, truncated bowl. We then watched her younger brother corkscrew the handle of

his fork from top to bottom, and the effect spread around the room, generally from the youngest to the oldest. People bent knives into knots, interwove the tines of forks, rolled the handles of spoons tightly into the bowls, and generally messed up twenty-three pieces of flatware.[6]

Although spoon-bending never became a part of the Monroe Institute's activities, or part of military training for that matter, Delta Company, in which the three officers served, continued for a time in its investigations into the possibilities of adapting certain potentials of human consciousness for military use.

There was more productive involvement from another area of the military. Lieutenant Fred Atwater was not the only member of the army who had read Monroe's first book and was attracted to the Institute. Another military intelligence officer, Warrant Officer Joseph McMoneagle, who had a distinguished record of service in several countries, including Vietnam and Thailand, also came into contact with Monroe through reading *Journeys Out of the Body*. He found a copy on the floor of a bookstore while he was stationed in the Washington, D.C., area. Joe picked it up to return it. Catching sight of the title, he said, "an electric shock ran through my entire body." Concealing the book from other customers lest they think it was inappropriate reading for a military man, he purchased it and read it avidly. It brought back to him an experience that had occurred in Germany nine years before. He had been dining out with friends when he began to feel ill. He left the table to go outside but collapsed by the door and went into convulsions, swallowed his tongue, was unable to breathe—and his heart stopped. Yet, he reported later, he observed everything that happened: his body lying in the street, the attempts to bring him around, the urgent drive to a hospital, doctors and nurses working on him—and then he moved from what he later came to understand as an out-of-body experience into a near-death experience in which he found himself absorbed by what he described as "a Being of Light." Gradually emerging from this, he was told he was not going to die—and he opened his eyes and sat up. The experience left him depressed, confused, and subject for some time to uncontrolled out-of-body experiences. It also left him with a gift of what he describes as spontaneous knowledge—an uncalled-for sensitivity to what people around him were thinking.

Once recovered, McMoneagle continued working with intelligence collection and operations in the European military theater for another seven years. While assigned to the headquarters in Washington, he was recruited into the army's secret remote-viewing project, then known as Grill Flame.[7] He was interviewed by the scientist in charge, Dr. Hal Puthoff of the Stanford Research Institute (who had visited Monroe at Whistlefield), and qualified for inclusion, having scored five out of six first-place remote viewings. Now a member of Grill Flame, where, as it happened, Fred Atwater was operations officer, he was to be recognized as its most successful remote-viewer.

Atwater suggested to McMoneagle that he might find it interesting to consult Monroe, who might be able to help him with a problem that had arisen with his remote-viewing. In October 1979 they drove to Roberts Mountain. McMoneagle called at the Gate House, where he was immediately impressed by Nancy, whom he described as "a wonderful sort of old-fashioned Southern lady." He found Monroe polite and friendly but clearly in pain, having recently returned from the hospital after surgery on his leg. During their conversation, Monroe discussed the paranormal as if it was an everyday occurrence, concluding by inviting McMoneagle to take part in a *Gateway* program.

McMoneagle's problem was the length of time it took him to prepare for a remote-viewing session. To begin with he needed about thirty-five minutes to move into the appropriate state of mind, but the more sessions he undertook the longer the period became. This, he felt, was due to the considerable stress incurred in working on cases often involving life and death and needing immediate responses. Moreover, everyday emotions, happenings, and problems kept getting in the way. He needed to ignore everything he had ever been taught regarding information-gathering, especially any feelings associated with targets such as kidnappings, bombings, and terrorist activities. As he said, "The concept with which you are dealing flies in the face of all that you have been imprinted with, by parents, siblings, friends, peer group, school, religion, etc. So you deal with it by increasing the time you spend before a remote viewing session in order to convince yourself that what you are about to do is okay." To do that was taking him two hours or more and it was becoming a major problem.

McMoneagle obtained the army's permission to sign up for *Gateway* in June 1982. The experiences he shared with his fellow participants and with the trainer, Melissa Jager, made him realize that at least twenty other people were able to feel and think as he did. In a break in the program he came across Scooter, recently returned from the West Coast. They talked for a while, a conversation that Scooter later described as the most noninformational meeting she had ever experienced. McMoneagle also took part in a second *Gateway* the following year, this time with Scooter as his trainer. He found that the skills acquired in these programs enhanced his remote-viewing ability, and, as he later wrote, "they also contribute a great deal to the mastering of one's environment, regardless of occupation." Joe soon became recognized as the most accomplished remote-viewer operating on what was eventually named the *Star Gate* program.

Because McMoneagle seemed to be well suited to the Hemi-Sync training, the *Star Gate* administration contracted with Monroe to work with him under Atwater's supervision for ten nonconsecutive weeks over a period of about fourteen months to see if this training might enhance Joe's remote-viewing abilities. Monroe first taught him to relax by focusing his attention on different parts of his body, directing them in turn to "relax, let go, sleep." Next he was required to breathe more slowly and imagine that his breath represented the flow of life-energy. Monroe suggested that Joe set his intent through a process of affirmation. Once these three ingredients were in place, he encouraged Joe to pay attention to his internal world, to become aware of his own mental realm without the "noise" of the physical senses. Next Joe learned to release stress and quickly enter a meditative state. Subsequently, he found his preparation time would last no more than five minutes. He later listed the skills that aided the remote-viewing experience: learning to achieve relaxation; meditation, or learning to become centered; opening your awareness and sensitivity; and communicating your intuitive perceptions. Lastly came the addition of certain Hemi-Sync frequencies, designed to alter the brain's cortical level of arousal. The effect of this training enabled Joe to report and record his remote-viewing perceptions to maximum effect.

Atwater, as *Star Gate*'s operations and training officer, conducted frequent audit remote-viewing sessions to try to determine any improvement in Joe's performance. On one occasion, he decided to use coordinates provided by Puthoff of certain unusual formations on the planet Mars. In preparation for the exercise Atwater had written "The planet Mars, one million years B.C." on a standard 3 x 5 index card, and sealed it in a small opaque envelope that Monroe placed in his breast pocket. Neither Monroe nor Joe had any idea of the target or the coordinates.

When Joe was ready, Atwater directed him to use the information in the envelope and then read him the first Martian coordinate. As Monroe adjusted the Hemi-Sync patterns, Joe's respiration slowed and his speech became slurred, with incomplete sentences—all signs that he was moving deeply into the process. When he began to describe an "arid climate" in "some distant place," Atwater knew he was probably on target. He checked the list of Martian coordinates and directed Joe to "move" from his present location to the next set of coordinates on Puthoff's list.

Perceiving the time period "one million years B.C.," Joe reported "the after-effect of a major geologic problem." Asked to move to a time before this problem (perhaps thousands or tens of thousands of years), he reported a "total difference" in the terrain. He also found "a shadow" of "very large people," and explained that by "shadow" he meant they weren't there anymore. Atwater then asked Joe to move to the time when the people were still there, no matter how far back that might be. He described "very large people" who were "wearing very strange clothes."

Altogether Joe described eight different coordinate-designated locations on Mars, including several unusual structures. He talked of a cataclysmic disaster that had destroyed the home of this ancient race. At one point it seemed to the listeners that he was in some form of telepathic communication with one of the Martians. During this deep-contact period, Joe's skin potential voltage, measured from the finger electrodes, reversed polarity (crossing the zero or null point), indicating a discrete shift in perception.

When the session was over, Atwater and Monroe debriefed Joe before revealing the contents of the sealed envelope. He remarked on what it felt to be such a long way off and declared, not surprisingly,

Joe McMoneagle, Cairn Holy, Galloway 2005

that this session had been very different from his previous remote-viewing experience.[8]

Whatever implications this remote-viewing may have for future exploration of Mars, its importance goes beyond that. It demonstrated that McMoneagle was not only able to lock on to a target of which he had no information whatsoever, but was also able to extend his consciousness across millions of miles and millions of years. This in itself adds a new dimension to our human potential.

Hemi-Sync training did not necessarily affect the overall remote-viewing quality, but it did improve the viewer's reliability. It provided a dependable tool that could be used to access beneficial states of cortical arousal, states conducive to relaxing physically and mentally, to connecting with the target, to listening quietly to internal perceptual processes, to becoming aware of the information of interest, and to reporting accurately such information. As it happened, Joe McMoneagle was the only remote-viewer to be trained personally by Bob Monroe. The *Star Gate* administrators found that the *Gateway Voyage* itself provided sufficient support for those selected to attend it, although as it turned out none of them performed as consistently as did Joe. It may be that in terms of reliability or dependability the ten weeks of individual training was the better preparation after all.

This involvement with the Institute attracted the attention of General Burt Stubblebine, at the time commanding officer of INSCOM (Intelligence & Security Command). Having studied McMoneagle's report on his experiences at the Institute, he proposed that a special course be arranged for certain INSCOM personnel. Monroe agreed and Scooter was given the task of adapting the *Gateway* program to suit this particular group.

This program was known as Rapid Acquisition Personnel Training (RAPT). Volunteers were interviewed to ensure they observed certain requirements. The first two RAPT programs were full, the participants including several senior officers. There were no negative reports and many highly positive responses. On the third program, however, one participant had to withdraw at short notice and was replaced by a man who had not been thoroughly interviewed and who also had concealed relevant personal details when he applied to join the army. He had to be removed during the program and taken to the hospital. Learning of this, the army chief of staff for intelligence ordered the program to be terminated. Stubblebine himself, whose interest in matters psychic and paranormal was regarded with suspicion by his seniors, retired shortly afterwards, to be replaced in the following year by an officer with a different outlook.

Another involvement with the military took place in the closing months of 1982, when the psychologist Ray Waldkoetter organized a project at the Defense Department Information School at Fort Benjamin Harrison to see if introducing Hemi-Sync to the training program would enhance the ability to learn. Monroe himself was scheduled to attend, but at the last moment he decided to send Melissa Jager and Rick Lawrence in his stead. The first results were promising, but the project came to an untimely end when an article on stress management in soldiers with reference to Monroe and the Institute appeared in the press. This came to the notice of several representatives, and the army authorities, concerned about possible political pressure, terminated the program.[9]

The Institute's periodical *Breakthrough* gave members of the Professional Division the opportunity to publicize the many applications of Hemi-Sync that were now being developed. The first three issues in 1983 included reports on using Hemi-Sync with an autistic child, the effects of music and Hemi-Sync on a child with a seizure disorder, a personal testimony on using specially designed Hemi-Sync exercises during several episodes of major surgery, and a report on a cognitive learning experiment in a community college in

Washington State. In the same year the first Professional Seminar took place at the Institute, the program including a presentation on using Hemi-Sync with alcohol-abuse patients and two presentations on what was being achieved by combining Hemi-Sync with music. A board of advisors was also established at the time, its membership having a strong academic slant with twelve of the seventeen members holding doctorates of various kinds.

By this time Director of Training Melissa Jager was living in her own house on the New Land, across the valley from the Institute buildings. Among her fellow trainers were Bill Schul, PhD, a social psychologist, and Dr. Stuart Twemlow, as at the time it was practice, when possible, to include a psychologist, psychiatrist, or other professional to mentor the programs. Psychologists and psychiatrists also often featured among the participants, as well as physicists and medical practitioners, with Elisabeth Kübler-Ross turning up now and again. Among the participants from overseas was Rupert Sheldrake, holder of a PhD from Cambridge University, whose ground-breaking book, *A New Science of Life: The Hypothesis of Formative Causation,* was published in 1981. "I greatly admire your scientific spirit of exploration and your great originality," Sheldrake wrote to Monroe on his return to the United Kingdom. "For not only have you explored regions of consciousness of which most people remain unaware, but you have also made it possible for others to enter them by means of your 'inner space shuttle.' I believe you are doing pioneering work of the greatest importance." He added, "I was helped a lot by the cheerful and reassuring presence of Melissa and Joe."

Now securely established on its new site, with its courses in demand, its reputation spreading, and research using Hemi-Sync beginning to produce results, the Institute had justified its move to Roberts Mountain. Melissa Jager was setting a high standard and related well with participants in her programs, being always willing to share with them her own wide range of interests. A paper she wrote in 1981 under the title "The Lamp Turn Laser" showed her deep understanding of the Hemi-Sync process. In July 1983 she began training her thirtieth *Gateway,* with Stuart Twemlow as her co-trainer. Then, midway through the week, for reasons known only to himself, with no prior warning or discussion, Monroe sent for her and fired her, adding that it was not professional for her to leave until the course was finished. Possibly in an attempt to justify his action, Monroe for the first time prepared assessment sheets for the course participants. Whatever he may have hoped for, the assessments contained nothing but praise for Melissa and her co-trainer as well as acclamation for the content of the program. "Melissa is superb," said one participant. "She meets you wherever you are and knows how to make the 'next step' appear easy, plain and fun." "The staff were excellent, the feedback tremendous, the support nurturing and timely," commented another. A further assessment expressed appreciation of the "wonderful" tapes, adding that the course provided "an opportunity to share and be shared with, to open up and question attitudes and beliefs in a free and encouraging atmosphere of support and love." This was to no avail. Following a brief, unfriendly meeting with Monroe, Melissa accepted that there was no future for her with the Institute. She sold her house as soon as she could and moved away.

What impelled Monroe to act as he did can only be a matter for conjecture, although it may be relevant that after the two previous programs, in April and June 1983, he had fired the trainers, both of them locally based, who had been working with Melissa. There were certainly other occasions when he acted in a way that seemed to defy explanation. Rosalind McKnight, whose nature was such that she tended to shine a kindly light on most situations, recalled an incident concerning George Durrette, Bob's "dream manager," as she described him, "since he was the main factor that helped Bob's dreams in his new location become a reality." She continued: "Bob would have an idea, such as building a fence in a certain spot, and George would manifest it. But sometimes George would have to unmanifest it until Bob decided for sure what he wanted. In fact, George was so patient with Bob's somewhat flexible energies that he should really be called Saint George." No more sympathetic expression than "somewhat flexible energies" could have been applied to such an event. Yet this does not seem to be an adequate explanation for Monroe's treatment of Melissa.

As the Institute now seemed ready for expansion, it was becoming clear that it was not only a new director of training that was needed but someone who was also able to take control of the day-to-day running of the Institute with the ability to transform ideas into action. Seeking a person to fill this demanding role, Monroe was persuaded by Morrie Coleman, a New Land resident who worked for a short time as an administrator in the Institute office, to recall the one individual who had enjoyed rich and varied experience during the years at Whistlefield as secretary, program coordinator, registrar, trainer, Explorer, and monitor. This was Bob's stepdaughter Scooter. In August

Bob and Scooter

1983, now aged thirty-one, she returned to the Institute as its director.

Scooter's appointment was regarded with suspicion by some of the staff, but it was not long before those who remained, and those recently appointed, became aware that a new dynamic was at work. On her arrival she found there were no trainers available. To begin with, she had to train the programs herself, with occasional assistance from Fowler Jones and Stuart Twemlow. They traveled in from the Midwest to co-train no more than twice a year, but Scooter also had to recruit and prepare new trainers to cope with the growing interest in *Gateway*. Hers was rather more than a full-time occupation.

Toward the end of 1983 Monroe drew up a flow chart entitled "Vision." Research and development remained the first priority, but he was now considering the possibilities of expansion, making use of ideas from professional members, *Gateway* participants, and Institute staff. Hemi-Sync should be made available "to as many people throughout the world as possible, to aid man in understanding and controlling his life." Another aim was "to integrate Hemi-Sync into all levels of educational systems," inspired by the progress achieved by Devon Edrington in schools in Washington State. Programs should be offered to prisons, nursing homes, and orphanages, and in the medical field Hemi-Sync should be applied "to upgrade present barbaric medical practices, e.g. overuse of drugs and consequent habituation; to aid in psychiatric treatment; to speed up and enhance the healing process." The only reference to finance was to have suffi-cient funds for research and development and to pay all the bills. It is clear from this document that Monroe's aim, now that he was aware of the potential of the technology, was not to make huge profits—there was not much prospect of that—but to provide help in some of the most important areas of life. Now that the expression "Hemi-Sync" was becoming more widely known, it was registered as a trademark in May 1984.

Later that year Joe McMoneagle retired from the army, having taken part in over 1,500 intelligence missions. He was awarded the Legion of Merit for "providing critical intelligence reported at the highest echelons of our military government . . . producing crucial and vital intelligence unavailable from any other source." Over the past two years Joe and Scooter had spent as much time as possible together, becoming very close to each other. In November 1984 they married. Then a few months later Joe suffered a major heart attack. Characteristically, part of his recovery program was building their self-designed house on the New Land. Joe was then hired by the Stanford Research Institute, which kept him in the remote-viewing program both operationally and for research purposes. He continued to act as a consultant to this program until it was closed down in November 1995. Although Joe took no part in the daily activities of the Institute, he did agree to give presentations at *Gateway* and other programs on request, and the added touch of glamour he gave to the occasion was much appreciated by course participants.

The following months saw a significant increase in the Institute's activities, many of them inspired and promoted by the new director. With the success of *Gateway,* it was becoming obvious that a second residential course was needed for those graduates who wished to continue and extend their forays into nonphysical reality. Incorporating ideas and experiences reported by Rosalind McKnight and other Explorers, Monroe created a new course entitled *Guidelines.* This was designed to enable participants to make contact with their inner guidance, or total self, to learn ways of accessing inner information and to use that expanded perspective to improve their daily lives. They would also learn to report verbally while in Focus 15 and Focus 21. In addition, several new tapes were created, all voiced by Monroe, as part of a series known as Mind Food. These were single exercises with various practical applications, including helping with relaxation, concentration, memory, and sleep. Tapes carrying musical compositions combined with Hemi-Sync began to be issued in the early 1980s, some composed by Alan Phillips and others by Monroe himself. The most popular of these early issues, Alan Phillips's *Midsummer Night,* still finds a place in the 2006 catalogue.

In 1984 an attempt was made to introduce *Gateway* to England by Harold Wessbacher, a psychotherapist and clinical hypnotist from West Germany. After qualifying as a trainer he organized three programs in England, but failed to attract sufficient participants to continue with the project. Harold also translated and voiced many of the exercises into German and for a time used Monroe materials alongside his other activities. As for England, in 1987 weekend programs began to be offered by The Russell Centre in Cambridge. These continued for about six years until the Centre relocated to

Nancy and Bob on vacation

South-West Scotland, where these programs are still held from time to time.

Seeking to expand the Institute's work beyond Roberts Mountain, in 1985 Scooter initiated the *Gateway Outreach* program, based on the first part of the residential course and designed by a trainer, James Jones. Those interested in becoming Outreach trainers could follow a week's course at the Institute and were then qualified to present introductory weekend workshops on the mainland or over-seas. In addition to the single exercises and Metamusic compositions already on sale, six albums of tapes in Focus 10 and Focus 12, many of them taken from *Gateway,* were made available. Expansion was in the air. This was also the year in which for the first time the finances of the Institute moved into the black. Then in December there was a major change in the Institute's financial structure when it was trans-formed into a nonprofit organization under U.S. law, thus enabling any contributions to be tax-deductible. The phrase "of Applied Sciences" was dropped from its name. Henceforth it was to be known simply as The Monroe Institute.

Notes

1. Joseph Chilton Pearce still lives in the same house on the New Land (2006).

2. This same donor, according to Nancy Monroe, returned early in 1980 offering to buy the entire place for $12 million (see *Catapult,* p. 136).

3. See, for example, *Fringes of Reason,* edited by Ted Schultz (Harmony Books, 1989) and *We Are the Earthquake Generation,* by Jeffrey Goodman (Seaview, 1978).

4. Both Dr. Gladman and Dr. Roalfe became members of the Institute's board of advisors. A more detailed account of Dr. Roalfe's Hemi-Sync trial appeared in *Using the Whole Brain,* edited by R. Russell (Hampton Roads, 1993).

5. See also *Focusing the Whole Brain,* edited by R. Russell (Hampton Roads, 2004): "Support for Surgery," by Marty Gerken.

6. See *From Magical Child to Magical Teen,* by Joseph Chilton Pearce (Park Street Press, 1985).

7. The program went through various changes of name. It became *Center Lane* for a time, as President Carter had inadvertently exposed the name *Grill Flame* during a press conference when he disclosed how a member of the program with psychic abilities had located two lost nuclear weapons on a Soviet bomber that had crashed in Zaire. Then it was retitled *Star Gate,* the name by which it is generally known.

8. See *The Stargate Chronicles,* by Joseph McMoneagle (Hampton Roads, 2000) and *Captain of My Ship, Master of My Soul,* by F. Holmes Atwater (Hampton Roads, 2001), which contains a CD-ROM including an audio recording of McMoneagle's remote-viewing of Mars.

9. Ray Waldkoetter reported that one not-quite-traumatic incident occurred when Colonel Billy Spangles, commanding officer of the unit working with the tapes, objected to the instruction in one exercise "to relax your genitals." Monroe assured the colonel (described by Waldkoetter as "a good old boy") that this tape would be appropriately edited to suit the sensitivity of the enlisted men.

CHAPTER 7

Far Journeys

Throughout the years of inquiry, investigation, and experiment at Whistlefield, Monroe's own out-of-body experiences continued quite regularly. However, he began to feel a sense of frustration; the experiences themselves now seemed limited, even boring. The question of proof no longer concerned him and he had lost interest in taking part in controlled tests. Also, he found it had become very easy for him to move into the out-of-body state. Refreshed after three or four hours of sleep, he was ready to slip out, as it were, but what was there to do? Everyone else was asleep and he saw no point in purposelessly drifting around. So, as he said, he would slip back in, turn on the light, read until he was sleepy again, and that was it.

Then, early in 1972, he realized that the limiting factor was his own conscious mind. To explore further he should stop attempting to control what was happening and instead remain passive, allowing his total self to take over. When he awoke on the following night he put this intention into practice. This is how he described what happened: "After waiting for what seemed only a few seconds, there was a tremendous surge, a movement, an energy in that familiar spatial blackness, and there began for me an entire new era in my out-of-body activities. Since that night, my non-physical activities have been almost totally due to this procedure."[1]

Unlike his team of Explorers, Monroe did not use his laboratory facilities or the sound signals he and his associates had designed to induce an out-of-body experience. Nor did he tape-record what was happening as it occurred. Instead, as with the episodes described in *Journeys Out of the Body,* he kept detailed notes, sometimes including mention of the time that elapsed while the OBE took place. Although he does not give the dates, it is apparent from the context that many of the experiences he describes in his second book occurred after the Institute moved to its new home on Roberts Mountain in 1979. Most of *Far Journeys,* perhaps all of it, was written while the Monroes were living in the Gate House at the time when their house on the mountaintop was being planned and built.

Far Journeys was published by Doubleday in 1985. The first part of the book includes an account of the research at Whistlefield with a description of the Hemi-Sync technology and extracts from the reports of the Explorers and some of the participants in the *Gateway* program. Monroe notes that over the eight years since the program was launched, 41 percent of participants were male, "double the norm for the typical self-awareness workshop." The average age of participants was thirty-nine, and 29 percent were professionals—scientists, educators, doctors, engineers, psychologists, psychiatrists—attending principally to determine how they might use Hemi-Sync in their own areas of interest. He also noted that 83 percent came to the program with one stated basic reason, but left with a different, more valuable, result.

Almost all *Gateway* participants are neophytes as far as the Hemi-Sync experience is concerned. They may have heard one or two exercises before commencing the program, but no more than that. What they experience during the program is generally unpremeditated and relevant only to themselves. On a very few occasions, however, a shared experience may be reported. One such report was from a young woman who had become aware that three of the men on the program were physically attracted to her. Annoyed by this, which she sensed had been distracting her during her experience of the program, she wondered how best to deal with it. She decided to ask what she described as the "divine forces" if it were possible for her to experience spiritual love, not to receive it but to learn how to give it to others. She kept that thought in mind as she commenced the next exercise. Then, as the exercise continued, she found herself moving out-of-body towards the one man on the course that she had not had a chance to talk with. Her report continues:

> All at once I had a knowing . . . that his vibrations were my vibrations. I had an overwhelming desire to meld, to feel a part of him—to become one . . . I gave to him both my body and soul until there was this tremendous energy surge that rocked and exploded in us. It was an experience that is beyond words, for love, total and absolute, surrounded us more strongly than can be earthly experienced or imagined. The more I gave, the greater I received and I didn't want to let go . . . It was like two energies becoming one at last. I can remember thinking how physical sex paled in comparison.

When the two participants spoke at the conclusion of the exercise, it became immediately clear that the experience of spiritual love had been shared by both of them. Their accounts fitted together "like puzzle pieces, matching perfectly and interlocking." From that time they began to share their lives, "growing and loving together."

Reports of such shared occurrences are very rare, although highly personal experiences are sometimes kept confidential and not placed in the Institute records. In contrast, another of the reports that

Monroe quotes seems to have a wider relevance. Reflecting on the possibility of perceiving ultimate reality—what he understood Monroe was referring to when he used the word *Home*—this participant felt that anything that could be formed into five physical senses, expressed in language or oriented thought, was an illusion. All that he was aware of was "blankness and bliss." Blankness, he explains, "not because it is blank, but because I attempt to experience it with mental processes that are geared to the five physical senses and that are in the habit of perceiving illusion. I am trying to use my biological illusion computer to perceive beyond the *apparent* limits of illusion. Like trying to smell a flower with your ear. I experience bliss because emotional feeling is the only perceptual tool that I am able to use to sense beyond illusion. If there are other perceptual tools that are available to me, they are either atrophied by lack of use, and must somehow be reactivated, or they must be initially activated."

This is not such an uncommon experience. Many participants in these programs find that words are inadequate to express what they have sensed or perceived and that their usual thought processes fall short of enabling them "to get their head round" what they have undergone.

Monroe was well aware of this. Throughout the published accounts of his own journeys, for the sake of his readers he seeks to organize and shape the material, as far as that is possible. In *Far Journeys* he no longer refers to Locales I, II, and III, but instead draws a distinction between two main types of out-of-body experience. One he calls "local traffic," defined as "events and activities that relate directly to here-now time-space." Local traffic includes such excursions as traveling around the neighborhood calling in on friends to see how they are doing, and he feels he has had enough of this. The second type he calls "interstate," implying moving from one state to another, with this description applying to experiences "where virtually all the rules, patterns, illusions, and the rest of 'local traffic,' with few exceptions, are non-existent." It is a selection of his travels on the interstate that he recounts in this book.

As a result of his own experiences and the reports of the Explorer team, by mid-1984 Monroe found it possible to state certain premises and conclusions. Here they are in outline:

- All humans move into the out-of-body state during sleep.

- A form of dynamic energy, so far unidentified, is present in all carbon-based organic life. It enters the body before birth and leaves it at death.

- The dominant waking consciousness is only a part of the various forms of consciousness available to man.

- Human consciousness is a manifestation of the dynamic energy already referred to. As a highly complex vibrational pattern it responds to and acts upon similar patterns from external sources.

- All patterns of consciousness are nonphysical and hence not dependent on time-space. "In short, like it or not, you're going to continue to do and be after you can no longer hang in there physically."

- From the work of the Explorers and their contacts has emanated an underlying mosaic of action that on examination becomes an astounding potential. It is the display and application of a science—or technology—that is totally absent from human culture. To this Monroe adds, "the application of this technology seems totally benevolent."

These are challenging statements. Because they are based on experiences reported by individuals in the out-of-body state they are open to rejection by those who have never knowingly entered into that state. With the exception of the second and third premises, they cannot at this time be scientifically validated. But in the world that Monroe and his Explorers were investigating, our present-day science—materialist science—has no relevance. We have no warrant to claim that our earthly science is the only science there is in the whole of the physical Universe—or within the immeasurable Universe of the human mind.

For readers of *Far Journeys,* and for anyone who seeks to understand Monroe's philosophy, two things need to be accepted, or at least considered. One is the existence of beings that employ the technology he refers to above. Some of these beings have never existed in human form, others walked the Earth hundreds or thousands of years ago, and still others have previously existed in nonhuman form elsewhere in the Universe. They seem to have some sort of individuality, but there is no way in which their numbers can be estimated. Some of them appear to have access to all knowledge and information. Some are interested in human life on Earth, although why and to what extent cannot be determined. They have developed a technology that forms no threat to humankind and is essentially benevolent.

The second requirement is acceptance of the existence of this technology, through which communication with human beings becomes possible. This is how Monroe explains it:

> This technology can produce a beam of energy, which is first translated as light, through which the human energy essence can travel back and forth, information can flow, and the operators of such technology can enter time-space earth environments. Once properly

perceived, they can endow the human mind with the ability to create (enhance?) such a beam of energy.

From Monroe's personal experience and the reports from his laboratory team and the thousands of individuals who had participated in his courses, experiments, and trials, it became clear, he writes, that "all other intelligent species, either in the physical universe or in other energy systems, use a form of communication that is total and certainly nonverbal." Nonverbal communication (NVC) is "direct instant experience and/or immediate knowing transmitted from one intelligent energy system and received by another."

There is nothing weird about nonverbal communication as such. All of us use it frequently, through body language, facial expression, and telepathy.[2] Saints and mystics especially place the highest value on nonverbal communications from nonphysical entities. But the nature of the NVC that Monroe and his Explorers were involved with is far more advanced. It incorporates the instantaneous transmission of emotions, sensations, pictures—information and experience in any imaginable shape or form. To engage in this type of communication necessitates moving into an altered state of consciousness. Monroe's own technology enabled his Explorers and *Gateway* participants to make this transition, while Monroe himself communicated via NVC while in his out-of-body state.

However, problems arise when it comes to translating NVC into language that others can understand. This is similar to the difficulty that arises when seeking to put into words a mystical or transcendent experience—the type of deeply felt experience that is essentially ineffable. In the areas that Monroe and the Explorers were venturing into, the resources of language were often inadequate, as can be gathered from the hesitancies, pauses, and corrections on many of the Explorer tapes. Monroe, with no monitor or recording equipment, could only make notes on his experiences and do what he could to put them into shape. These recollections form the major part of *Far Journeys,* some of them combining several out-of-body expeditions. But, he says, more than 90 percent of the events that occurred seemed impossible to translate into ordinary language. Whether he was successful in solving the problems of describing these events and translating NVC into everyday language has to be left to the judgment of his readers.

Monroe attempted to translate "non-time-space events and ambience into replicas of conscious human physical experience." While this might affect the accuracy of his account it should, he considered, help others to comprehend what he was trying to convey. Also, it was impossible to use terms such as "he said," "he walked," or "she smiled," as these implied physical activity that had no relevance. So he devised what he called a "replica vocabulary" of expressions that occurred frequently in his accounts, large parts of which involved passages of dialogue. For example, in his reports he used the word *blank* to indicate failure to understand, *vibrate* to show emotion, *dulled* for loss of interest, and *turn in* for considering or thinking something over. *Flickered* indicates uncertainty, *rolled* is being amused or laughing, and *smoothed* is getting it together, being in charge of self. It is helpful to have the list of these terms when reading his reports.

Some of the terms Monroe invented go further than these approximations. An especially useful one is *Rote,* meaning a thought ball—a packet of thought/mentation, total memory, involving knowledge, information, experience, and history, an idea or concept complete in itself. The term *Percept* indicates a combination of insight, intuition, and understanding. *Ident* is a mental name or address—the energy pattern of an item. *Curl* is organized energy, usually intelligent, and CLICK (printed thus) is an instantaneous change in consciousness.

One expression that occurs for the first time in *Far Journeys* and became an essential component in Monroe's interpretation of the Universe is the M Band. This, he says, is part of the energy spectrum surrounding the Earth that is commonly used for thought. It is not electronic, electric, magnetic, nucleonic, or anything else. M Band noise is caused by uncontrolled thought. Monroe perceived this as a sort of chaotic cacophony and learned to hurry through it as fast as he could.

The out-of-body experiences that Monroe describes in *Far Journeys* have a remarkable consistency. Although they took place over several years they fit into a sequence. They were, as he says himself, instructional sessions under the guidance of what he refers to as an "Inspec" (short for "intelligent species," with the implication that humans do not necessarily fit into this category). Monroe describes the Inspec as "an external intelligent energy source, helping, navigating, doing the driving." Similar entities appeared also in many OBE accounts from members of the Explorer team. Unlike some Explorers, however, Monroe never gave his Inspec a name, although he does give names or labels (idents) to some of the other beings he encountered. There is Bill, once his flying instructor, now fully integrated into nonphysical existence, and Lou, whose ident is now Z-55, a musician Monroe once worked with who died from the effects of diabetes. We are told that Lou has had two more lifetimes since then and has one more to undergo before becoming free from the illusion of time and space.

In one experience Monroe receives a Rote and opens it to find himself observing a tour of Time-Space Illusion (TSI), which encompasses the whole physical Universe. He follows the experiences of two entities, labeled by him AA and BB, who come from an area known as KT-95 and who participate in the tour. AA is attracted by the M Band noise, hearing it not as uncontrolled thought but as a mixture of resonance, beat frequencies, standing waves, and incalculable patterns. Suddenly, he feels a strong desire to be human, makes his way to the "Entry Station," and eventually emerges as a newborn baby in a New York tenement. He lives on Earth for forty-five years and, despite BB's remonstration, determines to return to Earth again, but this time as a woman. Monroe encounters BB many times in subsequent experiences. AA remains in the physical world, although frequently expressing a strong desire to rejoin his nonhuman friends. But as the ever-present Inspec says, he has to stay and perform his designed function—he has no other choice.

During this episode there is a helpful explanation of phrases that apply to those living forms who enter, leave, and reenter the Earth Life System. First-Timers are those, like AA in his manifestation as a newborn New Yorker, who enter the system for the first time because they want to, and soon forget everything previous to their life on Earth.[3] Old-Timers repeat entering and leaving the physical world several times and can recall some elements of previous existences there. Last-Timers are those on their final lifetime and when that terminates they leave forever—they go Home. Instances of all three groups are met with in Monroe's subsequent journeys. There is also a small number of Seekers who are able to make visits to the nonphysical realms while still possessing physical bodies.

A fascinating commentary on Monroe's account of these nonphysical realms appears in *Dark Night, Early Dawn,* by Christopher Bache, professor of Religious Studies at Youngstown State University. Bache comments that "Monroe's vision of reality assumes the concept of reincarnation, and therefore it is a vision that sees human beings developing across enormous tracts of time . . . According to him, our life before we began incarnating on Earth and after we stop is largely screened from our awareness by the heavy conditioning that space-time exerts on us while we are part of this system." The "between-life" existence takes place in a series of four rings that surround space-time, which Monroe learns about in detail from a Rote.

Bache points out that although these rings are described in spatial terms "it is clear that they represent not actual places but states of consciousness. The geometry of concentric rings is in the final analysis a metaphor for the different experiential possibilities inherent in different states of consciousness."⁴ Monroe's descriptions are so vivid and detailed that it is easy to overlook this and to fall into the error of treating his far journeys as if they took place in a geographical landscape.⁵

Among Monroe's out-of-body experiences are visits to occasions in his own childhood when significant events took place that helped in his later emergence into the being he became. There are also snapshots of climactic happenings in former lifetimes—as the father of a family dying in the desert, as a warrior in battle, as a priest about to perform a human sacrifice but finding himself unable to do so. He comes to understand these events as a series of demonstrations of the power of emotion, "the driving force, the creative energy which motivates human thought and action." A further experience shows him that aloneness is an illusion, that "our idents in one another are indelible." He is given to understand that it is his curiosity that motivates him in the search for completion, and he receives a detailed explanation of the functions of the entities, the Inspecs, who are guiding and informing him.

Some of his experiences resemble episodes from mature science fiction. In these, often accompanied by BB, he explores other realities and undergoes various adventures, all the time learning more about the immeasurable areas beyond the time-space continuum. On one journey he gives BB a tour of humanity, showing him how human activity is governed by the need to survive by visiting scenes of slaughtering a deer, cooking and eating, having sex, city life, and so on. They observe the behavior of people who are physically dead but are unaware of their condition. In contrast, Monroe, now much more confident and with better understanding of the territory beyond time-space, introduces BB to a friend of his, Charlie, no longer in physical state and totally aware of his situation, who is happily creating his own reality in a corner of this nonphysical universe. From there they move outward to an area of religious buildings and on the steps of a church meet a woman who tells Monroe that they are at the gates of Heaven. Finally, they encounter Monroe's one-time physical friend Bill, whose explanation of the massive importance of emotion and love quite stuns BB, who has never taken on physical form and has failed to understand that this "emotion and love energy stuff" is the inspiration for his adventures with Monroe and his concern for AA.

Occasionally during his journeys Monroe receives a Rote that he later unrolls and explains. A particularly complex Rote was thrown to him by BB, who described it as relating to a possible visit to the Time-Space Illusion. It is "about earth and humans, how it got started, what it's for . . . all that stuff." It consists of a lengthy parable with echoes of the Genesis creation story, moving on to a tightly compressed allegorical account of the history of the Earth and the creatures inhabiting it. It deals largely with the production of "Loosh," which Monroe explains as "an energy generated by all organic life in varying degrees of purity, the clearest and most potent coming from humans—engendered by human activity which triggers emotion, the highest of such emotions being—love?" The question mark is significant. While Loosh may serve as a comprehensive term for everything that grows or is made, and for the emotions that result from human activity, Monroe finds it difficult, if not impossible, to fit love into this concept. When the Inspec suggests that he define love in his own terms, he finds he cannot do so. A little farther on in this experience he comes up with the expression "a special energy waveform labeled love." He continues, "Yet we don't really know what it is and . . . how to really use it."

Then, towards the end of this particular journey, Monroe is granted a powerful visionary experience that he understands as revealing the source of the love energy. This experience leaves him with "the indescribable joy of knowing only that it did take place," and the realization that "the echoes would reverberate in me throughout eternity, whatever my eternity was." Shortly afterwards he feels pulled back into his physical body, with the memory of the visionary experience fading as he wonders what would have happened if there were no signal to return. He ends this account with a passage that movingly combines the two lives, physical and nonphysical, that he was leading at the time.

> It was then, lying there in the darkness, listening to the whippoorwill and the night crickets outside, the soft earth-scented breeze flowing in through the open window, feeling the hot warmth of our little dog Steamboat sleeping contentedly against the soles of my feet, the even breathing of Nancy sleeping beside me—that I felt the wetness of my cheeks and a few remaining tears in my eyes. And I remembered. Not much, but I remembered! I sat up in bed, wanting to jump up and shout in incomprehensible joy. Steamboat raised his head and looked at me curiously, then dropped back. My wife shifted position as I sat up, then gradually resumed her even breathing rhythm. I would not wake her, she needed her rest and recharge.

Monroe found that it took him several months to adjust his thinking to the contents of the Rote, but eventually he was able to accept the concept as "an explanation of total human behavior and history."

In another out-of-body experience, towards the end of the *Far Journeys* sequence, Monroe becomes aware that he is reaching a limit beyond which he cannot move until he has fully released his physical body. However, the Inspec tells him that he can be taken, as an observer only, "to a physical earth possibility at a point in your time measurement beyond the year 3000." The inhabitants are known as Humans-Plus, or H-Plus. From deep space he moves towards the Earth, aware that the rings that once surrounded it are gone. There is "no more random thought clutter." Descending above the Pacific he is aware that there are no ships or aircraft to be seen. As he surveys the land he observes that the fields resemble patchworks of bright colors, but he can see no roads, no buildings, no traffic, no power lines—no people. With the speed of thought the Inspec takes him three-quarters of the way around the Earth before bringing him down on a knoll in a field of rich green grass, with an oak wood behind him and in the distance lines of green-blue hills, a very familiar place to Monroe. The Inspec energy fades away, leaving him alone.

For Monroe, what follows is a remarkable learning experience. The humans he meets use nonverbal communication. One of them is his old friend BB, appearing now as a good-looking man in his late twenties. He is with a woman who is familiar to him, attracting him strongly and becoming more familiar as the episode develops, but whom he does not name. These individuals have bodies, but do not inhabit them all the time, storing them nearby until they need them—about twice a week, they tell him. They use the Reball– the resonant energy balloon that forms an impenetrable energy field—to protect their bodies when they are not occupying them.[6] They draw energy from the atmosphere and tell him they can create food from a handful of dirt. He asks for his favorite corn, Silver Queen. The woman takes a handful of dirt and stares intently at it. "The dirt began to bubble and boil, changing color, re-formed into a small full-kernelled mature ear of white corn. She handed it to me and I took it. It was hot to the touch. I carefully put it up to my mouth, took a bite. It was Silver Queen, the sweetest corn I ever tasted." He comes to understand that humans have taken over Mother Nature's work, with several improvements.

Next Monroe is taken on a tour during which he experiences being a fish, a plant, a panther, and a condor. Vividly described, this has similarities to a typical shamanic journey. Then towards the end of the episode he seeks for answers to questions that have been pre-occupying him both in and out of body. He learns that there is communication with other "civilizations" but nothing much is made of this, that there are visits to other nonphysical energy systems in order to cultivate them, that humans "graduate" from this point, never to return, and that the woman herself is shortly to graduate. He asks her what happens to graduates. She replies that she does not know—but that he does. At this he is suddenly aware that he has all the answers—or so he thinks. But it is time for the journey to end. He reaches out for the grassy knoll where he landed—and finds himself in the year 1982 close to the Monroe Institute buildings in Virginia. Back in his body and in bed he looks at the clock. The whole journey, one that has enormous significance to Monroe, lasted for just eight minutes.

If we can accept the conventional left brain/right brain distinction, it seems that the right hemisphere—emotional, spatial, subjective—is dominant in Monroe's out-of-body state, while the left hemisphere—rational, logical, objective—takes over when he comes to sort out and interpret the lessons of the experience itself. Once he has completed his reports of the out-of-body sessions recounted in *Far Journeys,* he turns to a study of the various Rotes he has received and then to what he calls "a crib sheet for the course," the course being how best to continue and expand one's daily life activities, physical, mental, and emotional. As with all three of his books, there are no references to any published authorities; everything he writes derives from his own experience and the conclusions he draws from that experience.

The Rote itself, a package of thought, knowledge, information, experience, and history, emanates from the nonphysical beings encountered in the out-of-body state. Reading, or rather "running" a Rote, as Monroe describes it, is like recalling the memory of a past event but differs because, as the process begins, every detail becomes immediately clear. You keep "your left-brain consciousness in the driver's seat."

The first Rote unrolled (or it may be more than one) deals with "the itinerary of human experience." This Rote describes what happens to those who are physically dead and who are lodged in one of a number of rings, the particular ring depending on their degree of awareness of their relationship to physical matter reality. Beyond are many more rings spanning an area from Human Time-Space Illusion on the inner side to Non-Physical Reality on the outer. From here the majority return to Earth for more lifetimes, while in the outermost ring are those, the Last-Timers, preparing for the departure into Non-Physical Reality, or graduation. They are on their way Home.

The second Rote is concerned with human existence on Earth. Life in the physical is "an intense learning experience, a school of a very unusual sort." There are strict conditions for entry into physical life. "The energy form must agree that time-space truly does exist," as without this agreement "it is impossible to have primary human consciousness." The existence of planet Earth as it is must be agreed and the nature of human consciousness must also be accepted. Previous experience has to be blanked out or sublimated so as not to interfere.

Once born, the new entrant (or First-Timer) undergoes a traumatic period while adjusting to the demands of the physical body and the signals flooding into it. Then the primary learning system takes over, "the focusing of conscious awareness." Input from the five physical senses "turns attention to the event being experienced and such experience is then learned and stored," a process enhanced if emotion is involved. Secondary learning occurs beyond our conscious awareness from input received where attention is not focused, affecting everything we think and do although we are not aware of it. Then there is a third type of learning that takes place during sleep. These learning systems are different from and ignored by the unnatural learning systems devised by human cultures, which are virtually confined to the knowledge, understanding, control, and application of physical matter and which, because they operate entirely through input from the physical senses, may effectively eliminate any last vestiges of originality from the individual.

The Rote continues to deal with the reasons why First-Timers desire to repeat their human experience time and again. Human physical life is addictive. It is imprinted with the drive to survive, with the need to protect and maintain the body no matter what. This leads to a form of distortion. Mere survival is not enough: luxury food and clothes, fully equipped houses, life-support systems, medicines, laws, nation-states—all and more distort the survival drive. Further distortion arises from the sensual emphasis on sexuality—"the original motivating drive to reproduce has long since become secondary to the temporary sensory peak of the act itself." All of this "adds to the glue that binds the human in low orbit."

The last part of the Rote is concerned with the overwhelming importance of emotion, "the key to and the driving force underlying every thought and action in human existence." Emotion, especially as it accumulates in and dominates the human ego, is seen as diffusion of the Prime Energy or Creative Force that is inherent in everyone. Moreover, it is inextricably involved in time-space physical matter events.

There is, however, an exception that accurately represents the original Prime Energy and that is essential if humans are ever to escape from the Time-Space Illusion. This, for the sake of clarity, may be called Super Love (SL) to distinguish it from love—a term so broadly used as to have lost any meaning. Super Love is indestructible, does not depend on physical matter, and has no object. It is "a continuous radiation, totally nondependent upon like reception or any other form of return whatsoever." Super Love just is. This is ultimately what we are on Earth to learn.

Monroe's crib sheet that concludes *Far Journeys* is a sequence of statements and recommendations that he has garnered from his nonphysical experiences. The four statements provide a baseline for the recommendations, or advice, that follows. They are:

- Reality is that which is perceived.

- Energy does not exist until expressed.

- Energy focused is exponential.

- Consciousness is focused energy.

Each of these statements carries a coherent explanation. The recommendations that follow are practical and forcefully expressed. Many of them are manifested in the exercises in the Institute's *Gateway* program. They conclude with a rare (if not solitary) reference to Monroe's father, the language professor, who used to quote what he called a famous old French proverb to stimulate his students, some of whom labored for hours trying to work it out. "Pas de Lieu Rhone que Nous" was the proverb. Say it in your mind or speak it with a French accent, Monroe senior suggested—and listen to what you are saying!

Some of the ideas and concepts elaborated in *Far Journeys* may not seem so very different from what can be found in certain esoteric writings or in various belief systems. As one reviewer wrote: "What is unique here is the attempt to remove the trappings of religious doctrine and mysticism and to simply describe the adventures of a man who has devoted the last quarter of a century to inner exploration." Christopher Bache makes the point that Monroe's account of the state between incarnations resonates deeply with the portrayal of this state in *The Tibetan Book of the Dead*. There is, however, no evidence that Monroe made any close study of this sort of material or that he was noticeably influenced by anyone in this field, including those he met such as Jane Roberts or Elmer and Alice Green. As a reviewer of the book remarked: "Monroe differs significantly from others who may propound such cosmic ideas . . . in that he is a contemporary American, a pragmatist with an unquenchable curiosity that propels him to explore the unknown. He became involved not from a philosophical standpoint, but from the need to make sense of his own experiences with OBEs."[7]

Among the appendixes in *Far Journeys* is a paper on "The OBE Psychophysiology of Robert A. Monroe" by Dr. Stuart Twemlow and Dr. Glen Gabbard, which first appeared in their study *With the Eyes of the Mind* (1984). The authors seek to find connections between Monroe's strong and lifelong interest in flying and the nature of his OBEs—the travels to distant locations and through "realms which are fantastic and inexplicable." They also used Rorschach tests (interpretations of inkblots) to analyze aspects of his personality, suggesting that "he has strong defenses against dealing with sexuality, defensive feelings, and especially aggression," adding that "by transcending the prison of his body," it allows him to steer clear of such potential conflict areas.

Yet the OBEs recorded in *Far Journeys* hardly bear this out. In these accounts he is taking a far more active role than in the experiences described in *Journeys Out of the Body*. Sexuality, depression, and aggression are not avoided, though it could be said that he still journeys through "realms which are fantastic and inexplicable." But he is determined to do his best to explain what may seem at first to defy any explanation. If we are looking to his OBEs for insight into his personality, we will find much evidence of courage and determination as well as a curiosity—a desire to *know*—that will not be denied. These qualities are often associated with the young, but as we read this book it is worth bearing in mind (from our own standing within the Time-Space Illusion) that Monroe was fifty-seven years old when the experiences recorded in *Far Journeys* first occurred and seventy when the book was published.

Far Journeys is not altogether an easy read. For those who have difficulty with the content of Monroe's narratives of his journeys, it helps to use (in Coleridge's phrase) the willing suspension of disbelief—for the time being at least. Moreover, Monroe's attempts to put nonverbal communication into ordinary everyday American sometimes descends into the banal, and expressions such as "Bill opened gently" and "I vibrated more" may affect the reader in ways that were never intended. Presumably he came to realize this and in his last book, *Ultimate Journey*, his interpretations of NVC are less demotic and he no longer employs his "replica vocabulary." Nevertheless, there is much vivid, explicit writing, for example, in the chapters entitled "Rainbow Route" and "Shock Treatment," both of which contain passages of considerable power and memorable content.

Yet there is more to *Far Journeys* than a series of accounts of several extraordinary out-of-body experiences and the information that may be extrapolated from them. In the final journey, "The Gathering," Monroe is brought to consider from "somewhere between the Earth and the Moon" a host of countless numbers of forms glowing in various degrees of expectancy that have come together to witness what the Inspec describes as "a very rare event—the conflux of several different and intense energy fields arriving at the same point in your time-space." The gathering is to observe the possible birth of a new energy that will, the Inspec continues, "offer human consciousness a rare potential to emerge rapidly into a unified intelligent energy system that will range far beyond your time-space illusion, creating, constructing, teaching as only a human-trained graduate energy is able to do." Should the opportunity be missed, humans would eventually lose their place as the dominant species on Earth and, the Inspec says, "we would just have to start up some action on some other planet in time-space with new humans."

There is, says the Inspec, one more process to perform. Following two rapid changes in consciousness, Monroe, still accompanied by the Inspec and now also by BB, finds himself in a place on Earth that is very familiar to him. Inside "a small structure in the middle of a grove of trees" is a man lying on a bed. It is, he is certain, the physical form of the nonphysical being known as AA. From time to time in his journeys Monroe has been aware of AA's presence in the vicinity and he feels that AA knows him at least as well as he knows himself. Now, as he watches, he becomes aware of a resistance emanating from the man. The Inspec tells BB to help the man separate temporarily from his physical body, which he succeeds in doing, and asks him to inquire as to his purpose. Monroe is aware of M Band screeching, indicating strong emotion. The resistance seems to be intensifying. Then the Inspec gives the man's response: "He stated he wished to serve humankind." "He wants to go with us," says BB. "Can he do that?" But Monroe knows the answer before the Inspec expresses it. "Inform him he must stay and perform his designed function. He has no other choice at this point." As the man sinks to his knees, Monroe, the Inspec, and BB move away. "It is done," says the Inspec. "The pattern is complete."

And here we come to the crucial point of the Hero's Journey— that other journey that Robert Monroe had been following unknowingly since those hours he spent many years before at the bottom of the well. As Joseph Campbell said, "The ultimate aim of the quest must be neither release nor ecstasy for oneself, but the wisdom and power to serve others." Now it was clear that the wish to serve humankind had become the chief motivating principle in Monroe's life and work. It was, in the words ascribed to the Inspec, "his designed function." He had no other choice.

Notes

1. *Far Journeys,* p. 6. All quotations from *Far Journeys* by Robert Monroe, copyright © 1985 by Robert Monroe are used by permission of Doubleday, a division of Random House, Inc.

2. See *The Sense of Being Stared At,* by Rupert Sheldrake (Hutchinson, 2003).

3. Readers may see a disconnection here between the memory of AA and of the other First-Timers. I regret that I am unable to resolve this!

4. *Dark Night, Early Dawn* (SUNY), pp. 126–31.

5. A simplified version of this was later introduced into the Institute's *Lifeline* course. An interesting comment on Monroe's rings from the Christian standpoint appeared in an article entitled "This World and the Next" by the theologian and parapsychologist Crawford Knox in *The Christian Parapsychologist* (December 2005): "Though Monroe describes the rings in spatial terms, they represent not actual places but states or depths of consciousness or

awareness. As we grow into the life of God . . . we can become aware of new depths of the life of God all around us. The geometry of concentric rings seems to be a metaphor for the different experiential possibilities inherent in different states of consciousness as people develop and grow deeper into the life of God. To think of the next world in spatial terms, therefore, is still to be under the influence of our space-time conditioning. Technically, one does not 'travel' in this reality so much as simply shift one's mode of awareness and attention."

6. The Reball became an essential component in the introductory exercises of the Institute course.

7. Ann Simpkinson, writing in *Common Boundary.*

CHAPTER 8

The Supernatural Fisherman

The publication in 1985 of the long-awaited *Far Journeys* brought a batch of favorable reviews and considerable increase in correspondence and inquiries about courses at the Institute. Around this time many of those who signed up were devotees of one or more of the New Age philosophies. The director's report in an Institute newsletter tactfully described these philosophies as "a number of 'disciplines,' tools, techniques and programs—many aimed at helping people obtain a desired state of being, many aimed at the commercial possibilities." While New Age thinking did not affect the program content, it did mean that some *Gateway* participants brought with them expectations that were not necessarily satisfied—as well as items of baggage that needed to be dumped before they could fully appreciate the Monroe approach. This approach, as exemplified by the trainers, was nonjudgmental, dispassionate, and objective. There was no belief system, no ritual (apart from handing in one's watch at the commencement of a course), no mystification. The participants were always in control of the process. The development and exploration of human consciousness, assisted not by substances, ceremonies, crystals, or chanting but only by scientifically designed, phased sound signals, were the only objectives of the Institute's research.

The "Supernatural Fisherman"

For the hundreds of men and women attending Institute courses (with increasing numbers coming from Europe, the Far East, South America, and Australia), special highlights were the sessions with Robert Monroe in David Francis Hall. Since his years as a high-powered, smart-suited executive in the world of radio and television his appearance and style had completely transformed. One participant recalled his first sight of him. "Dressed like a weekend sportsman in a sailor's cap, plaid shirt, baggy pants and beat-up loafers, he could have been a retired executive searching for a cocktail lounge in a resort hotel—only to stumble into some damn holistic seminar by mistake." Usually carrying a mug of coffee, he would wander into the hall, gaze around as if mildly surprised to find a number of people sitting there looking at him, take off his jacket, if he was wearing one, hang it on an imaginary hook (whence it would fall to the floor), and begin to talk. He would ask a question or two—"Are you having fun?" was a usual one—and then launch into an apparently rambling discourse more like a one-sided conversation than a lecture. Sometimes he would reminisce, with stories about events in his younger days, such as finding those two new, crisp dollar bills beneath the plank that had not been moved for years. Or he might recall episodes from his flying days, or anecdotes about a favorite dog or cat. Then he would move on to other matters: philosophical or psychological issues, ways of using Hemi-Sync, the importance of always being in the moment, assurances of surviving physical death. Whatever the subject, his audience sat there entranced—not so much by what he said but by the way he said it. Afterwards, although you might not remember the content, you never forgot what it was like to be in his presence with that resonant, rumbling voice echoing in your ears. Sometimes at the end he would take questions; other times it was "Dinner's ready," and off he shambled. It was, of course, a performance, and as with any good performance the timing was everything. But for his audience, to be in the presence of the great explorer of inner space, the man who had designed and voiced those exercises that carried you into realms beyond imagining—that was real magic.

The mid-1980s were years of development and expansion for the new Institute. In 1983 members of the recently formed Professional Division had assembled for the first annual Professional Seminar. In his opening remarks, Monroe emphasized the importance of producing research papers, designed to be appropriate for publication in professional journals, on specific applications of Hemi-Sync with references to control groups and accompanied by thorough statistical analysis. During the year, members contributed reports on using Hemi-Sync with alcohol abuse patients, in a vision improvement program, in focusing attention when learning, in increasing organizational effectiveness, and in working with two children, one diagnosed as autistic and the other with cerebral palsy and subject to seizures. There were also two very encouraging accounts on the value of the Emergency Treatment exercises during extensive surgical procedures.[1]

A further step forward was taken in 1984, when the laboratory was enriched with the installation of what became known as the "black box," designed for the most part by Joe McMoneagle and constructed by himself and Dave Wallis. This was an updated development of the installation in the Whistlefield laboratory. It consisted of a large sound-proofed booth, copper shielded, equipped with a waterbed and wired to a monitoring unit so that the monitor at a control desk and the subject in the booth would be in verbal contact via headphones throughout a session. Certain physiological readings, including temperature, galvanic skin response, and skin potential voltage, could be obtained from electrodes attached to the subject's fingers, which enabled the monitor to note, for example, the degree of relaxation of the subject and adjust the signals accordingly. The booth was to be utilized for the *Explorer* program and a session in it was later added for participants in *Guidelines*. It could also be made available to individuals for personal experiment or research. Monroe inspected this cozy and comfortable facility when it was completed and ready for use. He turned to Wallis. "Make sure everyone knows that this booth is not to be used for assignations," he said without a smile.[2]

In 1985 came another innovation, a portable Hemi-Sync synthesizer, a compact device able to create a range of selected Hemi-Sync frequencies that could be combined with music or the sound of surf. The synthesizer could be linked to external speakers or headphones, and it was possible to set the frequencies to create optimal learning conditions. Using this setting, it was tested in a number of schools in Washington State, under the supervision of Devon Edrington, who for several years had been using Hemi-Sync combined with music in his classes to help students improve their concentration and memory. Reports were uniformly favorable but, sadly, in 1986 Edrington died and the project lapsed. In the following year Michael Hutchison, a reporter for *Omni* magazine, toured the country trying out various devices that were claimed to affect states of consciousness, publishing his findings in *Megabrain* (Ballantine/Random House, 1986). He conducted a series of tests and workshops using the synthesizer, and became convinced of its effectiveness. He proposed that controlled studies involving larger groups would provide more compelling evidence, but before this idea could be put into practice Monroe decided to cease production. The reason for this is not clear; it may have been apprehension lest the device "fall into the wrong hands" or that, should its popularity increase, the sales of Hemi-Sync tapes would suffer.[3]

By 1985 it was becoming clear that one very important area of the Institute's operation, the production and duplication of the audiotapes, needed attention. Listening to music on a local radio program gave Monroe an idea. The presenter, Mark Certo, an impressively large individual with a warm personality and a caustic sense of humor, by profession an audio engineer and musician with a studio in Charlottesville, found a message on his answering machine to call Bob Monroe. He did so, and was invited to come to the Gate House, where he was greeted by "an elderly man wearing sweat pants fastened to his frame with multi-colored suspenders," smoking a Carlton cigarette with two inches of ash, which promptly fell onto his shirt. Mark was given a tour of the New Land and the Institute buildings. Finally, he was taken to the laboratory where, having listened closely to what Monroe was telling him, he expected to see a world-class recording facility complete with the latest equipment. What met his gaze, however, was, he recalled, "a collection of the most archaic recording equipment I think I had ever seen." He quickly understood that this equipment was Monroe's pride and joy and accepted the challenge to wire it all up to a console. Over lunch in nearby Nellysford, Mark outlined his experience and career goals, adding that he had no wish to work for anyone full time. Monroe smiled. "I just need you to mix about fifty tapes for me," he said. "The rest we'll take as it comes." So began Mark Certo's thirteen years with the Institute.

The fifty tapes that Monroe referred to were to form a new program under the title *Human-Plus* to be launched in 1987. The inspiration for this series derived from the OBE recounted in *Far*

Journeys, when he came across the inhabitants of a period in the distant future who were known as Humans-Plus. To begin with, Mark spent four days a week working on these tapes so that they could be duplicated for mass distribution. He was amused to find that the master that Monroe provided carried in the background the sounds of chirping crickets. It was impossible to edit them out without destroying the integrity of the tape so they had to stay. He began by approaching the task from a technical angle until he decided he ought to listen to one of the tapes through headphones. As Bob's voice counted up to ten he found himself in an extraordinarily deep meditative state—his first experience of the power of Hemi-Sync.

While Mark was not yet committed to working full time with Monroe, he was becoming increasingly involved with matters at the Institute. With the advent of Christmas he was invited to the staff party. As a gift to Monroe he created a spoof H-Plus tape, himself assuming the voice of Marlon Brando as the Godfather, Vito Corleone, and played this during the celebrations. Among the sound effects was Corleone shooting the noisy cricket. While everyone was laughing, he was disturbed to see Monroe leave the room. He went to apologize, but Nancy stopped him, saying she'd never seen Bob laugh so much. As Mark discovered, Monroe was wary of showing uncontrolled emotion, even hysterical laughter.

This episode seemed to draw the two closer together. For Monroe, Mark was someone he could joke with, who did not treat him as some sort of guru or New Age icon, or even as a somewhat unpredictable employer, but as a buddy with whom he could be at ease. They discussed various projects that Monroe had in mind, one of which was expanding the Metamusic program and improving its quality. Following Mark's advice, he decided to commission professional composers to provide the first tapes for a new series. While Monroe himself preferred dramatic symphonic compositions, Mark thought that an atmospheric style might be more appropriate. His own two choices, *Inner Journey,* by M. Sadigh, and *Sleeping through the Rain,* by M. Sigman and S. Anderson, quickly became best-sellers and have remained near the top of the list for almost twenty years.

Mark was now placed in charge of the Metamusic program. At the same time, however, his life outside the Institute was changing. He separated from his wife, with the consequence that he had to leave his house that contained his own recording studio. To improve his career prospects he applied for, and was offered, jobs in Chicago and Hawaii. Yet, on discussing his future with Monroe, he found himself persuaded that the Institute was the place where he belonged. He felt that Monroe really cared about what happened to him and accepted his offer of a full-time post, even though it was not as lucrative as the other offers he had received.

As a further task, Mark was required to do what he could to improve the audibility of the Explorer series of tapes. Many of these had been recorded at Whistlefield and their quality was poor. Mark had problems also with the content, having no previous experience of channeled material. When he later met some of the Explorers he found them to be pleasant, normal people, although on tape they sounded to him "like deranged beings with bogus English accents." Gradually, however, in talking with Monroe, who shared with him many of his own out-of-body experiences, his interest in topics such as channeling and reincarnation began to grow and he found himself more able to accept ideas and situations that hitherto had appeared bizarre. It was Monroe's ability to express himself in a way that every-one he talked with could relate to that enabled Mark to come to terms with what was being thought and said around him.

As the reputation of The Monroe Institute continued to expand it attracted an increasing number of talented individuals from all areas of the United States and from many countries overseas. Most came to take the programs, but there were others who felt they had something to offer to the Institute itself. One was the ebullient and energetic Leslie France, who had been involved in the early days of the hospice movement and had been strongly attracted by the work of Elisabeth Kübler-Ross. In 1986 she received a copy of *Far Journeys* as a gift from a friend, who said—shades of *Journeys Out of the Body*—that it had fallen on her from a bookstore shelf. Reading it, Leslie realized that Robert Monroe's fledgling Institute was where Kübler-Ross had undergone the transformational experiences she had described in one of her lectures. She contacted the Institute, took the *Gateway Experience* in-home course, bent all her intentions in the direction of finding employment there, and was amazed to be invited to an interview for the post of projects director. Once appointed, she proposed Kübler-Ross as the keynote speaker for the next Professional Seminar and felt that a circle had been completed when she agreed to come. Under Leslie's direction the Professional Division continued to grow, with its members feeding in increasing numbers of ideas and proposals as well as reporting on their own research into the uses and applications of Hemi-Sync.

A major asset to the training side of the Institute was Dave Mulvey. Mulvey had taken the *Gateway Voyage* in 1981 and had been attracted to the New Land as a place to live, moving into his own house there in 1983.[4] To begin with, he acted as airport courier from time to time; then Monroe invited him to help train some of the programs. He went on to fill several roles, including writing and designing the brochure, co-producing several tapes with Bob Monroe, editing the newsletters, and helping in the design of the *Guidelines* program and, later on, the H-Plus series. Dave proved an ideal trainer, never imposing his personal views and maintaining a keen sense of humor as well as a sympathetic approach towards all participants. In 1988 he was appointed director of programs.

Another individual drawn to the Institute was Fred Atwater, who had felt a strong compulsion to work there ever since his first meeting with Bob Monroe. Although no promise of permanent employment had been made, he was offered and accepted the role of technical consultant. In 1986, with retirement from the army beginning to loom, he bought a parcel of land some two-thirds of a mile from the Center and began to build a family house. Later that year David Lambert, a young researcher with a brilliant reputation who was working in the auditory physiology lab in the University of Illinois Medical Center in Chicago, contacted the Institute offering to barter his services as a computer programmer in exchange for a *Gateway* program. Lambert had read *Journeys Out of the Body* when at school and, as he said, "had been tremendously influenced by it." His interest had been reawakened by a magazine article on Monroe and the Institute, and further stimulated by reading *Far Journeys*.

The Gift House

Early in 1987 he visited the Institute, meeting Monroe, Dave Wallis, Leslie France, and Scooter. He offered to write software for them to help them make their research less anecdotal and more regimented, and showed them images of brain responses of gerbils to auditory stimuli at different depths over time as examples of recent research. Enthused by this new technology and Lambert's offer of help, Monroe arranged for him to return the following summer to develop the appropriate software.

In the summer of that year the Gift House was at last ready for occupation. The name proved appropriate. When the building commenced there was not enough money available to complete it. Yet somehow the money arrived, including checks from the sale of subsidiary rights to Bob's first book, from the closure of an escrow account on the sale of Whistlefield, from the sale of shares, and from other sources. After seven years in the restricted environment of the Gate House, to the Monroes the Gift House was almost a taste of Heaven. Bob said it was the nicest place he'd ever lived.

Bob Monroe and the waterfall in the Gift House

The Gift House is not what one might expect to find on the top of a mountain in Nelson County. The front elevation resembles a modest Spanish hacienda. The doorknocker is in the shape of a fox's head. (Nancy loved foxes and there are pictures of them throughout the house.) Inside to the right is a den, as at Whistlefield, with large, comfortable chairs, bookshelves, and an oversized television screen. To the left is an open-plan kitchen. There is a spacious formal dining room and a somewhat fanciful living room with one wall designed as a waterfall trickling over rocks. The Monroes' bedroom is also on this floor. To the rear the glass-walled garden room provides extensive views over treetops to the range of hills beyond. Downstairs are other bedrooms and outside a swimming pool. Music was piped into every room from an audio center in the den. Above, turkey buzzards and hawks ride the winds; inside, dogs and cats lived in comfort. Opposite stands the log cabin made of chestnut beams from an old barn on the property. One of Bob's pleasures once they had moved in was to wander out in his robe in the early morning, making sure he was properly covered lest Nancy comment, to watch the rays of the rising sun flickering through the trees. Then, after breakfast, he would cross to the cabin, where he spent much of his time, reading, writing, using his word processor with its huge screen for the sake of his weakening eye-sight—his third book, to be called *Ultimate Journey,* was already on its way—composing on one of the keyboard synthesizers, performing on his microchip-operated organ, or dealing with whatever Institute affairs found their way up the mountain and sending down

Bob's Cabin

instructions, proposals, flow charts, and memos, several of which might well be cancelled or amended the next day.

In her new house Nancy could entertain in style when the occasion arose. She delighted showing visitors around and welcoming members of the Professional Division on the last evening of their annual seminar. The house suited her natural elegance and she took pride in keeping it up to the mark. Now far from the distractions in and around the Gate House, she was able to relax, enjoy preparing meals in a kitchen of her own design, and spend more private time with Bob. One of her hopes was that she would now be able to complete the two novels that she felt inspired to write. One was to be a modern version of Scarlett O'Hara, the other a more mystical story under the title, "A City Not Built with Hands." Sadly, both remained unfinished.

The year 1987 saw the launch of the Human-Plus series, fifty exercises each dealing with a different function. The notion of using Hemi-Sync to create a simple learning system that could be of benefit to everyone, no matter what their educational background might be, and no matter whether they attended a residential program or not, had been in Monroe's thoughts for some years. At the Fifth Annual Professional Seminar in August of that year he introduced this new program to the largest group—ninety participants—that had so far assembled at the Center.

In his introductory talk, Monroe pointed out that so far Hemi-Sync had been used mainly for self-exploration. This, he now considered, was not enough, and he explained that the new program would provide a number of function exercises "that will teach individuals to develop control over physical, emotional and mental systems . . . one step at a time." This would be achieved by utilizing new multilayered Hemi-Sync signals to access a particular brain function, allowing the transformation of "beliefs" into "knowns," thus enabling those using the program to transcend their self-imposed limitations.

This "System of Planned Evolution," as Monroe described it, sounded very ambitious. To some of those present the idea that by listening to an exercise on audiotape you would be able, for example, to overcome pain, summon up extra physical strength, improve your arithmetical skills, or sharpen your concentration seemed far-fetched, if not incredible. Monroe explained that he never anticipated that every exercise would work for every individual, but that even if only 10 or 20 percent were effective it would be "an astounding step in human transformation." He added that you might need to listen only once or twice to a particular exercise. As soon as it was fixed in your memory, you were encouraged to give the tape to someone else—to anyone who might need it whether that person knew about Monroe, Hemi-Sync, the Institute, or not. He insisted that H-Plus was intended as a service to humankind, not as a means of creating profit for the Institute. In a letter to participants in the first H-Plus residential course Monroe emphasized "the obligation to be of service where and when the opportunity arises." He continued: "You will encounter others who need the help that H-Plus provides . . . It is a gift you can give, a service you can perform better than anyone else."

The initial residential course took place in October 1987. Two experienced trainers, Barbara Collier and Cathy Kachur, each blessed with a keen sense of humor, designed and conducted the first few programs. During the six days, participants were required to listen to thirty-six H-Plus exercises. Each tape included an identical "preparation" side, introducing and explaining the process, and a "function" side for the specific purpose of the tape. The idea was that you learned the "function command" ("plus focus," "plus see better," "plus relax" are examples) and then when you needed to enact the function you simply repeated it on a breath. To implant the function, as it were, Monroe created a new Hemi-Sync signal he called

Focus 11. This is recorded on every tape; the theory is that it is reactivated when the function is recalled.

Lying down listening to nearly forty almost identical exercises in six days was not altogether an inspiring or enjoyable experience. The trainers worked hard to devise activities to vary and lighten the program, and the Institute itself, together with the beautiful surroundings and prospects, cast its own special spell. Monroe himself learned much from the responses of the participants, whose experiences, to his delight, appeared to indicate a success rate approaching 40 percent. Before long, H-Plus weekend programs were being conducted by Outreach trainers in several venues throughout the United States, Canada, and England. The tapes were sold singly and many positive reports were received from individuals whose only contact with Hemi-Sync was through a single H-Plus tape. However, the six-day residential courses, originally intended for those who would become ambassadors for H-Plus, failed to attract sufficient applicants. This was not surprising, as the programs were repetitive rather than progressive, and it soon became obvious that it was much cheaper to buy those tapes that you felt that you needed, listen to them, and then, once the functions were embedded, pass them on to someone else. The residential courses were discontinued in 1991. In subsequent years some of the exercises in less demand were withdrawn, but the 2006 catalogue still included thirty-five H-Plus titles, now recorded also on compact disc.

While it is impossible to evaluate the success of the H-Plus program with any precision, published reports and personal testimonies provide evidence of its continued usefulness in a variety of situations, including dealing with pain, restoring energy postpregnancy, changing negative attitudes and emotional patterns, overcoming learning problems, sharpening the five senses, and as a positive element in learning. One surprising result involved a trial with two young women diagnosed with myalgic encephalitis (Epstein-Barr syndrome), who studied the H-Plus list and selected those exercises that they thought they needed. The choices they each made were found to be extremely helpful in coping with the difficulties presented by this condition. The wide variety of functions enabled users of H-Plus to develop their own ways of working with the system, usually by linking functions together to suit a particular purpose.[5] Much of the success of the process is due to the quality of Monroe's recorded voice, so powerful in conveying his own confidence in what he was saying. Transferred to the listener, that confidence is a vital element in encouraging belief that the process will actually work and its simplicity makes it easy to use and remember. It is a gift for which an incalculable number of people are grateful.

In the summer of 1988, work in the Institute laboratory began to intensify. David Lambert returned to continue his research. Atwater, whose house was nearly complete and whose retirement from the army was imminent, told Leslie France of his dream to be involved with the further development of Hemi-Sync. One of Leslie's aims was to create opportunities for professional members attending the forthcoming seminar to form interest groups so that research on specific projects might be continued after the meeting. She asked Atwater to organize a group on the effects of Hemi-Sync on the human brain and invited Lambert to participate. The topic attracted much interest, the group members, who included several scientists, concluding that the best tool currently available for this research was the standard strip-chart style EEG.

Meanwhile, Leslie received information about a team of scientists in Colorado who were developing a topographical EEG display system that, she thought, sounded as if it would be of interest to Bob Monroe. She suggested that this system could be worth investigating. Lambert visited the Colorado unit and returned convinced that it was what they needed. The system worked in conjunction with a then up-to-date desktop computer, an IBM-compatible 286. Atwater began generating binaural beats with his own Amiga computer, which was equipped with a sound card. He produced a simple program written in BASIC. Lambert was enthused by this and used the Amiga to develop a program that could be used to create multiple binaural beat patterns that could be mixed down to Hemi-Sync tapes. He was so impressed by the Amiga that he insisted on holding on to it, leaving Atwater to buy another one for himself. When this process was demonstrated to Monroe, he quickly appreciated how much more efficient this was than laboriously mixing layers of sounds through a multichannel audio mixing board.

Another development that came to the notice of the researchers was a technology known as BEAM (Brain Electrical Activity Mapping). This had been invented by Dr. Frank Duffy of the Children's Hospital Medical Center at Boston and David Culver of Braintech, a manufacturing company in New Jersey. It consisted of a neurophysiological diagnostic device that converted the output of a twenty-channel EEG into a color-contour map of the electrical activity of the brain. The data was gathered via noninvasive electrodes placed on defined positions on the scalp. The equipment converted this information into computer-readable form, analyzed the information, and displayed the results as a two-dimensional stylized color oval image of the head. Originally used to diagnose certain neurological conditions in children, the technology had been adapted by other companies for a variety of purposes. Having considered some of these purposes, members of the working group recommended that the Institute should purchase a BEAM-type device, the Neuromap System 20, from the NeuroMap Medical Corporation, Boulder, Colorado. The group also proposed that the Institute should provide funds for a research/laboratory effort to document the physiological effects of Hemi-Sync technology, develop improved Hemi-Sync processes, and provide individual sessions for those wishing to examine their own brain patterns while using Hemi-Sync. (All this was very different from Monroe's earlier attitude towards the purchase of equipment, which derived from his fascination with auctions. On one occasion he returned from a sale with a large item of outdated hospital equipment embellished with dials and switches. "What do you think we could use this for?" he asked Dave Wallis. Dave took one look at it. "Landfill," he replied.)

Ever since Hemi-Sync had first been developed, Monroe had been struggling to resolve a dilemma. He was wary of people with degrees, possibly because he himself had obtained one without doing much solid work. He also found it hard to trust scientists to understand a process that had come about largely through trial and error. In one way he wanted validation for the technology, but in another he did not think it was needed. Now he was put on the spot. He embarked on a series of discussions with Atwater and the Institute's senior staff members, including Scooter, Dave Mulvey, representing the trainers, Dave Wallis, Rita and Martin Warren, and Leslie France. All agreed that the project should go ahead. The one problem was shortage of money, as the Neuromap system was expensive to buy and install. Wallis proposed that the idea be introduced to a friend of his, a Canadian businessman who had recently taken the *Gateway* program and become an enthusiastic supporter of the Institute. Convinced by what he heard, the Canadian donated a generous sum of money towards furthering research. This enabled the system to be purchased and the laboratory to be updated. Atwater, who had been acting for some time as an unpaid technical consultant, offered for a token salary to manage the project for the first year, with renegotiation of his position after that, to which Monroe and Scooter agreed. In the following year Atwater joined the staff full time as director of research.

It is significant that two of the principals in the army's most innovative intelligence program, Captain Frederick Atwater and

Chief Warrant Officer Joseph McMoneagle, came on retirement to live as neighbors less than a mile from Bob Monroe and the Institute. Monroe has been described as a kind of supernatural fisherman, reeling in those who would be of value to himself and his Institute, no matter what they did or where they were. Some later slipped away; some were thrown back into the water. But these were two who stayed, each making distinct contributions to the old fisherman's projects.

In November 1989, in an open letter to supporters of the Institute, Monroe outlined "the mountain of information" that was being gathered from the operation of the Neuromapper. In using it "to identify and measure various levels of human consciousness in both normal subjects and those with special talents or training" spectacular results were being obtained. The equipment was now an essential component of the Institute's programs and was also available to anyone willing to pay for a personalized session. It was also an indispensable tool for a new venture, the *Gifted Subject* program, designed to investigate the brain activity of individuals with special gifts or talents. The purpose was to discover brainwave information related to subjects with special abilities to see if this information could be used to improve the Hemi-Sync process.[6] From this document it appears that Monroe's doubts about the necessity of validation were now finally resolved.

Staffing the Institute was always a problem, partly because of its geographical situation. If you could afford to buy or build a house on the New Land, then one problem was solved—for the time being. Most employees did not have that sort of money and were compelled to live elsewhere—but elsewhere could involve long journeys to and from work. There was no job security and few opportunities for promotion. Moreover, in its role as an employer the Institute might be described as erratic. Remuneration did not always match up to the dignity of the title of an appointment and working conditions were not ideal. While the registrar, Helen Warring, had a spacious office on the ground floor of the Gate House, on the floor above, where several people were dealing with matters such as accounts, orders, and

The Professional Division 1989

sales, conditions were cramped. It was not surprising that many employees remained for only a short time.

There were, however, two in particular who stayed on to provide especially valuable service. One of these was Dr. Darlene Miller, who joined the training staff in 1985. As a clinical psychologist she had directed a residential treatment facility for 160 violent juvenile offenders. She had also acted as a consultant with a number of management groups on effective team building. Monroe appointed her to direct the *Explorer* and *Personal Resources Exploration* programs and from 1991 she and Teena Anderson, an ex-social worker who had a notable gift for channeling, also facilitated the *Lifeline* program.

Dr. Miller was later promoted to director of training and was still holding that position in 2006.

The other long stayer was a locally recruited employee, Teresa Critzer (later Teresa West), who simply wanted a job closer to home. She knew nothing about the Institute, nor was she expecting, as she said, "the dramatic new and wonderful direction my life was to take." She continued: "Having considered myself a hard working country girl, the language and subject matter of TMI was like a foreign language to me." But hers was a real success story. She proved an efficient organizer and was soon promoted to take charge of personnel and administration. Then, in 1985, when the Institute became established as a nonprofit organization, it became necessary to separate the sales of products—tapes and, later, compact discs—from the Institute itself. For this purpose a new incorporated company was formed, to be relocated a few years later in Lovingston, some dozen miles distant from the Institute. Teresa moved across to work with this company. In 2004 this "hard working country girl" was appointed vice president of the Institute and also of the sales arm, now known as Monroe Products. While over the years the financial state of the nonprofit Institute fluctuated according to the uptake of courses, the sales arm was generally profitable and continued to expand.

Another complication—if that's the right word—was that Monroe was not the easiest person to work for. Leslie France thought that the best term to describe him was "mercurial."

"Among the staff," she recalls, "we often spoke of him in terms of which personality aspect he was expressing at the moment—Uncle Bob (or Dad), Businessman Bob, Good Old Boy Bob, Cosmic Bob, Paranoid Bob, Performer Bob. Those were the main Bobs I knew but not, by far, the only Bobs. One soon learned the advantage of determining which Bob was present before attempting communication. And it could change on a dime."

Leslie adds that "juggling Bobs" caused the staff much frustration. "Businessman Bob sent edicts down from the Black Hole, as we called his office in the cabin on Roberts Mountain, some other Bob refuted the edicts, and Paranoid Bob railed against the untrustworthiness of the staff who failed to follow the edicts." One interpretation, more sympathetic than some, was that he needed to stir things up to keep the energy moving and it didn't matter how this was done.

Businessman Bob, described by Leslie as "the personification of the 1950s ethic: sly, hard, unemotional in pursuit of the dollar," was whom Leslie expected to encounter when summoned to a meeting in the Center's dining room with Bob and Ron Harris, the recently appointed office manager. She was first to arrive and sat down to wait. The others came together, Bob carrying a yellow legal pad covered with his customary big black lettering.

"While we were settling in and Ron's attention was on his notes, I glanced at Bob," Leslie remembers. "At that moment he caught my eye and the most extraordinary thing happened. I felt as though he and I were transported into another awareness and a stream of communication issued from his gaze directly into my consciousness. The stream contained words and feelings. It said, 'Isn't this fun?' 'This' referred to the entire human drama as well as our little meeting and was accompanied by the lightest sense of fun and mischief, which I saw reflected in the sparkling eyes across from me. We giggled. Ron looked up and the moment was gone. I had encountered Cosmic Bob."

Now that the laboratory had been updated, Mark Certo began to work with Skip Atwater and Dave Wallis on a number of experimental projects. Being a very approachable person, he soon found himself questioned about the uses and possibilities of Hemi-Sync by those attending courses and by visitors, including doctors, psychologists, psychiatrists, engineers, and professionals in a variety of disciplines, all interested in ways of using the technology in their own practice or research. What principally motivated all of them, he concluded, was their desire to discover as much as they could about the enigma of consciousness.

One of these professionals was a young computer scientist, Paul King. Since graduating in 1970, Paul had been working commercially on designing computer systems. Among his interests were the study of human consciousness, psychic phenomena, philosophy of the mind, in which he had taken a course at Stanford, and meditation. After nearly twenty years he resigned from his employment, having become convinced that a change of direction was essential. He moved from California to an island off the coast of Washington State and began seeking a career that would enable him to contribute something worthwhile to humanity. Meantime, he had read Monroe's first two books and, his interest awakened, he attended a *Gateway* program in March 1989. He decided to take a year off to work as a volunteer for the Institute, developing computer tools for the exploration of consciousness. He brought his family with him and began work in the lab, where he wrote a much improved binaural beat generating program as well as a program to reverse-engineer binaural beats from brainwave data. His efforts led to the complete automation of the production of Hemi-Sync, saving much time and improving the quality. Paul's improvements also added to the flexibility of programs for the researchers and Explorers using the isolation unit. In return, Paul himself was able to make use of regular personal exploration sessions, which he found very rewarding.

Other professionals who were attracted to the Institute included a neurologist, Dr. Edgar Wilson, founder of the Colorado Association for Psychophysiologic Research, and Jungian psychotherapist Bernice Hill. Wilson had been researching consciousness since the late 1970s and was especially interested in the influence of sound on brainwave patterns, in particular, when binaural beat frequencies were employed. He also worked with healers, especially with Rod, a seventy-seven-year-old cowpoke from New Zealand, recording the changes in brainwave frequency both in Rod himself and in the subject he was treating. He noted with interest that when Rod was at work his and the patient's frequencies coincided, and when he stopped working the frequencies went their separate ways. Wilson discovered that the Institute was one of the few organizations with a laboratory where consciousness itself was studied and he worked there examining the effects of Hemi-Sync on the brain for what he described as "one of the most frenetic months I'd ever spent." In pursuit of this, he developed taped exercises based on the Fibonacci series, a progression of numbers derived from Pythagoras that is reproduced in the branching of plants, in DNA and RNA, and in the dendrites and neurons of the nervous system. Wilson also put together a small team consisting of Mark Certo, Skip Atwater, and Teena Anderson to see if they could emulate the structures of sacred geometry with the use of the Fibonacci series reinforced by Hemi-Sync.[7] Sadly this brilliant man died from cancer in 1992, his work incomplete. His fascinating essay, "The Transits of Consciousness," can be found in *Using the Whole Brain,* edited by R. Russell (Hampton Roads, 1993).

Confident in the ability of his audio engineer, Monroe began instructing Mark on the art and philosophy of Hemi-Sync application. This confidence extended so far that he felt sufficiently comfortable recording his voice tracks in the lab instead of in the privacy of his log cabin. Mark soon became aware of how hard Monroe was on himself and on the quality of his performance, at times blaming some ailment or illness for being, as he thought, inadequate. When things were going badly Mark would call a halt and both of them would drive out for a hamburger and an hour or two of casual conversation at Truslow's in nearby Nellysford. Monroe insisted that

Mark should read *Journeys Out of the Body* and told him about the problems he was having with the book he was currently writing, especially having to find time to focus on it while so much was happening at the Institute. These, however, were not the only problems he was facing. It was becoming clear to Mark and to others close to Monroe that certain personal concerns were beginning to wear him down. His own health was not good, but, more significantly, for some time Nancy also had been feeling unwell. Now they learned that the diagnosis of breast cancer was confirmed.

As the number of programs increased along with the sales of the tapes, the staff numbers continued to grow. By 1990 the Institute had twenty-one full-time employees, many with impressive titles including "director" and "coordinator." There were also eighteen trainers, many of them professionally qualified in their own fields, who visited to train the residential programs, and ninety-three Gateway Outreach trainers, with Maxine Lorence as coordinator, who were qualified to present two-day workshops in the United States and overseas. The physical fitness of course participants was catered to by Maxine's husband Larry, an ex-Olympic trainer, who conducted early morning fitness sessions in the Residential Center. With Monroe becoming less involved with the day-to-day management, Scooter now handled the tiller with a sure touch.

One of those who attended Outreach training was Stefano Siciliano, also known as Kala, an American living in West Germany with his German wife, Susanne. They were the founders and directors of the Rainbow Bridge Institute situated on a mountainside above Heidelberg. Stefano first came across Monroe in 1973, when his eye was caught by the jacket of *Journeys Out of the Body* in a southern New Jersey bookstore. He crossed paths with this book for many years, reading passages here and there, but avoided buying it until he noticed the title in a reading list issued at a seminar he attended in Munich in 1989. Acting on this, he contacted the Institute and ordered it, together with *Far Journeys.* He discovered that episodes in both volumes reflected and explained his own out-of-body experiences. His interest now fully captured, Stefano obtained the "Introduction to Hemi-Sync" demonstration tape. Almost immediately the recorded sound signals brought him, he said, into a profoundly coherent whole-brain state, and as a practiced meditator he was astounded at the effects of Hemi-Sync on his consciousness, especially the state of expanded awareness he experienced. He found that his out-of-body experiences became more frequent and more dramatic, and, he recalled, nonphysical beings began to visit him—or maybe he just became more aware of them. Now wholly enthused, he bought the in-home *Gateway* program, and shortly afterwards flew to Virginia, taking *Gateway, Guidelines,* and Outreach training within a year. Conversations with Bob Monroe and Scooter led to him suggesting that he should introduce Hemi-Sync to Europe. "Let's do it," was Monroe's reply.

To begin with, Stefano offered programs to some of the American communities then living in Germany. This proved disappointing, however, as their responses, he felt, lacked both freshness and openness. He then discovered an alternative group active in Poland that provided free meditation sessions and a variety of self-improvement modalities. He offered to introduce Hemi-Sync to this group, and his first demonstration to an audience of over fifty was well received. Encouraged by this and equipped with two nonverbal cassettes carrying Hemi-Sync signals created for him by Mark Certo, Stefano made repeated trips across Poland, being welcomed enthusiastically. At one point he was invited to Warsaw to take part in a televised program—a sort of "Good Morning Poland"—with a panel of physicists and two English-speaking hosts. In a twenty-minute slot Stefano was able to describe the effects of sound on consciousness and how that might apply to various disciplines. Much of Poland heard about The Monroe Institute and Hemi-Sync that morning, with special reference to sleep deprivation, accelerated learning, and expanded awareness.

Hoping to take advantage of the success of this program, and observing the success of the Silva Mind Control books recently translated into several European languages, Stefano proposed that Bob's books be translated similarly. Surprised by the lack of any response, he nevertheless continued to present seminars, moving into Slovakia and Hungary, followed by invitations to the Czech Republic, Russia, Greece, and Malta. Having to keep costs as low as possible, bearing in mind he was working alone and had to meet his own expenses, he was able to respond to only a few of the large number of inquiries. For a weekend seminar in Eastern Europe he charged each participant the equivalent of nineteen to thirty dollars, depending on the distance he had to travel. No one was refused for being unable to meet the cost. He sold what nonverbal tapes he could carry as cheaply as possible, with participants often pooling their meager funds to buy one tape to share between five or six of them. Groups varied from 40 to 120, many of whom traveled long distances to attend, sometimes sleeping out in the open or in the rented seminar room and carrying brown paper bags with a block of cheese and a loaf of bread for the weekend. Stefano ran these programs for about two years until, feeling exhausted and lacking the funds to continue, he decided to call a halt. His enthusiasm for promoting Hemi-Sync overseas did not evaporate, but the failure of the Institute to provide financial help made him aware that a different approach was needed. For the time being, however, this would have to wait.

While still living in the Gate House, Monroe had been able to keep an eye on the program participants as they came and went. Some were seminar groupies eager to try out the latest fad, seeking some sort of kick—some fantastic experience to equal or surpass their latest psychedelic trip. Most, however, were what he regarded as the "bounce-backers," those like himself who were not afraid to take risks or who had learned a few of life's rules and faced whatever confronted them with courage. With these he felt a strong affinity; it was as if they shared the seminars together. But one effect of the move to the top of the mountain was to detach Monroe from frequent contact with participants in the Institute's programs. With a competent senior staff under Scooter's direction now in place, including Programs Director Dave Mulvey and Projects Director Julie Mazo, he could afford to leave the running of the Institute to others. Apart from his two evening talks and his presence at breakfast on the last morning, he was seldom visible around the Institute buildings unless he was glimpsed entering or leaving the laboratory.

Yet, now in his mid-seventies, he was working as hard as ever. Aware from comments by some of the senior staff that the *Guidelines* program needed rethinking, he began voicing a revised and updated version, extending it by a day, incorporating more exercises in Focus 21, and adding an individual session in the laboratory's "black box" as part of a new *Personal Resource Exploration* program, designed by Darlene Miller. The new version was launched in February 1989 and was immediately in demand. Moreover, with *Far Journeys* now in the bookstores, Monroe was striving to complete his final statement, *Ultimate Journey*. Now that the H-Plus and the new *Guidelines* programs were up and running, he thought he would be able to put all his efforts into finishing the text, intending it to be published in 1990. But this was not to be.

Despite the progressive nature of her illness, Nancy continued to take as full a part as possible in what was happening at the Institute. After so many failed marriages, Monroe had found in her a partner with whom he could share his daily life as well as his paranormal experiences. He once remarked that people liked to think of him and

Nancy up on the hill spending their time thinking about and delving into "the mystic." "In fact," he added, "we're watching game shows like *Wheel of Fortune* and *Jeopardy* and wondering what to have for dinner—just like everyone else!" "Mystic stuff" was confined to the log cabin, when Bob wasn't amusing himself composing, playing with the idea of writing a novel, or practicing on the Lowrey organ.

To the Institute itself, Nancy made a huge contribution. "Were it not for her," Bob wrote, "there probably would not have been any such organization. She participated in all major and minor discussions and decisions, activities, and even research." Nancy had also taken major responsibility for the interior design of the Residential Center and David Francis Hall, as well as enhancing the surroundings of the Institute buildings with trees and shrubs. When in December 1988 it was decided to expand the Center by adding a new wing, incorporating a spacious dining room, an exercise room, and a treatment room, as well as more CHEC units and several shower-rooms and toilets, it was Nancy who attended to all the details and designed the dining area to the last detail, including the furniture and tableware. As Monroe said, "It is impossible to be at the Institute without encountering the result of her thoughts."

An outstanding feature of the improvements to the Center was the external tower housing a staircase leading from the base of the building to a railed open space on the roof. Its construction created a raft of problems. The first attempt proved disastrous, and Monroe invited Joe McMoneagle to take over. McMoneagle had taught himself how to build by trial and error supplemented by studying instructional books. It did not take long for Joe to discover that the best way to rectify the disaster and finish the task was to begin at the top and work down. The job was nearing completion when he arrived one morning to find a gang of builders beavering away on the final stages, hired by Monroe to complete the construction as quickly

Foulis Castle Tower

as possible. This, as it proved later, was not the best idea Monroe ever had, and fifteen years later the tower had to be rebuilt.

What was most remarkable about the tower, however, was not the manner of its building but its design. In 1990 Bob's younger brother and sister-in-law, Emmett and Alice, visited Foulis Castle, near Inverness, ancient seat of the Munro/Monroe clan, and took a number of photographs, including some of the castle's tower. Foulis had been totally rebuilt in the mid-eighteenth century, as the medieval building it replaced, which according to the records also had a tower although no illustrations of it appear to exist, had fallen into ruin. When Emmett received an Institute brochure including a picture of the Monroe Institute's new tower, he immediately mailed his photographs to his brother. Although the dimensions of the two towers are not identical, Foulis being larger, their proportions are similar; both have four stories, both are octagonal with similar pitched roofs, both are embedded into the main building, and both have access to the roof with similar iron railings at the access point. For Bob

Monroe this demonstrated an undeniable connection with what in *Ultimate Journey* he referred to as his "I Then," and he incorporated a description and photograph of the tower into the text.[8]

The Nancy Penn Center

Now as the months passed Nancy's state of health was cause for increasing concern. It was ironic that this was so, as she remarked to Laurie on one of her occasional visits from Florida where she now lived, as she had always thought that Bob would be the one to go first. When that happened, she hoped that Laurie would move to the Institute to do whatever was required of her. But now the situation had reversed and it was Bob who had to face the prospect that his partner might not have long to live. This being so, he turned his attention to an idea that had been around since February 1986, a proposal for a project that had never come to fruition. He discussed this with Nancy and with her encouragement resolved that the time was right for it to be revived.

This project was initially devised by Ruth Domin, director of volunteers at the Hospice of Chattanooga. This gentle and very determined lady had attended a *Gateway* program in 1983 and kept in contact with Monroe thereafter. It was her idea to investigate the use of Hemi-Sync tapes with hospice patients. The hospice nurses, together with other health professionals and a corps of volunteer support practitioners, introduced patients to selected taped exercises designed to promote relaxation. The purpose was to ascertain whether these exercises helped patients to deal with their pain, fear, anxiety, and loneliness, so that the end of life might be experienced as a natural event within the warm environment of the family. They were carefully monitored to ascertain what benefits, if any, these exercises provided. The project was headed by Ruth, who herself was later to be diagnosed with cancer.

After a number of trials it had become clear that the materials available were of only limited use. Ruth saw that exercises with more specific purposes were needed. During the 1987 Professional Seminar she headed a group under the title of "Life Transitions" to develop and test a package of Hemi-Sync tapes for the support of patients and their families, and also for health care providers who had to deal with terminal illness, death, and bereavement. Two pilot tapes were produced and used by hospice patients in Chattanooga. That, however, was as far as it went, as Ruth's own health was failing. In 1989 she died and the project fell into abeyance.

Recalling Ruth Domin's project, Monroe soon became aware that its scope was too limited. That was not all. As he records in *Ultimate Journey,* his more recent out-of-body experiences had presented him with what he described as a particular mission of service. He came to understand that Nancy's progressive illness demanded that this mission be defined and transformed into practical reality with no loss of time. In consultation with her he began work on a new program, to be called *Lifeline,* which he saw would be "a kind of death insurance." To him, this program might also provide what he described as "a way that Nancy and I could meet if one of us left the physical."

From many points of view, *Lifeline* was a risky venture. To begin with, the frequencies employed were designed to lead participants beyond Focus 21, hitherto regarded as the boundary of the time-space continuum and the farthest accessible stage within the compass of human consciousness. Then the program was based on the premise that consciousness was immortal, that when the body died consciousness simply continued to be. This was, to put it mildly, controversial, but that did not deter participants when, in June 1991, the program was launched. It proved an immediate success.

Lifeline was not the only program that stemmed from Nancy Monroe's illness. When Shay St. John, now a minister of religion, was visiting, she offered to drive Nancy to the hospital for a chemotherapy treatment, followed by lunch together afterwards. During the treatment the needle was misplaced and the chemo leaked into Nancy's hand instead of flowing into her bloodstream. The nurse warned her that her hand would turn black and she would be in much pain. It seemed there was nothing that could be done about it, so they decided to have lunch anyway before going home. As they settled at their table, Nancy's hand began to swell and showed signs of blackening. To distract her, Shay, knowing Nancy's love for dolphins, told her a story about how they have been known to assist whales during the birth process. Nancy closed her eyes, visualizing seven dolphins flowing through her bloodstream. Shay and Nancy together focused their thoughts on these dolphins, encouraging them to find and eat the chemo that would then transmute into their favorite food. During lunch they both continued to focus on Nancy's hand. The swelling began to decrease and the skin color to lighten. By evening the hand was normal.

As a consequence of this, the Dolphin Energy Club (DEC) was brought into being. This is a remote healing facility introduced by a

purpose-made taped exercise issued to those who have taken programs at the Institute and have signed on as DEC members. Requests
for healing are co-coordinated at the Institute by Shirley Bliley, who
succeeded Leslie France as director of the Professional Division, and
circulated to members who report on what they have visualized and
detail any impressions they may have received. It was never the intention that DEC healing would be analyzed or scientifically validated; it
is simply a method of directing healing energy wherever required.
The awareness that this is happening may in itself be of benefit. From
hundreds of reports sent to the Institute since the program was initiated, it appears that a majority of DEC recipients have received
positive results from the process.

Monroe was now seventy-six years old. The Institute's future
was secure, the courses were filled, and the sales of products continued to increase. *Ultimate Journey* was, he hoped, nearly ready for
submission to the publisher. But his mind was not at rest. Nancy's illness was not yielding to treatment—how much longer would she
have to live? And what would happen to the Institute when he was no
longer in control? Whom could he trust—and what did the future
have in store?

Notes

1. The accounts referred to are described in chapter 6.

2. To begin with the booth was equipped with a TV camera, which
   required low-level lighting, and with mechanisms for vibrating the
   waterbed, so it may have been these items that encouraged
   Monroe to suspect that it might be put to nonscientific use. In any
   event, neither proved necessary and both were soon withdrawn.

3. Although it was not a particularly sophisticated device, the synthesizer proved effective in many ways, including as an aid to meditation for a group meeting weekly for nine years in Cambridge, England.

4. New Land residents refused to have road names and signs until the county authorities said they were essential for the emergency services. Residents on each road collaborated on names, mostly descriptive or poetic. David Mulvey and Rick and Patty Lawrence were the only residents on their cul-de-sac. Dave asked Rick if he had any ideas. "Sure," said Rick. "Gasp Court." "What's that about?" asked Dave. "It's an acronym. It stands for 'Give a shit, people.'" "Gasp Court" it remains.

5. When learning to pilot a light aircraft, Outreach trainer Cheryl Williams linked seven H-Plus functions together to help her pass the various tests. She is confident that this helped her to pass all of them.

6. The *Gifted Subject* program did not involve the use of Hemi-Sync signals. The subject, wearing the twenty-channel brainwave transmitter, entered the "black box" in the laboratory unit and was asked to visualize using a unique talent—composing a piece of music, healing a patient, writing a poem—whatever it might be. The readings were recorded for later analysis. Interestingly, it was noted that at special moments of insight the brainwave frequency peaked, moving into the gamma band. At this time gamma frequencies were not employed in the creation of Hemi-Sync materials.

7. The Fibonacci series was discovered by the Italian mathematician Leonardo Fibonacci (ca. 1170–ca. 1250). It is a sequence in which each number is equal to the sum of the preceding two (0,1,1,2,3,5,8, and so on). It can be observed, for example, in the growth patterns of many plants. Thirteen patterns derived from Sacred Geometry are combined with two Metamusic compositions in "Light Source," an item of computer software issued by The Monroe Institute in 2004.

8. See chapter 10. The Foulis Castle tower photographed by Emmett Monroe dates from the rebuilding of the castle initiated by Sir Harry Munro after the 1745 rebellion and bears the date 1754. Monroe was mistaken in assuming that it was part of the twelfth-century castle, but that does not detract from the remarkable similarity of the two constructions nor from his belief that the Foulis tower builder-architect was a constituent of his own "I There" (or "I Then"), as described in *Ultimate Journey*.

CHAPTER 9

Ultimate Journey and Lifeline

Monroe was seventy years old when *Far Journeys* was published. His Institute was firmly established with an efficient director on site, and its programs were attracting participants from all across the world. His marriage was secure and all that was needed to perfect his domestic happiness was the completion of the Gift House on the top of Roberts Mountain. Now he could set to work on his final statement: *Ultimate Journey.*

His first two books had progressed from conception to publication with comparatively little difficulty. Sales of *Journeys Out of the Body,* after a slow start, had exceeded all expectations, while *Far Journeys* sold well if not spectacularly. With this eagerly anticipated final statement there should be no problems.

But problems there were. Thanks largely to his earlier books, the out-of-body experience was now a much more familiar phenomenon; therefore, what might be described as its novelty value no longer applied. Monroe himself had learned much from his more recent experiences, knowledge that he considered of great importance to the world at large. This had to be put into shape, welded into a philosophy that he believed would be of great benefit to humanity. On a different level, a widely selling book would provide a useful means for publicizing the work of the Institute. An account of this work would need to be integrated into the overall scheme.

And then, while the book was in progress, Nancy's health began to fail. Although Monroe makes very few references to her illness in *Ultimate Journey,* it affected him deeply and contributed to the direction his thinking was to take. In the draft that was first submitted to the publisher he introduced each chapter with a snatch of dialogue between himself and his wife, moving in the early chapters from friendly, everyday chat to acknowledgment of her illness and expression of their profound love. But for the great majority of those who would buy and read the book these dialogues would bear no relation to the chapters they headed. With one exception, they were omitted from the published version.

As time passed and Nancy's health continued to deteriorate, it seemed as if the undertaking of this final volume was beginning to overwhelm its author. There were frequent arguments with his agent and close neighbor Eleanor Friede, whose wide experience in the publishing world assured her that what he was presenting was not going to be saleable. Toward the end of the book he sought to include a lengthy extract from the Institute's brochure as well as no fewer than twenty-one addenda, a collection of miscellaneous items that made no contribution to the story he was telling. It was as if he was desperate to omit nothing that might in his mind have some relevance, no matter how distant, to the main text, but was unable to judge how the readers would respond to this.

Progress was very slow and it seemed as if the publishers might run out of patience and give up on the project. In desperation, Eleanor smuggled a typescript to an independent editor who managed to trim and shape the material acceptably for publication. The book eventually appeared in April 1994, four years later than first anticipated. Despite the difficulties Monroe experienced in organizing the material, the complexity of the subject matter, and the distress of Nancy's progressive illness, *Ultimate Journey* is easy to read, with much of it conversational in tone. Some of the ideas it contains are as mind-stretching as can be imagined, but nevertheless, considering the nature of the subject, Monroe succeeded for the third time in enticing his readers to accept his experiences and seriously consider his conclusions.

Over thirty years of out-of-body activity had brought Monroe to "a calm state of satisfaction"—or so he believed. He knew his origin, why he became human, why he "hung around," when he would leave, and where he would then go. He had mastered most of his fears and had formulated his purpose in life. This purpose was "service to humankind," as he declared to the Inspec in an out-of-body encounter. But he was surprised to be told in response that there were other goals, although what they were was not revealed to him. He was made to understand that this "service," as he had imagined it, would be soon forgotten and in effect was no more than mere ego-gratification. A new goal was required which, he concluded after some thought, was summed up in the very human yearning to go Home. This might be some favorite place on Earth, or the Heaven or Paradise held out as a target or destination in various religious beliefs. Or it might be understood as the place you came from—the place to which you desired to return.

In a subsequent out-of-body experience Monroe was enabled to make a visit Home. He had glimpsed this place before and was convinced that, after several lifetimes on Earth, it would be his ultimate destination. This visit, however, proved an enormous disappointment that took him several weeks to come to terms with. He discovered that the phenomena he experienced—the sights, the sounds, the energy—beautiful though they were, simply repeated themselves over and over again. There was no growth, no development, nothing but a kind of eternal boredom. He woke up tearful and depressed.

Further experiences under the tutelage of the Inspec eventually restored Monroe's spirits until the time came when he was told that they would no longer be meeting. He was made to understand that he had to follow a new path, and to discover and explore an essential knowledge, a basic, that hitherto he had missed despite the different overview that he had acquired through his decades of out-of-body travel. To prepare himself for this he needed to establish "a clear understanding of the here and now, of physical life just as it is without philosophical and emotional discoloration." In the following chapters this is what he attempted to do.

Monroe was not an academic. There is no reference in any of his books to anything that he had read, to any authority, to any specific religious belief or philosophical system. He was that very rare bird—an entirely original thinker. While there are strong resemblances to Darwin's theory of evolution in his account of the development of what he calls the Earth Life System, the use he makes of this concept, whether deriving from Darwin or not, is very much his own. Although some of his ideas may seem bizarre or far-fetched, he succeeds in integrating them into a consistent and comprehensive whole. Moreover, he was gifted with the ability to express himself clearly and succinctly. Certainly his fondness for acronyms (ASS—Animal Sub-Self; LIFE—Layered Intelligence-Forming Energy) at times brings the reader up short, but in *Ultimate Journey* he provides a helpful glossary for these and other idiosyncratic expressions.

Towards the end of his account of the Earth Life System, Monroe outlines the development of certain aspects of the Human Mind which, as he says, expresses and demonstrates "elements completely incompatible" with this System. Concern, empathy, and curiosity are three of these elements. He devotes a chapter to an examination of the many components—or facets—of the Human Mind, with suggestions for how to cope with problems presented by the Earth Life System. He considers the current concept that our thinking is divided into two categories, identified as left brain and right brain. Pointing out that the left-right distinction is only symbolic, he insists that it is what we regard as left-brain function that can make "Unknowns into Knowns, dissolve fears, enhance experience, open new vistas, clean out the false belief-system refuse." He continues: "It is the left brain that takes any idea, information or inspiration emanating from the right brain and puts it into action." The right brain, he says, has not grown or evolved; it is "the timeless, nonphysical part of us, untouched and unaffected by the Earth Life System." And he adds: "You should never abandon one for the other."

None of this, however, reveals anything about the "Missing Basic." So he decides to search in the area where he has been working for the past thirty years—the exploration of consciousness. In this regard, Monroe stands as far as can be imagined from the orthodox scientific view, prevalent in the last decades of the twentieth century, that consciousness is simply a product of the human brain and hence when the brain dies the individual's consciousness dies also. Monroe sees consciousness not as a function manufactured by and dependent on the brain, but as a continuum:

> The spectrum of consciousness ranges, seemingly endlessly, beyond time-space into other energy systems. It also continues "downward" through animal and plant life, possibly into the subatomic level. Everyday human consciousness is active commonly in only a small segment of the consciousness continuum.

Much of what Monroe discusses here is relevant to the work of the Institute. Yet as he expresses it, he is also aware that what has so far been achieved is not enough. He is aware that the Earth Life System is not the whole story, and his own purpose has not been fulfilled. It is clear to him that he had missed something—an

understanding, a "Known," as he called it—that was of vital importance. Perhaps it was only by moving out of physical reality into the
out-of-body state that he could find what he was searching for.

With this in mind, Monroe began on a series of voluntary out-
of-body journeys that he describes as "traveling the Interstate." No
longer was he guided by the Inspec; instead, he became an actor in a
series of dramas, each occurring at a different period in human history. In each of these dramas he found himself helping some
individual who was physically dead but convinced that he or she was
still alive. In one instance his help was rejected, but in the others he
was able to remove the individual from what appeared to be a dangerous or unpleasant situation and lift him out and upwards until,
without warning, he vanished.

In the final episode of this series, however, it happened differently. Monroe was now able to construct a map of the areas where his
out-of-body journeys were taking him. He saw the whole of time-
space, including the Earth Life System, as being permeated by what
he called the (M) Field, a nonphysical energy field that he had
referred to several times in *Far Journeys*. Now, however, he has a
fuller understanding of what it is. He uses the term *There* to apply to
the (M) Field energy spectrum in nonphysical form—that is, separate
from time-space. The route traveled from one state of consciousness
to another he calls the interstate, and those parts of the (M) Field
adjacent to the Earth Life System he designates the belief system territories. In these territories those who have completed physical life
come to reside according to which powerful religious belief they had
been attached during their days on Earth. In this episode he is guided
beyond these territories, finding himself among a multitude of souls
bound together by shared love. In this multitude he meets the friend
whom he first encountered in the experiences recorded in *Far
Journeys*—the friend he knew as BB.

While these experiences—the retrieval dramas and the explorations of the areas in and beyond time-space—seemed to Monroe to be moving him in what he felt was a new direction, he also sensed that he was in some way losing control. As he expressed it: "Some part of me that I wasn't aware of had taken over, and I certainly didn't understand it." That part he designated "I There," and he concluded that the exploration of this was to be the next stage in his journey.

Several events that occurred long before his first OBE returned to mind as Monroe began this exploration. But now they took on a deeper meaning, revealing to him more about himself. On investigating his "I There," he discovered what he interpreted as a multitude of personalities, each with its own life experience, each representing a past life. Of these personalities, one seemed especially significant. This was an architect/builder, involved with construction of cathedrals and castles many centuries ago. That so many workers were killed during construction caused him to object to his employers. One of these, an authority figure in a French cathedral, was so irked by what he saw as unwarranted interference that he ordered him to be beheaded. Monroe saw this as the reason why on a recent holiday his visits to cathedrals in France and England had made him physically ill. He claimed to have found direct evidence of this previous personality in the similarities between the Foulis Castle tower and the tower he designed for the Institute's residential center. All this and more convinced Monroe that he was an element in a continuum of personalities, "more than a thousand lifetimes," he suggests, that combined to form his present being, his "I Here," as he called it. Those past personalities combine together to become components of what Monroe (with his fondness for acronyms) describes as the EXCOM that all human beings possess—the Executive Committee of our I There, "emerging from the many life personalities that each of us contain." What binds these personalities together is love.

In a subsequent out-of-body experience Monroe received further information about the (M) Field. He emphasized that this energy field was unrecognized in the present civilization. However, about this time a number of scientists were beginning to show interest in what became known as the Zero Point Field. This was described by Lynne McTaggart in *The Field* (HarperCollins, 2001), a popular and controversial introduction to the subject, as "a field of energy connected to every other living thing in the world. This pulsating energy field is the central engine of our being and our consciousness, the alpha and omega of our existence." That Monroe knew of the research and experiments over different branches of science that led to the concept of the Zero Point Field is unlikely, especially as most of this work was published after *Ultimate Journey*. Nevertheless, his description of the (M) Field would have fitted neatly into McTaggart's study, even though his information came from his EXCOM during an out-of-body session and not from controlled experimentation in laboratory conditions.

By now Monroe felt that he was establishing what he called a "good, solid Different Overview." He was, however, concerned that he might have overlooked certain discrepancies so he determined to make one more out-of-body inquiry. In this it was revealed to him that his old friend the Inspec was none other than elements of his "I There"—that, in effect, he had been talking with an aspect of himself during all those journeys. It was also becoming clear that he was approaching a climax in his investigative experiences. For the first time for many years he records the date and time when this full-scale approach, as he describes it, took place.

So we know that it was at three in the morning on November 27, 1987, that this apotheotic experience, Monroe's ultimate journey, began. It took him away from the Earth Life System, through the belief system territories, on to an encounter with the entity he knew as Miranon, and farther still. This was a journey of self-discovery, the final one in a series of journeys that he had taken for the past three decades. The farther he traveled, the more was revealed to him about himself. Ultimately, he was able to perceive the source of the energy that creates the physical Universe and to sense the power of its radiation. This source he calls the Emitter.

Monroe's experience is personal yet he seems to imply that he is both Bob Monroe and at the same time a significant representative of humankind. He is made aware that as an individual he is incomplete. In a kind of mystical revelation he is filled with the knowledge of what he truly is: not simply an individual but a part of what he calls a cluster made up of all his "I Theres," all his previous personalities. Every individual soul is part of such a cluster and for what he calls "completion" all lost parts—souls who have wandered astray—must be retrieved. When completion is achieved, humanity will take its final journey—into the Unknown.

The physical Universe that includes all living creatures, as Monroe understands, is a continuous creative process, designed and adjusted by a Creator who makes no demands, inflicts no punishments, remains aloof from human's life activity, and has a purpose which we are unable to comprehend. Incorporated in this design is the need for all of us to become truly One, ready to move on to whatever lies ahead "with a multitude of gifts of experience and love." This, he says, is a Known firmly fixed in his mind-consciousness. It is the "missing Basic" for which he had been searching.

Before returning to full, physical, waking consciousness Monroe asks, "What happens when we enter and rejoin the Whole?" He receives no direct answer. As yet, he is told, he is incomplete and he has to return. But the new consciousness he has acquired will return with him. "What is it to become complete?" he asks. In reply he is given a poem. "It may help you to be patient," he is told, "you and the sum of you."

There is no beginning, there is no end,
There is only change.
There is no teacher, there is no student,
There is only remembering.
There is no good, there is no evil,
There is only expression.
There is no union, there is no sharing,
There is only one.
There is no joy, there is no sadness,
There is only love.
There is no greater, there is no lesser,
There is only balance.
There is no stasis, there is no entropy,
There is only motion.
There is no wakefulness, there is no sleep,
There is only being.
There is no limit, there is no chance,
There is only a plan.

It took Monroe several weeks, he says, before he could absorb what he experienced on this traumatic journey. It stands as the most profound experience recorded in any of his books. While he rejects the word *spiritual*, it is hard to find another term with which to describe it. *Transcendent* is as close as one can get. It owes nothing to the teachings or vocabulary of organized religion or to the extensive literature dealing with reincarnation and past lives. What makes it especially remarkable is its originality, with nothing derived from any belief system or ancient text. He is now convinced that "there is indeed a Creator" who is beyond human understanding and yet is "the designer of the ongoing process of which we are a part." The "Knowing" he has acquired, he says, cannot be transferred to another human mind. It can come only through direct individual experience. Now he wonders how this experience might be provided.

At the same time Monroe was aware that Nancy's time was limited. He felt that what he called "a personal inventory" was necessary and decided to investigate, so far as he could, what had happened to some of those friends whom he had already contacted in an out-of-body state after their physical deaths. In a further exploration he discovered that those he had known were no longer where he had previously found them. Then he came across what appeared to be a doctor's office where two men were talking. He asked if they knew anything about his old friend Dr. Gordon, as this resembled the place where he had previously met him in an earlier out-of-body exploration. They told him that this "office" was where many medical professionals paused for a while to calm down after their transition. One of them referred to the Park—and this brought back to Monroe the memory of occasions many years ago when on out-of body journeys he had arrived at the Park and was warmly welcomed. That was the place he was looking for.

He left the office and found himself walking through a forest. Everything he encountered appeared real; he could feel the breeze, hear the birds, taste the leaf he plucked from a maple. Suddenly, he was aware that all this—the wood, the doctor's office, the places he had visited—was a continuing human creation, the product of human mind-consciousness over countless thousands of years. He walked on, turned away from the woods, and found himself in the Park, "with winding walks, benches, flowers and shrubbery, different colored grass lawns, clusters of stately trees, small streams and fountains and with a warm sun overhead among small cumulus clouds." There he was greeted by a woman whom he was certain he had met before. She greeted him as Ashaneen, a name he remembered from another lifetime, and explained to him that the Park was where those who died could rest and be guided as to what might be their next stage.

Many of them were moving on to become part of what Monroe understood as their "I There."

Back "in the body," Monroe turned to consider the concept of the Park. He concluded that it was "an artificial synthesis created by human minds, a way station designed to ease the trauma and shock of the transition out of physical reality. It takes on the form of various earth environments in order to be acceptable to the enormously wide variety of newcomers." This differs considerably from his first impression of what he once called Home, with its music, fluffy white clouds, curls of energy—a sort of New Age vision of the landscape of Heaven without any religious connotations or connections. The Park is not Home. It is a place where you have the opportunity to decide on "the next step to take along the path to growth."

Viewed from a different perspective, Monroe's Park has much in common with the twelfth-century Sufi concept of the next world, "a world created solely out of the subtle matter of *alam almithal,* or thought . . . a plane of existence created by the imagination of many people and yet one that still had its own corporeality and dimension, its own forests, mountains and even cities."[1] This is the "imaginal realm," as Henry Corbin, the great authority on Sufi thought, called it, "a world that is created by the imagination but is ontologically no less real than physical reality." In Monroe's second visit to the Park, he was told that it was "a creation that is here and will be here whatever your beliefs. It will not disappear if you don't believe it exists."

Monroe expresses no theology. His experiences, especially those recorded in *Ultimate Journey,* convinced him that "the physical universe, including the whole of humankind, is an ongoing creative process." For him, "death" is simply a label for another energy system, and he would have no argument (except possibly for the inclusion of the word *spiritual* in the quotation) with the doctrine of the Baha'i' faith that "humans are essentially spiritual beings who undergo a temporary physical experience on this planet." He is not critical of the teachings of organized religions and is not into the business of conversion. These religions he sees simply as belief systems, with no sense that they are divinely inspired but simply existing to provide a haven for those who subscribe to them. His experiences also showed him that there are countless numbers of individuals who are no longer in physical existence but are unable to accept that this is so. These individuals, although no longer in physical form, continue to act as if they are still alive. There are also, he discovered, countless others who seem to be lingering in an in-between state, comatose, heavily drugged, or semiconscious.

After much reflection, Monroe's task became clear to him. He was to be a facilitator. He was to use his Known—the knowledge and understanding he had been vouchsafed—to find a way by which others could travel into the areas beyond the physical and provide help to those who, for whatever reason, were unaware that they were no longer alive and were stuck or marooned in a kind of no-man's land. This was what everything he had been doing in the past twenty years had been leading to. So far the results of his research had shown that it was possible to enable human consciousness to move to the very boundary of time-space. Now he understood that he should return to what had become his life's work, to see how much farther he could take it.

Monroe was well aware that what he had in mind ran counter to what the majority of scientists and medical professionals believed. As the scientific approach to death depended ultimately on measurement, when measurement was no longer able to record any response then the conclusion was simply "Nothing." Although he points out that some of the greatest scientists have deduced that we are more than our physical bodies, nevertheless "the bulk of our scientific knowledge is not germane to any approach that tries to make Something out of Nothing." Therefore, it is only personal experience that could provide the evidence that death does not equal finality.

With the knowledge provided by that experience, fear would be eliminated and lives would be transformed.

In this way Monroe put together the results of his recent out-of-body experiences with his left-brain logical approach. With the resources of the Institute at his disposal, he determined to see if it was possible to enable the individual mind-consciousness to move beyond the point of physical death and, having accomplished what he was now convinced was to be a mission of service, to return safely. This involved research into frequencies that could enable the body to rest in a state as near suspended animation as possible while the consciousness was free to be guided into this other energy system beyond physical life. He invited Mark Certo to his cabin and explained to him what he had in mind.

Monroe began by outlining his concept of the Park as he had encountered it in his out-of-body journeys. Using his now familiar numerical system of identifying states of consciousness, he equated the Park to Focus 27. To reach the Park you had to pass through the H Band, the designation he gave to the cacophonous region of human thought that surrounds the planet. Having done this, you arrive at Focus 23, where those are found who are still trapped in the Earth Life System—physically dead but unable to comprehend that this is so. From there you pass through the various belief systems centered on Focus 25. Finally, you arrive at the Park, the way-station where you may rest and be helped as needed, creating your own space in this illimitable paradise. This program would be called *Lifeline.*

Mark's task was to create the tapes to which Monroe would later add his voice. First came the "H Band noise," with Monroe checking almost daily on the effects and complaining that more sound and more drama were needed.[2] When at last he was satisfied—although Mark felt that no one would be able to maintain an altered state of consciousness while listening to such sounds—they moved on to Focus 23. For this a medley of human voices was needed and various members of staff came in to contribute. Listening hard, you might be able to discern the voice of Monroe himself. Then for the next stage you follow a light that leads you through Focus 24, Focus 25, and Focus 26. These are the areas of the belief systems. As markers, it was decided that snatches of music appropriate to various religions, ranging from the primitive to the major current faiths, would be utilized. At Focus 27 you pass through the light and before you is the Reception Center, the Park.

On one occasion, having studied the scripts and read some chapters of an early version of *Ultimate Journey*, Mark asked Monroe what his experience was beyond Focus 27. "Beyond that . . . mmmmm . . . you couldn't go beyond that and come back to tell about it," he replied. Mark was puzzled. "You mean you would somehow get absorbed into that strata?" he asked. "No. It's an existence that as I perceive it cannot be translated into anything that we humans can relate to or translate into words." That was what he thought at the time, but it turned out not to be the end of the story.

Once all this was completed, Monroe began to lay down the voice tracks. He was tired, anxious about Nancy, and, according to Mark, who edited the tapes to wipe out any mistakes or intrusions, frustrated with the sound of his voice. Listening to the unedited versions years later, Mark was impressed by the way Bob used his voice to move the participant into the next highest Focus level, noting how he was able to guide and direct you while leaving you to have your own experience. Mark recalled how, in one instance, he was leading the listener "from the familiar territory of Focus 25 into the Park of Focus 27. As he was encouraging you to move 'more and more through the light' he stumbled on a word and said 'Ah, shit!' It cracked me up to the point of tears. Perhaps because I was remembering my now departed friend, or perhaps because Bob rarely used expletives of that sort! Probably Nancy's influence."

While all this was in process, Nancy's health was causing increasing concern. Monroe very seldom referred to personal matters in his books. In all of them his out-of-body existence is kept apart from his daily life so that it is rarely possible to detect how the one impacts on the other. Apart from this, there is only one reference to Nancy's illness where, in a later chapter, it is referred to as "the Variable." This term Monroe explained as "a change that occurs in an individual life experience that was not planned or necessarily fore-seen." Among the examples he gives are winning a major lottery or moving to a different area. Death of a loved one, perhaps the most traumatic lifetime event, is not mentioned. It is as if Monroe is con-cerned to conceal or suppress any emotional response. The most he can do at this stage is to admit that the Variable "forced a new direc-tion," compelling him to face the prospect of her "transition from physical life," as he put it. This prospect impelled him to intensify his efforts to complete his new program as quickly as he could.

While Mark was working on the production of the *Lifeline* materials, he would take time out to listen to each completed exercise as if he was a participant in a program. Having finished the Focus 23 tape, he put headphones on and relaxed. He found himself moving into what he described as an exotic state of consciousness and in a space that was amber in color and misty. His grandfather had recently died and Mark wondered if he might be in such a space. In his mind he called his name but there was no response. He tried again.

> I felt some sort of movement and all of a sudden
> there was my grandfather's face, looking very stone-like
> in expression but with a hint of pain. I had no idea of
> what to do or say . . . I tried to speak to him but he
> seemed unaware of my presence. Then I said the silliest
> thing to him, almost in a panic. "Grandpa, I have no
> idea what to do for you, but if you wait here I'll come

back and get you. I haven't made the tape yet that will help you get where you need to go." I heard Bob prompting me to return back now to full physical waking consciousness. He began to count backwards but I was already back.

Feeling sad and confused, Mark resumed working on the rest of the series. It never occurred to him to ask Monroe for help. He completed the rest of the tapes, calling his grandfather's name at each Focus level but with no response until he came to the final tape, Focus 27. Then, as he listened to it, he found himself entering the Park, that for him was an extensive grassy field. There he saw Winslow, his golden retriever, running towards him, followed by his grandfather. He was surprised and also greatly relieved, but curious to see his dog who, unlike his grandfather, was alive and well and living with his ex-wife and stepson. He talked with his grandfather, who said that his wife, who was still alive at that time, had helped him to get where he was and visited him quite often. Mark decided that he had some psychological need to connect with his grandfather, but he could not understand what the dog was doing in the Focus 27 Park. After his grandfather left, saying he would make contact again, Mark looked at the dog, assuming this was nothing more than a Freudian wish-fulfillment vision, and asked: "So is there any message you have for me, O product of my subconscious mind?" The dog looked at him, and in his head Mark heard quite clearly: "Yes. When we meet next time around, for God's sake give me a better name than Winslow!" Then he heard Monroe prompting him back to ordinary everyday consciousness.

Two days later, a Sunday, Mark met his stepson as usual for an outing. "Over breakfast he looked at me and said 'I have some bad news,'" said Mark later. "'We found Winslow in the woods on Thursday. He died.'"

The *Lifeline* program was launched on June 22, 1991. Monroe was unusually anxious before the launch of the first program and his anxiety continued throughout the week. His concern was twofold. He was not confident that the Hemi-Sync exercises and the new frequencies he had developed for the program would be the correct mixes to support participants in their explorations of these new territories and in their rescue and retrieval operations. His second concern was that the potential emotional reactions to the situations the participants encountered might prove overwhelming. Darlene Miller recalled that he would come into the control room several times a day—something he never did in other residential programs—to check with the trainers on how things were going. His concerns were needless. When the program ended and the trainers reported that all had gone according to plan, his relief was evident. At his final meeting with the group Monroe brought Steamboat with him and together they led the company in a robust round of resonant howling.

A requirement for taking part in this program was that participants must have previously attended *Gateway* so that they were already acquainted with Hemi-Sync and therefore could move easily into the higher Focus levels. It was notable that, while *Gateway* participants came from a variety of backgrounds, those who elected to take *Lifeline,* including Monroe's daughter Laurie in the first program, were largely drawn from professional or practical occupations. The third program, for example, included five doctors or other medical professionals, three educationists, three therapists, an Alaska pipeline worker, a baker, a script writer, a telecommunications worker, a physics professor, an author, a librarian, a psychologist, a public relations consultant, a machine shop worker, a detective, and Elisabeth Kübler-Ross.

By the time *Ultimate Journey* was published, there had been thirteen *Lifeline* sessions involving some 250 participants. The program as designed differed from *Gateway* and *Guidelines* in one important respect. In the two earlier programs those taking part were enabled to move into different states of consciousness, being provided with simple tasks or exercises to perform but not given an environment in which to perform them. In *Lifeline,* Monroe provided the environment: the three "belief system territories" and the Park, described as he had seen it himself. It seemed as if participants might be conditioned by this, with the result that the reports of their experiences would have many features in common, and their accounts would resemble those of a group of visitors to a foreign city who had read the same guidebook and undertaken the same sightseeing tours. Yet this did not happen. The responses were wholly personal and often idiosyncratic.

Submitting written reports on their experiences was a requirement for all participants and these reports, some of which are included in *Ultimate Journey,* demonstrated that for almost all of them the process worked. Interestingly, and without any briefing from Monroe, several reported that what they had found or retrieved were not other individuals but parts or aspects of themselves that they had neglected or forgotten and were now able to reabsorb. One wrote that it had been a week of growth and expanding. "The very thin phase between what we know as reality, Here, and what Monroe calls 'There' becomes apparent. Life as a whole has begun to take on a different perspective." Now sixteen years after its inception, the *Lifeline* program remains unchanged and is usually oversubscribed.[3]

As Charles Tart points out, throughout *Ultimate Journey* Monroe holds his position as the objective reporter while he struggles to convey his experiences as accurately as words will allow. As in his previous books, he strives only to tell it as it is. Reviewing *Ultimate Journey* for the journal of the Scientific & Medical Network, David Lorimer described it as "the most accessible and profound of Monroe's books" and ranks it as "one of the most important books I have read in this field," adding that it is "required reading for anyone interested in the inner horizons of consciousness."

The final chapter of *Ultimate Journey* includes a moving tribute to Nancy Monroe, whose death, Bob said later, "cut off twenty-three years of daily sharing in total love and devotion."[4] Shortly after she died, he made two attempts to visit her out-of-body. He found the experience too much to handle and resolved henceforth to restrict himself from any form of nonphysical activity. At one time he questioned if it were possible to meet a new challenge: to adjust himself so that he could live simultaneously with Nancy in Focus 27 and with his seven cats and two dogs in a lonely house. Then he realized that it was no challenge at all and to his question there would be no answer.

Notes

1. See Michael Talbot, *The Holographic Universe* (HarperCollins, 1991).

2. It is a moot point whether any distinction can be made between M Band noise, explained in *Far Journeys* as "uncontrolled thought," and H Band noise, "the peak of uncontrolled thought that emanates from all living forms on Earth, particularly humans," according to *Ultimate Journey*. If there is no distinction, we may ascribe this apparent confusion to a cosmic alphabetical slip.

3. Soon after the launch of *Lifeline*, a small team was formed from those in and around the Institute who felt that they were able to help individuals who had died but might need assistance to find their way to the Park. Members of this team were on call when

Nancy Monroe died and were able to describe how they helped her on her way to Focus 27.

4. Quotations from *Ultimate Journey* by Robert Monroe, copyright © 1994 by Robert Monroe are used by permission of Doubleday, a division of Random House, Inc.

.

CHAPTER 10

End Game (1)

Reflecting some sixteen years later on the time she had spent at the Institute, where she had worked in the office as well as being an Explorer, Ria Ericson recalled a conversation she had with Monroe. He invited her to lunch at a local restaurant and, much to her surprise, asked her if she could anticipate what the future might hold for the Institute. She told him that she had not given any thought to it, assuming that its future was well established in his own mind. But it did not seem to be so, and as the conversation continued she became aware, as she remembered, of "his puzzlement as to what had really made TMI and all the programs as large and important to so many people throughout the world." The Institute, she felt, " had grown around him, through and from him, but somehow he still, in his own natural, humble way couldn't quite decide why." Self-deprecating, many would think, might be more appropriate than humble, but otherwise Ria's comment is perceptive. In the earlier years of the Institute there is no evidence of long-term planning, nor any indication that Monroe had foreseen the impact that the programs would have on their participants. He had managed to keep a grip on the tiger's tail, but the tiger would never eat out of his hand. With the turn of the decade, however, there were signs of a change.

In the spring of 1990, two-and-a-half years after his culminating experience recorded in *Ultimate Journey,* Monroe wrote an article for the Institute's newsletter on his current understanding of the out-of-body state. He noted how his attitude towards his experiences had changed over the years. Now the out-of-body experience, as he understood it, is "part of a 'phasing' process that all of us perform without awareness of what we do . . . The OBE is simply another stage of phase relationship to time-space." Other examples of phase relationships, he added, are hallucinations, meditation, visions, mystical events, ecstasies, "and a long list of other phenomena humankind looks upon with distortion or tries to ignore."

The next two paragraphs in the article provided his answer to questions he was asked many times by participants in Institute courses.

> What is my OB action in 1990? Indescribable. I don't sleep now in the usual meaning. I haven't for several years. When I relax physically to a certain point, I phase out of being conscious physically and I'm off somewhere and somewhen to do and be. I don't even bother attempting to record and report such activity because there seems to be little counterpart here and far too much of it to translate. Try writing down and reporting second by second every thought and activity you may have in an hour of wakefulness. That same hour of "sleep" to me may be the equivalent of a year or a century, most of it unrelated to human life on earth past and present.

> What keeps me here? Loves. Friendships. The beauty of Earth-nature. Curiosity. Ability to help others in one way or another as long as I can give more than I take. But I don't at all feel superior in the process. It's

more like a monkey who found a hole in his cage and sneaks out to revisit the Forest.

Although Monroe's perception of the OBE had changed over the years, he insisted that this change did not affect the reality of his early experiences. "They stand very much exactly as reported and remain very accurate," he commented. He had changed. He no longer had the time, energy, or inclination to replicate them.

Besides Nancy's progressive illness, other pressures were building on Monroe. His physical energy was deteriorating—he felt that his body was betraying him—and his mental acuity was not what it had been. Much of his own fortune had been spent creating and maintaining the Institute, but the number of programs that could be offered was limited by the space available. Expansion of the premises would cost far more than he could afford and he suspected that others with far greater resources at their disposal were planning to buy him out. He began to think that among those who attended courses at the Institute were some who had sought to copy the Hemi-Sync process or had adapted it to their own purposes, even setting up their own residential centers and advertising their products. His suspicions in this regard had some justification, although very few of the imitations or derivations survived for long.

However, to *Gateway* participants he was, as always, the wise old man from the mountaintop, descending once or twice a week to share with them his thoughts, his humor, his amazing stories. Most regarded him with awe. They were familiar with his voice that had led them into experiences that they had never imagined were within their reach. Now here he was, the great explorer into the farthest reaches of consciousness, joking with them, teasing them gently, leading them on, sometimes into realms beyond thought, sometimes up the garden path.

One observer recalled watching Monroe at the time and noting that "his energy seemed to fluctuate like a lamp on a dimmer switch controlled by an unseen hand. One moment his gestures were feeble, his voice almost inaudible; the next his movements were forceful, his voice strong. It was otherworldly, as if his energy were divided between this reality and somewhere else." He described this as mesmerizing. Was there some force renewing his energy at certain times? Or was it part of a performance, beautifully timed and expertly delivered?

The Monroe that course participants saw was rather different from the Monroe as he related to the Institute staff. Some of his decisions seemed arbitrary or inexplicable, depending, it seemed, on emotion rather than reason, and not everyone who decided it was time to move elsewhere felt that their efforts had been fully appreciated. Towards the end of 1990 an especially difficult situation arose when Scooter became aware that Monroe's attitude towards her was changing. She felt that he was undercutting her authority as director, giving her the responsibility but rejecting her recommendations, in particular over the major issue of investigating ways to cut costs and increase income. She sensed that he no longer trusted her and was disturbed to find that he was countermanding her instructions to other employees. The situation for her was becoming intolerable. In November of that year she asked for an appointment with both Bob and Nancy and told them she had decided to resign. In the following January, she broke off all contact with the Institute.

Scooter's contribution to the development of the Institute was incalculable. Her ability to handle people with humor and tact, no matter who they were or where they came from, was remarkable, and her organizational skills were outstanding. But in her own interest it was time for her to move away, although in her role as director she was, as it turned out, irreplaceable, and no successor was appointed. Nevertheless, the parting was especially painful for her. Monroe had seen her through college, given her a car and taught her to drive, taught her about business, treated her as a partner in the creation of what became The Monroe Institute, made special tapes to help in her studies and to enable her to move into different states of consciousness, so that she learned how to control her emotions and her out-of-body experiences. He had introduced her to new philosophies of life and to the achievements of people such as Amelia Earhart, Duke Ellington, James Michener, Robert Heinlein, and more. As she later said, she was immensely grateful to him for his incredibly profound effect on her life—the good, the bad—all of it!

For a time Monroe himself took on some of the director's responsibilities. One priority was to take action to improve the Institute's finances. He asked Mark Certo to examine the production system of everything they sold, to investigate all costings and discover where economies could be made. Mark's report indicated that some $150,000 might be saved annually by adopting alternative measures for the duplication and packaging of tapes. However, he had not anticipated that Monroe would use this report to criticize some of his senior staff. Their response, while not actively hostile, was certainly discouraging. It caused Monroe to feel that his control might be slipping. He now suspected that some of those he was employing felt it was time for him to move to the sidelines, confining his activities to delivering his evening talks to program participants. But he had no intention of so doing.

At about this time, Director of Programs David Mulvey began to feel that it was time for him to move on. While he remained on good personal terms with Monroe, he was finding him more difficult to work with. He noted that whenever he or any other of the senior staff made some suggestion or proposal it was, in the first instance, usually well received. Monroe would ask for more detail and for the proposal to be put in its final form. But when this was submitted to him, his usual response was "Well, that's not what I had in mind," and the matter was dropped. Nevertheless, because of his interest in the future of the Institute and his concern for his own career, Dave was prepared to take on more responsibility himself. He asked if it was possible for him to become a member of the board of directors. Monroe said he thought that was a good idea, but as no further word on the subject was forthcoming for several months Dave became convinced that this cause was lost. Now believing that there was no future for him at the Institute, he resigned. Shortly afterwards he sold his house and moved away, although his interest in the work of the Institute was such that during the next few years he returned to train programs from time to time.[1]

While Scooter had been well aware of the Institute's financial problems, she had usually been frustrated in her attempts to do something about them. Monroe accepted that the ultimate responsibility was his, but he felt that his age and state of health, together with his emotional state, meant that these problems needed someone else to solve them. He could see that what was required was a full-time director to take on the day-to-day management of the company and to sort out the finances, but have nothing to do with programs, trainers, or course participants. Yet it could be that he now lacked the confidence to make the right decision when it came to making an appointment. He called his daughter Laurie, then a high-flyer in real estate in Florida, and asked her to join him within twenty-four hours to interview a candidate for the post. This was Ron Harris, a bluff local businessman who looked happier out-of-doors than behind a desk. In the event, Harris proved an effective manager, reducing both the running expenses and the number of employees, and helping to establish the company on a stable footing. One new appointment was made: that of an ex-IRS agent, Dick Savigny, who joined the staff as accountant. Neither of these newcomers could be described as metaphysical types, which was no drawback considering the type of work they were required to undertake.

Perhaps in the hope of improving the Institute's finances by expansion overseas, Monroe invited Stefano to return to the Institute as a full-time salaried member of staff with the title of international project coordinator. He also offered to sell Stefano a parcel of land in which he had previously shown interest but—Monroe had then told him—was not available. This was a prime site of three acres across the valley from the Institute building, where the one-time peach packing shed was sited and where the old homestead had once stood. Even though the amount Monroe demanded was something like two-and-a-half times the going price per acre, Stefano accepted. Some time later he admitted that he had been so focused on the possibilities of Hemi-Sync and the potentials of his new appointment that he had temporarily lost touch with reality.

Never enthusiastic about spending much time behind a desk, Stefano expressed his willingness to travel on the Institute's behalf wherever needed. In return, Monroe offered him 10 percent of everything "off the top" that resulted from international sales. Now that it looked as if progress was in sight, Stefano developed an ambitious plan to train others to present his two-and-a-half day program to non-English-speaking people worldwide, using specially designed nonverbal tapes and CDs that could be duplicated in different countries for ease of distribution and sales. He thought it might be possible to set up centers in those countries, and as demand for the program increased it would be essential to have the texts of the exercises translated into the appropriate languages. In the meantime, however, they would have to make do with the nonverbal tapes that he had previously used.

An opportunity arose through a German friend of Stefano's, Peter, who had married an Argentinean girl and was living in Buenos Aires. Peter had a business partner, a retired banker interested in introducing "brain machines" and similar technologies into Argentine society. This seemed to Stefano a good opportunity to introduce Hemi-Sync to Latin America. It so happened that a large-scale trade fair was being organized in Buenos Aires as part of the celebrations for the five hundredth anniversary of Columbus's landing. Peter and his business partner proposed to become vendors at this fair, intending to introduce the public to various devices and methods that claimed to enhance human consciousness. They sent Stefano a glossy brochure with an aerial view of the site, a circle indicating the booth where Hemi-Sync could be available. He passed this to Monroe, who responded favorably. Stefano planned to have non-verbal Hemi-Sync tapes on sale, hoping that this would enable him to get his foot in the Latin American door. Unfortunately, he discovered that taxes imposed by the Argentine authorities, added to shipping charges, would so increase the cost of the tapes that to make any sort of profit they would need to be sold at about thirty-five dollars each. The only way to make overseas sales economically viable was to arrange for the tapes to be duplicated in the countries in which they were to be sold. As it was impossible to do this in time for the fair, he decided to ask that a hundred nonverbal tapes, labeled as samples, should be shipped over for sale. There was, however, no precedent for anything like this and the request was refused.

Despite this unpromising start, Stefano was intent on going ahead. He had already initiated the process of having the texts of several tapes and CDs translated into Spanish and arrangements were in hand for duplication in Federal Capital, the industrial park of Buenos Aires. Contact was made with a number of potential distributors in Argentina, Chile, and Uruguay, and individuals who could be trained as Outreach trainers were being sought. Everything was now in place. All that was needed was the release of the master tapes carrying the Hemi-Sync frequencies so that duplication could begin.

However, Monroe refused to agree to the release unless Stefano guaranteed that his royalties would be paid in full and that no one would cheat him, a guarantee that Stefano felt it was impossible for him to give. He also demanded that credit checks be run through the U.S. Embassy in Argentina on everyone involved. Time was now running short, and Stefano realized that it was pointless to pursue the Buenos Aires project any further. It was dropped, leaving behind disappointment and expense for those involved. For the time being the International Project went on hold, leaving Stefano with the opportunity to concentrate on building his house.

As the months passed, despite various surgical procedures Nancy's health continued to deteriorate. She carried on, as far as possible, with her usual pattern of daily life, and almost all of those who saw her found it hard to believe that she was as ill as she was. She faced her situation with courage and dignity, supported by the philosophy and promise of the *Lifeline* program that she had helped to create. Then on July 31, 1992, having great difficulty with breathing, she was taken to the University of Virginia Hospital. Four days later an operation was performed to relieve the pressure on her lungs. But the progress of her illness was not halted. Darlene Miller visited her as often as she could and, with Teena Anderson working with them at a distance, Nancy and Darlene used the methods of *Lifeline,* traveling together into a postphysical state of consciousness, Monroe's Focus 27, into the Park, defined as an area of rest and recovery beyond the time-space continuum. Shortly after midnight on August 15, quietly and peacefully, Nancy died.

The life that Nancy Penn was thrust into on her second marriage was about as different as could be imagined from her earlier years as the wife of a serving officer. To begin with there was plenty of money, together with a fine country house surrounded by extensive grounds in one of the most upmarket counties in Virginia. Before long, however, her new husband had disposed of most of his assets and was spending much of his time closeted in his laboratory creating and listening to patterns of sound. The visitors who came to see what he was doing might have originated from a different planet compared to the officers' wives she used to entertain. However, she soon proved that she could cope. Resourceful and tactful, she was a

delightful hostess and at the same time progressively more interested in what her husband was involved with, including taking part in several laboratory sessions.

On the move to Roberts Mountain, Nancy had become a full partner in the fledgling Institute, devoting much time and energy to making the environment as attractive as possible for the many hundreds who came to take the pro-

Nancy Monroe outside the Gift House

grams. When her new home on the mountaintop was built, she was able to apply her creativity and sense of style to its décor and furnishings. These qualities are also manifested in the improvements, especially the fine new dining room, in the Residential Center, which was renamed the Nancy Penn Center in her memory. Her love of plants and trees and her understanding of how best to display them are evidenced around the Institute buildings. She was an exceptionally talented lady.

Two days after Nancy's death a close friend of hers had a dream in which she saw her about to leave home on a journey to a new assignment. She left three items behind: a small plant in a pot, which the friend identified as thyme, a package containing sage, and a gift-wrapped glass ball like a paperweight. Awakened from the dream, the friend looked again at these three items, with the understanding that they were gifts from Nancy for everyone. In folklore, thyme is a symbol of strength, and the souls of the dead were once thought to dwell in the flowers of thyme. Sage is the symbol of domestic virtue, flourishing where the woman rules, and it grows best for the wise. The gift-wrapped glass ball, she concluded, stood for all the gifts that Nancy gave—her wholeness, her clarity, herself.

The confidence and serenity with which Nancy faced the world were qualities much needed in coping with her husband's preoccupations and fluctuating moods. While Bob had come to regard all organized religions simply as belief systems, Nancy was both supported and strengthened by her Christian faith. Among her best-loved authors was C. S. Lewis, and her favorite among his many books was his fable, *The Great Divorce,* in which he rejects any idea that good and evil can ever be reconciled and denies any possibility of William Blake's suggestion of a marriage between Heaven and Hell. This book in particular seemed to reflect Nancy's own beliefs.

Although Monroe often found it difficult to express his feelings verbally, he was able to do so in writing. *Ultimate Journey* especially has a strong emotional content, apparent even more so in some of the early drafts when he sought to include snatches of dialogue with Nancy that re-created their mutual love and the gradual progress of her illness. But when it came to openly expressing their love, he seemed to find this beyond him. This was publicly demonstrated at Nancy's funeral. After her two elder daughters had spoken movingly about their mother and their love for her, all that Bob could bring himself to do was to read out a list of what she had achieved from notes he had made on a yellow legal pad.

Monroe was seventy-six when his wife died. Their marriage had lasted for twenty-three years and they had known each other socially for seven years before. Since his early twenties, Monroe had never lived alone for more than a few months and now, with no one to make the coffee or drink it with him, and only the dogs and cats for company—sadly, his favorite cat Fusby had died just three days before Nancy—he found it very hard. George Durrette came up the mountain to chat with him from time to time and Ed Sturz brought him catfish from the lake, but he had no close neighbors and, apart from Rita and Martin Warren and his agent Eleanor Friede, few friends of his own generation. He joined the Warrens for dinner once a week, usually driving to the café in nearby Lovingston, and sometimes had lunch with Rita on a Saturday, while on Sunday mornings he might visit Ed and Ruth Sturz for breakfast at their home on Rainbow Ridge. When the lack of company became hard to bear, he would drive down to the Warrens and sit in their living room, talking with anyone who happened to look in. He would call Cindy once a week, conversations that brought them closer together than they had been when Cindy was living on the New Land. A. J. and his wife Shaaron moved in to the lower floor of the Gift House and did their best to keep him on a healthy diet. While he was grateful for their presence, they had little in common, especially notions about food. "Have you ever heard of pesto?" he asked Mark one day. "It's green! Doesn't make sense to me to eat green," a remark that accords with his distaste for most vegetables. One positive move he made was to buy an adjustable bed he had seen advertised on television, and he appreciated the ease with which he could raise or lower either end to make himself comfortable.

Having alienated himself from Scooter and thereby also from Joe, Monroe had no one nearby to confide in. When Joe had moved to the New Land he had become a close personal confidant to Bob, meeting with him most days, acting with power of attorney when required, and helping him also with various personal matters. That relationship was now over, with no prospect of its being renewed. However, there was one employee with whom he felt he could share at least some of his concerns, and whom he did not suspect of angling to take over the Institute when the time came. This was Mark Certo. Moving into a nostalgic frame of mind, he asked Mark to digitize and catalogue hundreds of reels of tapes of the radio shows, such as *High Adventure* and *Nightmare with Peter Lorre,* which he had produced in the 1940s and 1950s. Since the move to Roberts Mountain these reels had been stored in a barn on the New Land, slowly deteriorating in an old chest covered with dust and rodent droppings. For Mark, working on these recordings provided entertainment of the highest order, especially those orchestral interludes in which Bob could be heard interacting with the musicians and conductor. The whole experience, he said, provided a fascinating journey through the history of broadcasting in America. For Monroe, listening to these tapes provided a relief from his unhappiness and he especially enjoyed answering the questions that arose as they listened to these recollections of times long gone by.

Another source of entertainment for Monroe and Mark Certo were the Wednesday evening sessions, when Martin Warren, A. J., and occasional visitors from the neighborhood—strictly men only—joined them in the dining hall to play poker. For Monroe, a longtime poker player with a handful of tricks as well as the ability to read his opponents' minds, this was a special pleasure. Away from the loneliness of his cabin he could forget his responsibilities and the concerns of the Institute and enjoy the challenges of the game and the jokes of his companions.

A special bonus at this difficult time was the success of the revised *Guidelines* program, which was received with acclamation by both staff and participants. Many of them thought it the best work that Monroe had done. Listening to what was being said, Mark Certo determined to join the course himself. As he had not taken the *Gateway* program, a prerequisite for attendance at any other Institute course, this request was technically out of order. Eventually, however,

Monroe was persuaded to agree. For Mark it turned out to be in effect a life-changing experience. As he said many years later, "I carry the tools with me to this day and utilize them almost daily."

Although the courses continued to be in demand, matters at the Institute itself were not running smoothly. Besides those whose services were dispensed with for reasons of economy, others associated with the Institute, including some with talents as Explorers, departed suddenly, sometimes without leaving a forwarding address. They had found that doors hitherto open to them were now firmly closed. One senior member of staff had no idea that his time was up until he read an advertisement for his job in a local paper. There were also those who had offered their help or expertise and whose offers had been accepted only to discover when they arrived that it was as if they no longer existed. A psychologist who was working with the juvenile justice system in Montreal moved his family south to Virginia in the expectation of employment with Bob Monroe—an expectation that was never fulfilled. Another who was especially unfortunate was a highly qualified medical doctor who sold his practice after being invited by Monroe to join the Institute as director of research. On arrival he discovered that the laboratory was not available as far as he was concerned and Monroe was not interested in meeting him. He stayed around for three months with nothing to do and then, totally disillusioned, left. Another doctor, a member of the board of advisors, was invited to participate in research on sleep. She took leave from her post and drove many hundreds of miles to stay with her dog in a caravan on the New Land. But there was no research in progress for her to pursue. Her experience turned into an extended holiday with friends nearby and a creek in which to swim.

Why was this? It seems that as he aged Monroe was finding it increasingly difficult to trust anyone. Although he made use of professional scientists to help in the creation and testing of the Hemi-

Sync technology, he became increasingly wary of people with degrees. Perhaps it was because he thought that, if science could explain Hemi-Sync, it might go on to explain it away. Part of him wanted Hemi-Sync to be scientifically validated, while another part was opposed to this. This conflict led to a kind of frustration. While he found it difficult to reject an offer of help or to cancel invitations extended to individuals who impressed him by their sincerity and willingness to work for modest financial reward—or even none— when it came to the point he simply could not face up to the possible consequences. If they validated Hemi-Sync, then he would no longer be the only one who really understood it. If they were unable to validate it, then they had failed to understand it so their time and his money had been wasted. And there was something else, occasionally hinted at but never put precisely into words. When it was time for him to die, he wanted—or he might want—to take it with him. If he was not able to control it Here, then it should not be Here at all. So he took refuge on the mountaintop, hoping it would not be long before those who offered to help or work with him ran out of patience and went back home.

There are two possible explanations for Monroe's behavior at this time. His own experience may have disenchanted him as to the value of a college education. A more likely explanation is his need to be in control at all times. This derived from his career in the entertainment field, as director, producer, and owner—all positions in which for maximum efficiency one-man control is essential. This may be the reason why those he appointed to senior positions were in his opinion not the sort of ambitious characters that might in time present some sort of threat. Should he suspect that he was in error, he would soon find a reason to terminate their employment.

There were other difficulties. Following Nancy's death, Monroe became increasingly concerned about his own health. Narrowing of the arteries in his legs made walking any distance painful and a respiratory infection affected his breathing. His eyesight was poor: he suffered from macular degeneration but hated wearing glasses. He was no longer able to enjoy those pursuits—flying, sailing, composing, and playing music—that had given him so much pleasure in earlier years. His sleep pattern changed also. He said he could not face the emotional trauma of drifting in Nancy's direction even in the deepest sleep. He felt that he was facing a new challenge, a massive adjustment, as he expressed it in *Ultimate Journey.* "Can I live in two worlds at the same time? With Nancy in 27, and Here with our lonely fur family—seven cats and two dogs—in a lonely house? I don't know."

For a time it seemed as if his creative ability had begun to fail. To attract more participants to the Institute and encourage *Gateway* graduates to return for further experiences it was important that new programs be launched every few years. But since the revision of *Guidelines,* inspiration appeared to be lacking. It began to look as if Monroe was desperately searching around for ideas. In 1992 he came up with what he called the Timeout Project, described as a learning system rather than a method of treatment, intended to provide "noninvasive tools that are designed to assist greatly in such cases where psychological factors disturb the sleep process." He declared expansively that the project "has the potential to alter constructively and completely the lives of every living human." However, this concept never developed into a program, although the Institute's sleep-inducing exercises, "Catnapper," "Sound Sleeper," and "Super Sleep," and the Metamusic composition *Sleeping through the Rain,* which were already in circulation, all continued to prove effective as single items.

In the same year, Monroe announced a new residential program, *Hemi-Sync 2000.* This, he proclaimed, was to be "the long-awaited learning system that provides the individual a way to begin complete self-control over all personal mental, physical, and emotional energies."

It was, in addition, "a new and companion learning system for *Lifeline* . . . open to anyone because it can be of immense benefit to any person who desires progress." Despite the enthusiastic prose, this learning system was no more than a spin-off from Human-Plus. No matter how energetically they were presented, these repetitive exercises were simply inappropriate for a residential course. A few programs were scheduled, but the response was disappointing and after a couple of years they were quietly dropped.

Some months later Monroe tried again. He announced another new program, *Lifespan 2000,* that, he claimed, "will provide an all-encompassing structure that will help any individual exist and grow . . . It can be termed a new way of being and knowing, perhaps truly a new kind of human, where one is totally in control of one's self." The purpose of the program was "to provide means and methods for the human mind-body to live progressively and constructively in a rapidly changing world environment, and to assist profoundly in adaptation to such changes whatever they may be." Such grandiose claims strongly contrast with the modesty with which the successful programs, *Gateway* and *Guidelines,* were introduced. At the core of *Lifespan 2000* was, by this time unsurprisingly, "the entire library of the Human-Plus exercises." But this program was no more successful than its predecessor in attracting participants. Seven sessions were scheduled and that was all.

There were disappointments also with the Outreach projects. Despite the failure of the Buenos Aires enterprise, Stefano continued to develop further schemes for expanding the use of Hemi-Sync overseas. However, plans and proposals continued to end in frustration. A German journalist/entrepreneur, a friend of Stefano's, was appointed by the Music Group of the international media conglomerate Bertelsmann to create a label for "Healing Sounds," to be retailed in doctors' offices and pharmacies across the German-speaking countries. Stefano reported that the Hemi-Sync technology was under consideration for the new Bertelsmann Music Group label. At first Monroe's interest was aroused and he told Stefano to enter into negotiations. But before action could be taken, matters came to a halt. Monroe called a meeting of what was known as "the boys' club"—senior staff members of whom Stefano was one—to discuss the proposal. He instructed Stefano to provide Ron Harris with all the details and to do whatever was needed. In subsequent meetings with Harris, however, Stefano was ordered to provide a report on his German contact and to ask him for references. Hearing of this, Stefano's friend was furious, declared that he had been grossly insulted, and refused to have anything more to do with the Institute.

Something similar occurred with a wealthy Austrian business-man, who had come across *Journeys Out of the Body* while on holiday. His interest captured, at the first opportunity he flew to the States and called at the Institute. He met Monroe, who introduced him to Stefano. After a lengthy discussion, he said that he was willing to provide Monroe with whatever help he needed. He arranged to stay in the area for several weeks and, after touring the buildings, offered to reequip the kitchen and to bring in a professional chef to improve the catering. Those fortunate enough to attend the 1993 Professional Seminar enjoyed a veritable banquet. All seemed to be going well until, for some reason, he and Monroe came into conflict. The visitor's enthusiasm suddenly vanished; he sold the top-of-the-market Jeep he had bought to travel the rough roads of the New Land and moved out. The chef soon departed also, the catering reverted to its previous standards, and Monroe was left with an impressively large bill.

There were also two competing Japanese companies that expressed interest in Hemi-Sync. Representatives of each visited the Institute and were impressed by the presentations of the technology. Each company wanted to have exclusive rights in handling the Institute's products, but the matter never came to competitive bidding.

The terms that Monroe proposed proved too steep; negotiations were broken off and the representatives of both companies packed their bags and returned home.

Monroe's dealings with those who offered to support the Institute by promoting the spread of Hemi-Sync beyond the borders of the United States reveal much about himself at this time of his life. While he was willing to listen to the proposals of the wealthy entrepreneurs who were attracted by his magnetic personality and were convinced of the value of his audio technology, when it came to the point he backed off—and was quick to find reasons for doing so. He became, or so it seems, suspicious of their motives; it was as if he saw them as exemplifying the predator theory he described in the opening chapters of *Ultimate Journey*. Again, he seemed to be fearful of losing control and, driven by this fear, was unable to trust anyone, except for those who were content to align themselves with the Institute as it was and demanded nothing further. As Stefano saw it, Monroe repeatedly sabotaged himself.

But there is another way of looking at this. It may have been that the time for such expansion was not yet right. There had been attempts in the United States to copy Hemi-Sync and although none of these had been successful in that the copyists, or imitators, had not made large profits thereby, the chances of such action being effective overseas were far greater. Also, there would have been little chance of successfully launching lawsuits against copyists or imitators in Central Europe, Japan, or South America.

There is another argument. Those who, like Stefano, came from overseas to take courses at the Institute and returned to their native countries to present Outreach workshops maintained a high degree of loyalty to Monroe and his creation. Almost without exception, their policy was to keep Hemi-Sync pure. The only tapes or CDs they sold were produced by the Institute and the question of making copies for sale and profiting personally therefrom did not arise. But who could guarantee that if the technology passed into the hands of those who had not taken any of the accredited programs, had not met Monroe or heard him addressing course participants, that this purity would not be sullied? Who would then be responsible for bad experiences, or even the failure to have any experiences at all, that might befall users of such products?[2]

Nevertheless, Stefano was disappointed at the failure of his attempts to promote Hemi-Sync overseas and resolved to return to his original goal—to share Hemi-Sync with others wherever he could. There being no place in the organization for an international project coordinator without any international projects to coordinate, he handed in his resignation. Monroe still wanted him to remain focused on international affairs rather than to restrict his activities to training, but Stefano refused. For the next few months he directed his attention to training programs at the Institute and raising Raphael, his two-year-old son. By this time his house was almost complete. It was a log house, constructed by what was known on the New Land as the SBA (the Slow Builders Association), a small, informal group of local craftsmen with various practical skills. The work, not altogether surprisingly, ran into some problems, particularly when it was found that the structure was in danger of collapsing unless stronger internal support was installed. As soon as the house was secure and habitable Stefano with his wife and son moved in. They had been living there for just twelve days when, with no warning, in the space of twenty-four hours Stefano's domestic life collapsed around him. Shortly afterwards he sold the house and left the Institute, never to return. It was to be many years before Hemi-Sync was to obtain more than a toehold in the world beyond the United States.

Notes

1. No explanation has been offered for Monroe's occasional inconsistencies and contradictions, which occurred more frequently in his last decade. An earlier example that disturbed those involved was when he handed cases of the original *Gateway* tapes to Melissa Jager and Bill Schul in appreciation, he said, of their work with the Institute. Two days later he demanded their return, saying he certainly never meant they should keep them. Bill refused, saying that they were honored to have been given them, had accepted them in good faith, and intended to keep them in good faith.

2. A bad experience could be very bad indeed. I was once asked to try a nonverbal tape said to carry Hemi-Sync signals but of uncertain origin and found it induced a feeling of absolute terror.

CHAPTER II

End Game (2)

In the past, Monroe's judgment with regard to the residential programs had been inspired. *Gateway* and *Guidelines* had stood the test of time and the *Lifeline* program was in high demand. Sales of tapes continued to increase and the new Metamusic compositions were proving popular. In his relationships with program participants Monroe was, as ever, informal, friendly, willing to listen and take notice. Many were devoted to him and most of those who worked for him or with him admired his achievements and regarded him with great affection. But now that his judgment seemed less sure, those who knew him well, including most of the members of the board of advisors, felt a growing concern both for his own well-being and for the future of the Institute.

This concern was expressed at the board meeting in July 1993. In the past Monroe had shown scant enthusiasm for these sessions—in a previous meeting he had walked out halfway through—and the discussions had little or no effect on Institute policy. Now, however, he declared that he intended to draw the board into greater participation. Many words were spoken and many issues and questions raised, although few conclusions were reached. Observing him, it was clear to those present that Monroe's health was failing. He looked tired and older than his years. The meeting was shadowed by the question that no one was prepared to ask: "What was to happen to the Institute after Monroe's death?" The best that the advisors could do was to tighten up their own organization, voice their questions and concerns, and propose a further meeting in six months' time.

Although this was not the happiest of times for the Institute, one of the most effective items of publicity appeared midway between the dates of the two board meetings. This was an article entitled "Notes from the New Land," by Murray Cox, published in the October 1993 issue of the glossy magazine *Omni*. Illustrated by fine photography—had Bob Monroe ever looked more relaxed or Skip Atwater more beatific?—the article took the readers through the author's own experience of a full *Gateway Voyage*, together with extracts from his journal and a clear and informative account of EEG brain mapping of the Hemi-Sync process. Cox also makes a provocatively thoughtful comment that, he says, occurred to him early in the week:

> Lying in my cell on the second day I thought of Don Quixote whom Monroe reminds me of. Where the Don saw giants, Sancho Panza, his sidekick, saw windmills. Gazing into a simple barber's basin, the Don saw the Shield of Mambrino, and Sancho wondered, How can these things be? Monroe, I think, is a descendant of the Don, telling us there's more to reality than what we see or touch.

At the end of the course he summed up his thoughts and experiences:

> For a week we knocked on doors, our own doors of perception, our belief systems—what we say is real or possible, what we dismiss as ridiculous, impossible.

Some of us traveled out of our bodies on tours of the known universe—the coveted OBE. I didn't. Others encountered "entities" out there, beyond the known. I may have. Most of us opened worn steamer trunks and rummaged about in old memories. And each time I opened the trunk I was rewarded . . . After my brief sojourn at the Institute, I know I have the capacity to "see" beyond flesh or physical reality.

In December 1993 Monroe circulated a year-end report to all staff, advisors, and others associated with the Institute. The report opened with an admission that attempts to attract major grants had failed. While accumulating profits was not the prime goal, the vital need was "to maintain a solid financial base that not only provides tools for expansion, but at least a symbolic reward for outstanding performance."

The report continued with a description of three long-term goals:

- To redefine and verify a new understanding of the process now identified as sleep.

- To identify and isolate the patterns of human thought that incite and control (M) Field energy.

- To bring forth practical solutions to the above that can be used to create a massive evolution in the human species.

With regard to the first of these, Monroe declared that the sleep state was not simply one of "physical restoration and rejuvenation" but that it had been proved and demonstrated "that human mind-consciousness can indeed exist . . . without signal input from the physical body," and that such mental activity was fully retained in memory upon awakening. He listed a number of questions to do with dreams and nightmares, the unconscious, intuition, ideas and precognition, and channeled information as reported by the Explorers. The answers to these and other questions, he added, "may provide a profound change in the knowledge and behavior of Humankind."

In *Ultimate Journey,* Monroe described the (M) Field as "the only energy field common to and operational both within and outside time-space and present in varying degrees in all physical matter." Here he defined it as "the contemporary label for the power behind certain phenomena induced by the human mind with or without willful intent and awareness." These phenomena included telepathy, prophecy, healing, affecting physical matter by using the mind, remote-viewing, and the measurable reduction of gravitational fields. Hitherto, he said, these had been almost always dismissed as fantasy, hallucination, fraud, or "help from a source beyond the capability of human mind-consciousness." He now proposed that the Institute would organize research into (M) Field energy applications and make those results available to anyone who desired them.

What was going on in the mind of this elderly man, his physical capacities in decline, sitting lonely in his log cabin, seeking to find means to change "the knowledge and behavior of Humankind" and to create "a massive evolution in the human species"? Was he suffering from delusions of grandeur—believing that he was the one marked out to perform this massive task? Had he been affected by the attitude of those who attended his courses, some of whom regarded him as a kind of guru, or as a prophet to whose words the closest attention had to be paid? Or, as he recalled his experiences recorded in *Ultimate Journey,* had he been marked out as one chosen to know the Ultimate Truth? Yet in that book he had declared that he had no desire to become a guru or "spiritual" leader; that fame and fortune were not his motives; and that his role was merely that of a facilitator. Had his attitude changed since those words were written?

There can be no firm answers to these questions. Without Nancy to provide love and companionship, as well as sound common sense, without Scooter to talk with and confide in, isolated on the mountaintop with, apart from brief interludes, his own thoughts and his animal friends his only company, only too aware of the weakening of his physical body, it is not surprising that from time to time he lost contact with the realities, and also the limitations, of the audio technology he had created.

Seeking to fulfill his intentions, he propounded a number of practical solutions embodied in Interim Goals for 1994 and 1995. For 1994 these included promotion of *Lifespan, Timeout,* an idea for a new series to be called *Going Home,* reworking of the *Gateway Experience* albums, research into using Hemi-Sync with hyperbaric oxygen and with ultrasonic sound, and a raft of public relations proposals, including books, magazine articles, videos, conferences, and so on. The following year would see an expansion of *Lifespan,* to include among other areas past-life regression therapy and "penal inmate behavior modification." Seven books or workbooks were proposed as well as "sonic and elf gardening," which unfortunately was never explained. Reading this document gives the impression that Monroe was desperate to find new programs to encourage more participants, and also to sponsor publications that would bring in grants for research. It is as if he was casting here and there to fish up ideas and jot them down without having the time, or possibly the inclination, to think them through. Yet it was already obvious that programs based on the H-Plus concept, such as *Lifespan,* failed to attract participants, no matter how enthusiastically they were presented.

However, recent years had provided one undoubted success. The *Lifeline* program was in constant demand. It attracted would-be participants by providing the opportunity to experience Focus levels beyond the hitherto impassable barrier of Focus 21, thereby opening up a means of exploring the realms beyond the physical, freeing participants from the bonds of time and space while still enabling them to act as required and report on what they observed and did. Such reports were treated seriously, being collected and filed in the office; others were mailed in by *Lifeline* graduates who had continued their explorations back home, and who had met together in groups or teams with the intention of helping those approaching their transition or guiding others who had already moved on.

Whatever advisory board members thought of the goals set out in the report, these concerns were excluded from the discussions in the meeting in January 1994. For the first time since its formation Monroe did not take the chair, yielding it to Dr. Suzanne Morris, a long-standing member of the board. The primary purpose of the meeting, she explained, "was to explore alternative structures and functions for the Board and its members," so that the advisors could support the Institute more effectively and efficiently.

Monroe outlined the changed structure of the Institute, commenting that the financial health of the nonprofit element was not good, adding that he was no longer able to subsidize it himself. While the Institute was never profit-oriented it had to become self-supporting, although he gave no clear indication as to how that could be achieved. Board members then questioned him about the internal organization, to which he replied that he had been working on this for six months with the intention of producing a formal organization chart, including job descriptions for all employees and setting out lines of communication between them. There was a pause and then—at last—he admitted to the severely depressed state he had been in since Nancy's death. There was more to come. He acknowledged that he had lost trust in many of those who were associated with the Institute and referred to certain "subtle take-over attempts" that he had become aware of during the past two years. As the Institute was not a profitable undertaking, he claimed that he could not understand anyone's reasons for wanting to have it. Board members suggested that to put an end to these attempts he should develop a long-range plan of succession to create continuity within the organization after his death, adding that it was important to deal with these matters when death was not the issue. To this, for reasons that became clear later, Monroe made no response.

Although not all the advisors may have been aware of it, Monroe's suspicions had some justification. Owing to the uncertainty about the future, some of the senior staff members had discussed plans to take over the running not of the Institute itself but of the laboratory after Monroe's death. They believed that there was far more potential in the laboratory setup than was being realized, potential that Monroe himself might not fully appreciate, and they wished to ensure that research, experiment, and their own employment would continue. They may have been misguided in avoiding any discussion of their plans with Monroe and were terrified lest he discover their intent—which almost happened when they spotted Monroe approaching the lab while they were holding a meeting there—and possibly also naïve, as without knowing the contents of Monroe's will and without the blessing of the surviving directors they would have no knowledge of how the company structure operated and no control over financial matters.

However, what Monroe seems to have told no one was that a successor had been in his mind at least since 1985, when on the flyleaf of Laurie's copy of *Far Journeys* he had expressed the hope that she would "take on her inheritance" when the time came. He felt he could not ask her formally because she was married, both she and her husband were working in Florida, and he could not be certain that she would agree. The question of succession was a cause of great worry for him, and he frequently discussed with Rita Warren the reasons why each staff member in turn was not up to the task.

Nevertheless, the hope—a card that the old poker player had kept close to his chest—that on his death the Institute and its associated companies would pass to Laurie remained alive. Eventually it was fulfilled.

The Institute staff knew little or nothing about Laurie, although some of them had met her on one of her rare visits. She had a successful real estate business and, although she had taken several *Gateway* and *Guidelines* programs over the years and had been a participant in the first *Lifeline,* she had never held any position in the Institute structure. Then, in 1989, Monroe, who had kept her updated on what was going on, appointed her to the board of directors. But it is doubtful that any of the Institute's employees or advisors envisaged that it was Laurie who would be Monroe's chosen successor.

All this served to intensify Monroe's depressed state. While he was very hopeful that Laurie would accept her role when the time came, he had no clear idea of what might happen to the Institute should she reject it. His depression was becoming obvious, although he could still sparkle in his evening talks to program participants. Darlene Miller recalls that he would often be feeling tired and unwell when he arrived at the hall. One evening when she met him out of sight of the group to help him put on his lapel microphone, he seemed so weary that she asked him if he felt up to doing his talk. "I'll be fine," he said. "Willy will help." (Willy, Darlene later discovered, was the old-time showman aspect of Bob.) She watched him walk down the stairs into the hall. "In a kind of awe I observed the transformation which occurred," she continued. "His shoulders straightened, his steps became purposeful and confident, the trademark twinkle returned to his eyes, and by the time he reached the front of the room and picked up his coffee cup he was clearly ready for 'show time' and proceeded to deliver an energetic talk and engaged enthusiastically with the group for an hour or more. As he left the hall that night he winked at me and whispered, 'That Willy's really something, isn't he?'"

While Willy, or "Performer Bob," as Leslie France named this aspect, was able to entrance the program participants, Monroe himself was becoming increasingly pessimistic about human beings in general. The predator theory that he had developed and had surfaced previously in dealings with apparently wealthy entrepreneurs from overseas now came to dominate his thinking. He felt he was being pressured by members of the board of advisors to name his successor and he became suspicious about their motives. He continued to think that certain staff members were plotting to take over when the time came. "I feel like a man dying on a desert plateau and watching the buzzards circling," he once said to Mark. One of those who attracted his attention was Dave Wallis, whom he suspected was cooperating with others to assume control of the Institute after his death. Hitherto, Wallis had been one of the most valued members of the Institute and his warm, outgoing personality enabled him to gain the confidence of course participants and assuage any qualms they might have about what lay ahead of them. After he had spent many years as a consultant, Monroe had acknowledged his contribution by appointing him in 1989 to both the board of directors and the advisory board, and in the following year making him full-time systems engineer in charge of Hemi-Sync development.

As time passed, however, Monroe became concerned that Wallis was not producing the results that he had hoped for. This put him in a difficult position. He felt indebted to Dave for the valuable work he had done as a consultant and for the service he had provided in maintaining and improving the physical environment of the Institute, but as a full-time senior member of staff on what was, for the Institute, a generous salary, Monroe thought—or persuaded himself to think— that he was falling short of what was needed. It was not that Wallis lacked experience or technical ability but that, possibly because of his past experience at Lockheed, where ample funds for research were available, he sometimes acted as if problems could best be solved by spending more money on them than the Institute's funds could meet. In the hope of finding a way out of what was becoming a difficult situation, Monroe sent him on a course on fundraising, from which Wallis concluded only that the Institute lacked the structure and experience to succeed in this area. Then, without warning, early in 1994 Monroe sent him a devastating letter outlining the areas in which he claimed that Wallis had failed to merit his salary, dismissing him from his position and informing him that he was only permitted to remain on the payroll subject to certain restrictions that removed any authority he once had and reduced him to what was in effect a part-time member of the maintenance staff.

Wallis was deeply hurt. He considered that he had given many years of faithful service to the Institute and was responsible for much of the creation and success of the technology. He claimed not to understand what had happened. As he had been dealt with in writing and referred to Ron Harris if he had any questions rather than to Monroe himself, he felt that there was no point in taking the matter further. He resigned immediately—which was what Monroe had hoped he would do.

This episode reveals certain features of Monroe's management style at this stage in his life. If he was so unhappy about Dave Wallis's failings over the past three years, why had he not called him in to discuss them? In his letter he refers to various memos that Dave had sent him, but there is no sign that he responded to them at the time. He also refers to people who were plotting to deceive, cheat, and manipulate the Institute for their own personal gain and the implication is that he believed Wallis was among their number. But no evidence has been revealed that this belief had any justification. For the thousands of program participants who had met him, Dave Wallis was the warm and welcoming face of the Institute and his presence was greatly missed.[1]

In his address to the Professional Seminar in July 1994, Monroe seemed to be fumbling for words and to have little idea of what to say next. Only when he spoke of the two Buddhist monks who had attended a recent *Gateway* did he seem to recapture some of his old energy, referring to their acceptance of everything they had learned in the program, all of which, they declared, dovetailed with Buddhist philosophy. One other ray of sunshine that managed to penetrate the gloom was when the *Wall Street Journal* printed a front-page three-column piece on the Institute. Most of the journalists who came to Roberts Mountain worked for New Age, local, or specialist publications. To be taken seriously by such a prestigious journal, in a well-researched article with references to Du Pont, a member of the U.S. Senate, the military, and the head of a Buddhist temple, was something very different.

Replying to a question from Bob Ortega, the *Journal* reporter, Monroe declared that he no longer traveled out-of-body. Two days after Nancy's death, he said, he had made an attempt to visit her, but the experience had been so traumatic that he was unable to cope with it. He had described this in more detail in *Ultimate Journey:* "The result was an emotional explosion that included every nuance existing between two humans deeply in love, all up-front and simultaneous, without the limitations of time and physical matter." It took him, he said, a week to recover. Then he made a second attempt, with a similar result. It was all too much. He resolved from then on to desist from out-of-body travel and to put up a shield to restrict any kind of nonphysical activity. Thus thirty-four years of exploration into the farthest reaches of consciousness came to an end.

Monroe's past experiences had made him aware that only those heavily addicted to physical life remained for long in the area of

Focus 27. Nancy, he was certain, was not so addicted. That part of him he called his "I There" was assured that the freedoms she would be attracted to would draw her onward. By the time he had completed what he had to do and was ready to leave physical life, there was no telling where she might be. All he was certain of was that they would be reunited in the totality that, as he wrote in the final paragraphs of *Ultimate Journey,* would "wink out and pass through the Aperture" when Earth-time reaches the thirty-fifth century.

Mark Certo, because Monroe believed that he had no ambition to take over the Institute, still retained a good measure of Monroe's confidence. He told Mark how greatly he regretted spending so much time on Institute concerns instead of being with Nancy, and how sorry he was that he had never fulfilled his promise of taking her to Hawaii. He talked about his fascination with the Pacific islands. Years ago he had spent several months in Fiji, but eventually he became aware that the motivation that drove his need for success was melting away there and he had never returned. Reminiscing over his past made him feel the need to recover something of it, and he decided to make a visit to his childhood home in Lexington, Kentucky. This was the longest drive he had undertaken for some years and Ron Harris and Dick Savigny agreed to accompany him. He arranged to meet Emmett and Alice in the town, but the trip worked no magic. Monroe had been looking for something of the Lexington he remembered from the 1920s. They found the horse farms and the golf course where Bob once caddied, and then drove up and down the streets in the town center looking for their old house, the school they once attended, and the routes they walked when they were young. Watching him, Ron was moved by the innocent and childlike way Bob remembered and cherished those memories. Sadly, most of the district they once knew so well had been razed to the ground and replaced by a large shopping mall. Bob's spirits began to droop and he cut the visit short. As Emmett commented, he wasn't able to accept one of his basic quotes: "There is one thing that's certain—change."

Then a few days later, much to Mark Certo's amazement, Monroe burst into the lab with a huge smile on his face. He had at last managed to knock into shape his idea for the new project, *Going Home*—one he was convinced could not fail. This was the Outreach project for which the seed had been sown years before by Ruth Domin of the Hospice of Chattanooga. Monroe now saw this program as one of self-controlled change, "designed to enable you to remember better how much more you are." In addition, it would offer a means "whereby the individual can be helped to overcome the common fear of physical death." As he explained it, the program would incorporate the basic structure of the *Lifeline* program, including the higher Focus levels. It was intended to provide a personal journey both for the person who was dying and for the family, friends, and caregivers who would be helped to understand and accept what was happening when a loved one was approaching death and would thus be enabled to provide appropriate support. Each would have their own set of taped exercises, allowing them to share their experiences of the afterlife as envisaged in the *Lifeline* program and affirmed by many of that program's participants. Hence, fear and apprehension need no longer be a part of the dying process.

This proposal created something as near an uproar as the Institute ever approached. The cost was prohibitive, as the series as originally envisaged would occupy twenty-four tapes. The release of higher Focus levels to the general public who had no previous experience of Hemi-Sync was running an unjustifiable risk. As Mark Certo put it: "It seemed as if one of the Ten Commandments was being shattered by Moses himself!" Monroe would have none of this. By recording different content on each side of a tape, the total required for the series could be reduced to twelve. And as for the higher Focus levels—they were no more, and no less, than markers for certain different states of consciousness within anyone's compass. All arguments were dismissed: *Going Home* would go ahead.

To provide authority to this concept, Monroe asked two old friends to record their views. Dr. Elisabeth Kübler-Ross, whose best-selling books, lectures, and life-changing workshops had created her worldwide reputation, had been a participant in the November 1991 *Lifeline* program, which she attended equipped with bars of Swiss chocolate, home-made cookies, and slices of Swiss cheese. She had responded enthusiastically, having on the last day of the program made her own contact with a woman and a child who had been killed by the Khmer Rouge in Cambodia and whom, she said, she had been able to escort to the Park in Focus 27. She came from her farm near Headwaters in the Shenandoah Mountains and joined Monroe and Mark Certo in the recording lab. With Monroe putting in the occasional question, she gave her views on how people should be allowed to die with dignity and in character according to how they lived. Their one disagreement was on the question of suicide. While Bob supported the right-to-die issue much discussed at the time in the press, believing that no rules or regulations should be imposed on anyone who wished their life to end, Elisabeth was adamant that suicide was not an option, maintaining that there were strong karmic repercussions that would come into play in the afterlife. This part of the conversation, while fascinating, was omitted from the final recording.[2]

The second contributor was Charles Tart, now professor of psychology at the University of California at Davis. Although commitments prevented him from traveling from the West Coast, Professor Tart spent several weeks working intensively with Monroe on the design of the series, scrutinizing and suggesting revisions on all the scripts sent to him, followed by lengthy discussions via telephone. One particular suggestion he made was to tone down some of Monroe's instructions from the authoritarian to the permissive. Tart submitted his contribution on tape, with Mark editing in Monroe's questions and the occasional affirming grunt or comment. Then Monroe added his own introduction. The three talks fill two sides of a cassette tape and are altogether fascinating, providing as they do the opportunity to hear three very different minds—leading minds of their day—discussing their ideas on this all-important subject.

With regard to the *Going Home* program itself, it is doubtful whether many individuals who are aware that they are approaching death have actually used the materials specifically intended for them. But the support exercises, especially when employed in a group setting, have proved of much value to relatives and caregivers, and even more so to those who have been bereaved. Like its parent program, *Lifeline,* it challenges assumptions, relieves anxieties, and, as many of its participants testify, enables contact to be made with those no longer in physical form. There are instances in both programs where participants have reported entering into each other's experience. Some have told of retrieving aspects of their own selves and reintegrating them into the whole. Both programs also tactfully demonstrate the limitations of certain belief systems.

In October 1994 a *Lifeline* program was in progress with Franceen King as lead trainer. During his evening meeting with participants, Monroe asked, as usual, if there were any questions. The first question came from the back of the room: "In which Focus state is the Gathering taking place?" (The Gathering is referred to in *Far Journeys* as "a very rare event—the conflux of several different and intense energy fields arriving at the same point in your time-space.") Franceen was surprised as questions about the Gathering had often been asked soon after the publication of *Far Journeys* but hardly at all in recent years. To questions such as this Monroe's usual answer was "go find out," but this time he gave a direct reply. "The Gathering is taking place in Focus 34 and 35." Chatting with Monroe and another trainer a few days later, Franceen casually mentioned that it might be time to create a program that would take participants to the Gathering, but Monroe did not respond.

Some two weeks later Franceen, who as well as being a trainer was a licensed psychotherapist and an ordained minister in a church in Tampa, Florida, was asked to sit in on a psychic development class at her local church. During the evening a student declared that she had received a message for Franceen herself. To her astonishment, the essence of the message was that it was very important that she approach Bob Monroe as soon as possible about the new course she had suggested. Knowing that Monroe did not take kindly to being told what to do, Franceen was at first hesitant, but eventually she decided to send him a casually phrased memo including some ideas that had come to her and suggesting that he seek guidance about the possibilities. This she did in December when she returned to the Institute to train another program. Again there was no response, so towards the end of the week she asked him if he had read the memo. He had already decided to create such a program, he told her, and she could announce to the course that this new program would take participants to the Gathering in Focus 34/35. He asked the office to arrange and publicize dates for the new program, to be called *Exploration 27,* and referred to it in his talks to *Lifeline* groups, arousing so much enthusiasm that the first two programs were immediately fully booked. In the last piece he was to write for the *Focus* newsletter he explained that the program was designed for *Lifeline* graduates, adding that "it will truly examine in detail, and with as much documentation and validation as possible, human life beyond the physical." He told Franceen that he would write all the scripts himself. But this was not to be, and in the event it was Franceen King and Darlene Miller who completed the task.[3]

One of the very few who occasionally ventured up the mountain to spend time with Monroe was George Durrette. For a while he failed to appreciate how unwell Monroe was, seeing that he drove to his office every day. But during the summer of 1994 he became concerned, noting on one occasion the difficulty Monroe had in trying to open a packet of doughnuts. Several times George's offers to drive to Nellysford to collect something to eat, or to take him down to his office, were rejected, Monroe insisting he was able to do this himself. Then during the summer months George, who was now visiting more frequently, became aware of a change. "I know he was failing because he wanted to get everything straight," he recalled. "I knew he was going . . . because he was wanting me to stay there and he'd tell me you don't need to go anywhere, you sit right here and talk to me. He said, go over there and get your guys doing something and then you come on back."

One evening about eight George drove up to spend time with Monroe and found him in a deeply depressed state. "He said there weren't no use in him hanging around no more with short days, sleeping all the time." Monroe complained that no one came to visit him and he had no friends. George refused to accept this. He told him to ask Ed Sturz if he'd like to go out to breakfast and then Ed would invite him down to his house. Then he added: "Tomorrow you get up and I want you to call Dave Wallis and say, 'Dave, let's go out to lunch.'" While Monroe was always on friendly terms with Ed, and breakfast with him presented no problem, it says much for the respect he had for George that he agreed to reestablish contact with the man he had so recently downgraded. Wallis, who had hoped above all else for reconciliation with Monroe, whom he had always regarded as a friend rather than a boss, accepted. The lunch went well, neither of them mentioning their parting, until Monroe himself raised the subject, implying that he had acted as he did because someone—he did not say who—had persuaded him to do so. Although the reason for this was not made clear, it was as good as an admission that he had been in the wrong. For Wallis, this meant more than words could say.

For several months Monroe had been communicating regularly with Laurie, calling her two or three times a week to share his problems and update her on matters at the Institute. As Christmas approached, Monroe invited her to visit. For four days they sat in the cabin and talked from morn until night. "It was a time where we laughed, cried, shared memories and related to each other as pure essence," Laurie wrote afterwards, adding that her experiences during these sessions led to her creation two years later of a new program called *Heartline*.[4] Since her childhood they had spent little time together as father and daughter. Laurie had followed her father's pattern in striking out on her own to make her way in life, but now it was as if they needed, even at this late stage, to get to know each other more thoroughly. Laurie had a record of success in her chosen career and Monroe, appreciating this, suggested that after his death she should stay in her occupation and oversee the Institute from Florida. It was clear to her that this was not possible. She was employed by an organization that managed forty-five shopping centers in Florida and elsewhere and she also ran her own real estate company. Combining all this with presiding over The Monroe Institute and its associated companies was a likely recipe for failure in both regards. In any event, her choice had already been made.

At a board of directors meeting, Monroe asked Laurie if she would accept the nomination of president of the Institute. She agreed, and became its president on January 1, 1995. From then on she traveled from Florida whenever she could to spend three or four days talking with Bob in the cabin. He had first told her about his out-of-body experiences when she was ten years old and, as with many children, she thought that everyone flew around out of his or her body so she was in no way surprised. In the early days of experiments she had acted as a kind of unofficial Explorer, trying out new procedures in the laboratory, but since then they had spent little time together. These visits now enabled them in many ways to rediscover each other.

Towards the end of February Monroe paid a surprise visit to

Laurie Monroe

Scooter and Joe. Since Scooter's resignation he had spent little time with them, feeling, quite unjustifiably, as if he himself had been slighted. For many years they had been paying him monthly installments on the acreage they had bought from him to build their house. Now he absolved them from the remainder of the balance that

they owed, handing over a document showing that he had been repaid in full. To Scooter it seemed as if he was putting his own house in order, ready for his final journey into nonphysical reality. While he never said so much in words, she understood this gesture to mean that everything between them was now well.

Early in March, Monroe developed pneumonia. He was driven to hospital in Charlottesville, returning home after a few days with a supply of medications and sufficiently recovered to work in his cabin. Then, on Tuesday, March 14, he called Mark Certo to have lunch with him at Truslows'. Saying he wasn't feeling too good, he asked Mark to drive. They had burgers and fries as usual, which seemed to revive his energy. They crossed the road to the grocery store. Mark grabbed a basket, expecting that Monroe would fill it with essential items such as butter, eggs, and so on. They walked up and down the aisles with Monroe stopping now and then, murmuring, "Hmmm, this looks good," and filling the basket with a selection of junk food, finishing with a jar of cold remedy and a bottle of Phillips Milk of Magnesia, grumbling that he was having a hard time with indigestion. Mark drove him home and helped him unpack what he'd bought and put it away. It was then time for his afternoon nap. "I'll see you tomorrow," he said to Mark as he turned to leave.

That same day Laurie was due to fly out of Tampa at seven in the morning to arrive at Charlottesville by eleven. The flight was cancelled, so she called her father to say she'd be late. He was, she said, furious—a very unusual reaction—and kept repeating that she had to come. She arrived late in the afternoon and found him in the cabin making out his "to do" list for the week. He insisted that he felt fine, although she did not find this convincing.

A *Lifeline* program was in progress and, as was his usual practice, Monroe drove down to the Center on the Monday evening to have dinner before talking to the participants. Franceen King, who was one of the trainers for the program, went to the employees' dining room to see how he was. He said that he felt Nancy had been visiting him during the previous two weeks, but he would not allow her to come close to him as he was afraid of what might happen. Franceen had been reading an article on a process known as instrumental communication and asked him if he would be more comfortable in seeking to communicate with Nancy in this way. This seemed to attract his interest, although he said he had never had any success with this in the past.[5]

Franceen noticed that he seemed very weak and was unable to steady his hand to light a cigarette. She left to prepare for the program, expecting him to follow in a few minutes. But he did not appear. The second trainer, Bob McCulloch, went to see what was happening, returning to say that Monroe would be along shortly. But he did not arrive. Having checked again, McCulloch told the group that Bob needed to rest that evening but would try to come and talk to them later in the week. He drew Franceen aside, saying that Bob had fallen twice after leaving the dining room and he had told him to go back home.

The next day Laurie arranged to bring her father to the evening session. They met the trainers in the dining room, where he asked them how Barbara Brennan, the well-known healer who was taking part in the *Lifeline* course, was doing. Then Laurie took him across to the hall, where Franceen helped him fix his microphone and said he could lean on her for support when descending the stairs. "Well, we don't want to make this look too bad," he murmured, declining her offer.

Laurie joined the course participants, deeply concerned by the cautious way Monroe walked over to his chair and by the weakness of his voice. He talked about the history of *Lifeline*, answered various questions about the higher Focus levels, and told the group that three of the H-Plus exercises had been sustaining him in his weakened state. Suddenly, he asked if there were any healers present. Some of the participants pointed to Barbara, who said she would be willing to do a session with him although he might prefer to have this in privacy. Bob said he was happy to do it there and then. While a massage table, pillows, and blankets were being fetched, one of the participants walked over to Bob and began energy healing work with him.

When all was ready the overhead fluorescent lights were turned off. Monroe was helped onto the table and the course members watched as Barbara's hands moved over his body. Looking closely, Franceen observed what she described as "massive releases of various kinds of energy formations from Bob's body." Barbara talked quietly to Monroe throughout the treatment, explaining that she was clearing and restructuring the lower chakras of the auric body and clearing the pancreas and liver organs. She also told him that she was untangling, organizing, and rebuilding some of the "cords" that he had attached to various people and events in his life. He said that it was fine for her to do whatever she had to do, adding that he was willing for his life to be open and assuring her that he was basically a good person. It seemed to Franceen that Barbara was clearing old patterns of guilt and judgments.

At one point Barbara said quietly, "You see who's here, don't you?" Monroe nodded. "Do you hear what she's saying to you?" He nodded again.

After about forty-five minutes, Bob indicated that he wanted to end the session. He asked Barbara if she knew where she had learned her healing approach, but before she could reply told her that it was very many thousands of years ago in a civilization where she was a healer named Chiana. He now seemed stronger in both speech and energy. He joined in a closing circle with the group and thanked them for their patience and participation.

Laurie drove her father home to find that Maria had driven over from Richmond and had prepared his favorite meal of fried pork chops, mashed potatoes, country gravy, and a salad. He ate little. In reply to Laurie's question if he felt any different after the session, he uttered only one word: "Somewhat." The three of them sat around talking about the past, comparing memories and contrasting viewpoints. At eleven Monroe went to the counter to take his medication. As he stood there it seemed to Laurie as if his energy was draining away from his physical body. Then his knees gave under him and he began to sink to the floor. Maria and Laurie caught him, helped him to his bedroom, gave him his medication and a glass of orange juice, and made him comfortable in bed.

When his daughters entered Bob's room next morning, they found him sitting on the edge of his bed staring out of the window. It was, they both felt, as if he was having a nonverbal conversation with someone unseen. He took his medication and said he wanted to stay where he was. Barbara Brennan had offered to do a follow-up session with him if he so desired and he agreed to see her early that afternoon. A massage table was found and set up in the room next to his bedroom. When the treatment was finished there was a period of silence. Then as Barbara rose to leave she turned to Bob and said, "See you later, Ashaneen." "See you later, Chiana," he replied. It was a moment of recognition, Laurie later wrote, "a recognition of a part of the wholeness from where we originate . . . a recognition of spirit."

Monroe seemed exhausted, lying on a sofa, drifting in and out of sleep. He roused himself to insist that he should go down to the Center to give his Thursday night talk to the program participants. This was clearly out of the question. Laurie, having studied him closely, decided to call his doctor, who told her to take him to the hospital immediately for a blood analysis. Bob, who always hated the thought of hospitals, agreed to go on condition that Laurie and A. J. would take him and stay with him there.

They arrived at the hospital at 6:45 P.M. After some delay an examination room was found and oxygen was administered. Bob's spirits quickly recovered. He grumbled half-seriously about how hospitals always kept you waiting and then complained that he was hungry. The doctor agreed to admit him, but there was another lengthy delay while the nurses searched for a room where he could stay overnight. The only vacancy turned out to be a private room in the cardiac ward. Unhappy at this, Laurie recalled the feeling of loss she had experienced as an eight-year-old child when her father suffered his heart attack. Then, as he was settled in, this feeling was replaced by a sense of gratitude that she was able to be with him. Before she left, they expressed their love for each other—the last words they shared in physical existence.

Laurie and A. J. arrived back at the Gift House about 12:30 A.M. Maria had already left to return to Richmond. A. J. went to bed while Laurie, anxious but at the same time feeling that she had support, prepared herself a cup of soup. Standing at the kitchen counter she suddenly felt the presence of what she sensed as "a familiar energy."

She turned around and felt as if "a vast number of sparkling lights" was moving towards her and surrounding her. To Laurie this signified the presence of Nancy assuring her that everything would be all right. It was a sign to her, she believed, that her father was making his conscious choice to die.

At 4 A.M. the hospital called to say that Monroe was now in Intensive Care and on a respirator. Angry and upset because she knew that he was wholly against any artificial means of life support, having said that he wanted to die on his own terms and conditions, Laurie asked for it to be removed. This, she was told, could not be done without her signature. She woke A. J. and they called Scooter and Maria as they drove to the hospital. On arrival, Laurie, A. J., Scooter, and Joe gathered in the waiting room, talking, making a few jokes to relieve the tension, reflecting on how they all felt that Nancy was ready to welcome him. Maria, who had just gone to bed when Laurie called, drove back from Richmond to join them. One by one they went into the IC unit to have time with him, to express their grief and thank him for all he had done for them. The respirator was removed. Monroe was unconscious, although the monitors showed his body was still active and alive.

After the family had made their individual farewells, they gathered together and held hands around the bed, wishing him a good voyage as he crossed over. Some time later he stopped breathing and the monitors flat-lined. They called a nurse, who went to fetch a doctor to certify that he was dead. After a couple of minutes, to the surprise of the watchers, Monroe suddenly took a huge breath and the monitors began to register. The watchers wondered if he was about to come to, but after a few moments his breathing once more stopped. Again the nurse was called—and again his breathing resumed. It began to seem as if Monroe was doing what he used to do—going out of his body, checking what it was like out there, and then coming back. Three times this happened until, shortly after nine on the morning of St. Patrick's Day, Friday, March 17, his breathing finally ceased. The family hugged him one last time, hugged each other, and pledged to keep strong as a family, deeply sad but also relieved that he was free from his physical troubles and reunited with his beloved Nancy. Laurie said later that she felt he made the decision to leave his physical body three hours earlier.

Towards the end of *Ultimate Journey*, reflecting on Nancy's death, Bob Monroe had questioned if it was possible to live in two worlds—with Nancy in Focus 27 and Here in a lonely house. Then he recalled what another voice from his "I There" had insisted: "Once the transition is made, only the heavily addicted remain closely attached to the physical life they have just departed, according to your data and others. For most, the resonance/interest/attachment begins to fade almost immediately, some slowly, some rapidly. But it does."

For the first half of his life it seems that no thoughts of there being anything that might be described as an afterlife ever entered Monroe's head. He was focused on earning money and on enjoying himself—indulging himself perhaps—flying, gliding, sailing, driving fast cars, and, it might be added, getting married. "How many times have you been married, Ron?" he once asked Ron Harris. "Just once," was the reply. Monroe burst out laughing. "You're a smart boy, aren't you?" he rejoined. Perhaps late in life he could afford to laugh at his earlier marital ventures. But it was not only his out-of-body experiences that caused him to change direction. Without the love, support, tolerance, and consistency of Nancy Penn, he might still have created the Institute but it is very unlikely that it would have radiated the warmth, the style, the feeling of "a home with a heart" that not only welcomes and embraces those who visit it but calls so many of them back time and again.

It is not easy—perhaps it is not possible—to categorize Bob Monroe. Ron Harris made a bold attempt at summing him up:

"Author, musician, businessman, land developer, cattle farmer, poker player extraordinaire, naturally curious scientist, philosopher, etc. . . . in short, a true renaissance man!" Like many renaissance men, as history demonstrates, he could be intolerant, peremptory, and capable at times of serious misjudgment. Unlike many of the New Age gurus who were his contemporaries, he was unpretentious, was unassuming, and had no desire to be set on a pedestal—or even on a soapbox. He was essentially, as Harris says, "a man of simple tastes whose favorite lunch was a cheeseburger and fries, followed by a cigarette or two, at the local 'greasy spoon,' rather than any 'high end' fare available nearby."

For George Durrette, who knew him for over thirty years, who began by cooking his hamburgers, who accompanied him to auctions, ran his farms, played poker with him, and always told him what he thought, "he was the best friend I ever met in my life."

And for Leslie France, "he was the most frustrating, perverse, childish man to work for at times. I once calculated that up to fifty percent of my creative energy on the job went to dealing with the 'Monroe Effect.' When it tipped over the fifty percent mark, it was time for me to go." She continues: "As consuming as those moments were, they are the little picture. In the big picture, Bob Monroe changed my life in a major and positive way. His books, Hemi-Sync, the Institute, his brilliance and creativity—there are no words that can accurately evoke the depthless thanks I owe, and gladly give, to Bob for sharing himself with me in a meaningful way. I am so much more myself than I would have been without his influence and guidance. Wow! I really can't imagine my life without Bob Monroe." There are countless thousands who would echo that last sentence.

In his final decade Monroe had developed two major aims: to demonstrate that death was not a terminus but a gateway, and, using his own words, " to create a massive evolution in the human species." In the first of these aims he succeeded, as far as many of his readers and the great majority of his *Lifeline* graduates were concerned—and to those can also be added many of those, in the United States and countries overseas, who have experienced *Going Home.* In the second, it looked as if he had failed. His attempts to develop the H-Plus material into comprehensive programs that would radically affect those with the good fortune to experience them came to naught. Yet it may be that the failure was more apparent than real. He placed in the hands of others the audio technology known as Hemi-Sync that he had discovered and developed. These others—doctors, teachers, psychologists, research scientists, composers, and other professionals among them—took this gift and worked with it. The applications of Hemi-Sync, when allied to their professional skills, proved to be manifold, including such areas as pain management, learning and memory, hyperactivity, support for cancer patients, stress relief, sleep patterns, pregnancy and childbirth, depression, and many more. While "massive evolution" may be an overstatement, the benefits of this discreet and noninvasive technology are already apparent and increase exponentially year by year.

As for Monroe himself, consider some words of William James.

> I have no doubt whatever that most people live, whether physically, intellectually or morally, in a very restricted circle of their potential being. They make use of a very small portion of their possible consciousness, and of the soul's resources in general, much like a man who, out of his whole bodily organism, should get into a habit of using and moving only his little finger . . . We all have reservoirs of life to draw upon, of which we do not dream.

Bob Monroe was one who was able to draw upon those reservoirs. More than that: he gave others the encouragement and the means to do likewise. This was the gift he brought back from his hero's journey.

Notes

1. Dave Wallis remained on the New Land, continuing to build his new house on a wooded slope overlooking the creek. He became involved in an ambitious and potentially dangerous project to contact the afterlife that required some complicated electrical engineering. In January 1998 he crashed his car on the approach road to the Institute, and, while hospitalized, it was discovered that he had been suffering from a tumor on the brain. He made a good recovery, but he had to undergo a second operation in midsummer. His condition deteriorated in the fall and he died the evening before Thanksgiving Day, 1998.

2. Elisabeth was both hated and feared by many of the local backwoods fundamentalists, who tried to force her to leave by such actions as covering the entrance to the drive to her farm with broken glass and even shooting from the hill above at the log cabin she had built for visitors to stay in, in the belief that she slept there herself. When she was involved with seeking to remove babies of parents with AIDS from the hospital ("pincushion babies" she called them, as they were subject to many investigations and procedures), they refused to follow her into the local store, terrified of receiving in their change any money she had handled lest it carried the AIDS virus. In October 1994 her house was burned down and her llamas were shot. No one was ever convicted, although a customer in the store was heard to say, "We've gotten rid of the AIDS lady!"

3. Darlene Miller commented that while she was working on the scripts she was aware of the presence of Bob and Nancy helping her.

4. *Heartline* is a graduate program, described as "for those who are serious about looking within. It is about creating 'heartspace': self-love, self-trust, and non-judgmental acceptance. It is about allowing, understanding, and moving beyond feelings into the transcendental."

5. Instrumental transcommunication (ITC), which incorporates electronic voice phenomena (EVP), studies the various ways in which, according to the survival hypothesis, "the dead"—that is, those of us no longer in our physical bodies but existing in nonphysical reality—seek to communicate with the living, including through the media of audio recorders, telephones, television, computers, and video recorders. Listen in, and draw your own conclusions.

CHAPTER 12

Legacy

Until shortly before he died, Bob Monroe had kept the expansion of the Hemi-Sync technology under strict control. Focus 21, the edge of here-now, was *ultima thule.* No one knew what perils might lie beyond this level. However, much to the amazement of most of the Institute staff, with the *Lifeline* and *Going Home* programs the boundary was crossed. The Park in Focus 27 became familiar territory to those who had qualified as *Gateway* graduates and hence were able to explore it. The last program Bob authorized, *Exploration 27,* extended the territory still farther. Now it was possible for others to venture into, explore, and return safely from areas that Monroe himself, as he described in *Ultimate Journey,* had only recently discovered.

All this, of course, is metaphor. We talk of boundaries and territories, but what we are experiencing are states of consciousness that most of us seldom, if ever, encounter in our daily lives. When under Monroe's guidance we venture into these states, we are given signposts, so that not only may we safely return but we also now have the ability to recognize and reconnect with them whenever we are moved to do so.

Yet that is not the whole story. The books, the programs, the power of the audio technology make us face the massive question that humankind has sought to find an answer to from the dawn of recorded history. What happens to us after we die? Monroe took this question away from the teachings of religion and placed it squarely before us. Convinced that human consciousness is not extinguished by physical death, he used his own experiences in the out-of-body state to create a multidimensional map of the afterlife. This map has several editions. As his inhibitions and fears fell away, he was able to revise and extend this supernatural cartography until in the expeditions recorded in his final book he seems to have reached the very edge.

In *Far Journeys* Monroe bravely—or some would say rashly—sought to portray what he calls "the itinerary of human experience" in the form of a flow sheet "of where the action is in which all of us are involved." This, he wrote, "is a summary based upon several hundred individual explorations, most of which are beyond literal translation." The flow sheet demonstrates both the strengths and the weaknesses of Monroe's attempts at the time to convey the lessons of his personal experiences in the out-of-body state. He felt he was under an obligation to share his discoveries with the world at large, as far as that was possible. But at this stage in his life he did not have the equipment to enable him to do this. While his straightforward recounting of his experiences carry conviction, his attempts in *Far Journeys* to draw conclusions from them, sometimes expressed as if those conclusions are absolute, do not have the same force.

By the time he began to write *Ultimate Journey,* however, Monroe had arrived at a simplicity of expression that enabled him to carry his readers with him throughout the book. Three short paragraphs towards the end of the first chapter bring readers and writer very close together.

The highways and byways of out-of-body adventures and exploration are broad and varied, for the most part beyond ordinary time-space concepts. We can understand only that portion which relates directly to the Earth Life System. We may attempt to report the rest of it—and it seems limitless—but we have no acceptable or comparable baseline of knowledge and experience to do this accurately. The problem lies in trying to understand it and to translate what you find—to bring it back. Never be surprised when you return to the physical to find tears running down your cheeks.

What has happened is that you have gone off the edge of the Known map, and have returned with some previous important Unknowns now converted to Knowns. You may or may not convince others of this reality. Most do not try; the individual knowledge is enough.

Think how such knowledge—not belief or faith—would affect your own life pattern; the knowledge that you are indeed more than your physical body, that you do indeed survive physical death. These two Unknowns converted to Knowns, with no conditions or contingencies—what a difference this would make!

"One can acquire a belief in the possibility of life after death through either faith or experience." So said Peter and Elizabeth Fenwick in *Past Lives,* their study of reincarnation memories.[1] With Monroe, that experience came from his out-of-body explorations—no faith was involved. Once described as a bold explorer rather than a spiritual practitioner, he was untrammeled by any religious or New Age spiritual belief systems. Through his experiences in the second half of his life he came to accept that physical death was not a terminus but simply a kind of way-station. He does not talk about an immortal soul, but uses the term *mind-consciousness* for the element that continues after the physical body has died. He does not discuss regression into past lives, although in his reports of his own out-of-body experiences there are several instances where he appears to be reliving episodes from previous existences. In many of these episodes these previous existences appear to be those of his ancestors from remote periods of time. There are instances where he identifies specific past selves, such as the architect-builder responsible for the original Foulis Castle tower. "I was I after all!" he declares. There is also what he describes as "the deep sadness, amounting to physical illness" that he felt when, following the publication of *Far Journeys,* he and Nancy were visiting cathedrals in England and France. He ascribes this to the same previous personality who was beheaded after protesting against the lack of safety precautions during the building of a cathedral on which he was working.

Reincarnation is a term he seldom uses but it is clear from his books that his out-of-body experiences have revealed to him that some kind of reincarnation does occur, and that it may take very many visits to this corporeal world before an individual is ready to make the final journey as part of the cluster of lives that Monroe calls "I There," a journey that he suggests will take place in the thirty-fifth century. Heaven and Hell are not part of Monroe's postphysical life structure, but belong in what he describes as the belief system territories where those wholly committed to a particular belief or faith receive whatever reward or penalty is appropriate.

Fear is not evident in Monroe's vision of the afterlife. One of the goals of the *Lifeline* program was "to release all fears related to the physical death process." It is as if by accepting the message of the program you are assured that on cessation of physical life your mind-consciousness will shift without interruption to another form of existence. *Lifeline* presents a model that participants in the program may find helpful in their journeys into nonphysical realms. Their reports have similarities to the reports of those who have undergone a near-death experience, who almost with one voice declare that death no longer has any fears for them. Monroe's vision is, on the whole, gentle: there is no mention of sin or judgment, but only of enrichment of experience. There is, however, an exception, as those who are unable to recognize and accept that they are no longer in physical existence, or, to use his own words, "are unable to free themselves from the ties of the Earth Life System," find themselves stuck in a kind of limbo, unable to move on until the nature of their situation becomes clear to them.

Reports from the tens of thousands who have attended his residential programs, and the hundreds of thousands more who have participated in Outreach courses and workshops or made use of the materials in their own homes, provide evidence of Hemi-Sync's effectiveness in enabling access to nonordinary states of consciousness. But did Monroe ever foresee the many different practical ways in which his audio technology would be applied? This has proved to be an ongoing process. With every passing year, new applications for his audio technology have been discovered, tried, and tested. Some of the areas in which this technology has proved its usefulness include autism, Asperger's syndrome and other learning difficulties in adults and children, pediatric physical therapy, improving sleep patterns, helping children with feeding problems and their parents also, psychiatric practice, education and business seminars, stroke recovery, psycho-oncology, strengthening the immune system, and ameliorating the side effects of chemotherapy and radiotherapy. Additionally, Hemi-Sync signals have been shown to have a calming effect on certain animals, notably dogs recovering from illness or injury and nervous or high-strung horses.[2]

During Monroe's lifetime, almost all research took place in-house, following a policy that he framed himself:

> All research conducted by The Monroe Institute is directed solely toward the development of methods and techniques that will aid others in the evolution and growth of human consciousness and perception. The Institute uses conventional scientific procedures whenever feasible but does not limit itself to such processes.
>
> Thus much of our research has not been designed to conduct studies in form and protocol that will insure acceptance by orthodox segments of our culture. The Institute has recognized long ago that such efforts may not be possible within the area of investigation covered in our work.
>
> Conversely, when we do find data that may be of interest to conventional research groups, we are happy to release such information in the hope and expectation that it will be of help or interest to others in their particular area of endeavor. We also encourage other organizations to conduct studies that may offer additional or extended verification of our own work.

Since Monroe's death, however, the direction of research as conducted in-house has changed. Director of Research Skip Atwater expresses it thus: "No longer will the Institute's research interest be on proving whether or not Hemi-Sync works or alters brainwave states, but on the far-reaching implications of the evolution of human consciousness that have been at the core of our work all along." He continues: "What is it that will define humanity itself as the discovery of boundless consciousness emerges? The answer surely must be in the understanding of first-person subjective experience and the apparent interrelation with the corporeal quantum." The emphasis, says Atwater, is shifting from quantitative research, based on measurement, cause and effect, and reductionism, towards qualitative research, based on hermeneutics and phenomenology (concerned with the experiences of the self). He states the reasons for this shift of emphasis:

> Exposing people to various conditions, even in the name of quantitative science, may undermine their self-respect, their psychological integrity, their sense of self-determination, or even their physical health and the very first-person experience they are seeking with the Hemi-Sync process. In such studies it is the reliance on measurement that is disturbing. While reducing everything to numbers may be justified in the physical sciences, doing the same to human experience seems to dismiss the other, non-quantitative dimensions of that experience. How do you quantify meaning, for example, of love, or anger, or confusion? You can describe the Grand Canyon using only numbers—but somehow that wouldn't capture the essence of it.

Research involving the practical applications of Hemi-Sync and binaural beat frequencies has moved into the hands of members of the Professional Division and their colleagues, who are able to make use of the extensive facilities available in universities, hospitals, and other institutions in several countries, including the United States, the United Kingdom, Canada, Norway, Italy, and Denmark. Results from their completed projects are published in a variety of professional journals, and thus the applications of Hemi-Sync may be extended farther.[3] Accounts of these projects and of work in progress are reported at the Professional Seminars, which have attracted a number of notable keynote speakers, including Elisabeth Kübler-Ross; Dr. Beverly Rubik, founder and president of the Institute for Frontier Science; Edgar Mitchell of Apollo 14, the sixth man to walk on the Moon and the founder of the Institute for Noetic Sciences; the futurist and author Peter Russell; and Jeffrey Mishlove, author of *The Roots of Consciousness* and holder of the first PhD in parapsychology awarded by a major American university. An increasing number of colleges are prepared to accept projects involving Hemi-Sync as elements in courses leading to the award of degrees. While Bob Monroe occasionally claimed that what he was doing in his work was merely satisfying his own curiosity, his stated belief that he was providing those who attended courses or made use of Hemi-Sync materials with "something of value" has been justified time and again.

It is not only in research that Monroe's Hemi-Sync has proved its value but also in the everyday lives of those who have used it. This is clearly expressed by author Michael Hutchison, founder of the Neurotechnologies Research Institute in San Francisco, in summarizing his response to the *Gateway* program:

> The goal was not only to experience quite distinct domains of consciousness, but to learn how to enter them at will, and to use them in everyday life, accessing specific mental realms for purposes ranging from enhanced creativity to accelerated learning to self-healing to tapping intuitive powers.

In this regard, the impact that Hemi-Sync has had on individual lives cannot be overstated. To take just two examples:

Suzanne Morris, PhD, a speech-language pathologist internationally known for her work with children who have significant feeding problems due to sensorimotor disorders such as cerebral palsy and autism, took her first *Gateway* program in 1981. She repeated the program twice more, after which time she moved to live on the New Land. For five years she trained *Gateway* programs herself. She bought an adjoining property and converted it into a residential clinic where families could stay while she was working with their children. She integrated Metamusic into her work, finding that, to use her own words, "it opened the door to learning for many children with developmental disabilities." Suzanne has published two authoritative books on her work and has contributed papers to several professional journals and collections of papers. During the past twenty years, she has incorporated information and videotaped examples of her use of Hemi-Sync in over a hundred continuing education workshops attended by some ten thousand professionals throughout the world, thus bringing the value of Monroe's audio technology to the notice of the wider therapeutic community.

Hemi-Sync had a marked effect on Suzanne's personal life also. Using it, she says, brought home to her that she was more than her physical body and also relieved her of her fear of death. She found that she could move into Focus 10 or Focus 12 on a thought, thus enabling her to access information on whatever she was involved with. It demonstrated to her that, while we shift consciousness all the time, we can do so intentionally and efficiently and for long periods. By so doing our lives become more focused—we become more of whom we really are. "I can pilot the ship of consciousness," she once said. "I am more in tune—more connected."

In contrast, there is the experience of Gail Blanchette. Gail grew up in a family "plagued by addictions, violence, and acutely dysfunctional behavior," and her childhood and youth were "a living nightmare." For many years she was haunted by her traumatic experiences in her early years. Seeking to change her life, she searched books on self-help and personal growth and attended seminars and workshops, but found no answers. She kept falling back "into old traps and dysfunctional behavior patterns."

Gail's serious self-discovery work began in her late thirties, when she consulted a clinical psychologist specializing in the problems she encountered. She had lost her ability to cry and was unable to speak or write about her deeper thoughts and feelings. "It was as if a part of me were frozen solid, like an iceberg," she said. Her sessions continued for nearly ten years, but she was still unable to escape from the haunting of her past.

Then a friend lent her several Hemi-Sync tapes. These helped in creating a calmer state of mind, but they did not effect the kind of change she was seeking. However, using them encouraged her to attend a *Gateway* program. Here, feeling safe and secure, Gail began to experience emotions and responses that were hitherto unknown. She found that she was able to cry for the first time in many years and could review the appalling experiences of her past without being overwhelmed by them. She added, "There was a new sense of emotional freedom and well-being I had never experienced before."

Returning to her psychologist, Gail found that unlocking the past and understanding how its negativity had affected her present life had opened the path to change. Yet she was still not at peace with herself and was troubled by terrifying nightmares and negative emotions. It was as though she had traveled far in her search for self-discovery but had arrived at a plateau whence she could go no farther.

Gail returned to the Institute two years later to take the *Heartline* program. During the week she discovered that she had disowned parts of herself from her earlier years. She had, she says, "rejected the severely traumatized and raped three-year-old . . . and disowned the awkward and demoralized sixteen-year-old who had no friends." She had not understood how to reconnect with those parts of herself as she was not aware they existed. Her experiences during the program, she said, "were life-altering and profoundly healing."

Since then Gail has made many changes in her life and enjoys a sense of freedom and serenity unknown to her before. She uses Hemi-Sync in her professional work as a business coach and trainer and has written and published a book about her life and how she learned to grow and change.[4]

The affirmation at the commencement of many Hemi-Sync exercises begins with the words "I am more than my physical body." That to most people is simply stating the obvious. Then the affirmation continues: "Because I am more than physical matter, I can perceive that which is greater than the physical world." This is really the starting point. Working with this audio technology enables the individual to explore the whole spectrum of consciousness. But it is important to realize that once you are familiar with the Hemi-Sync process you no longer need to listen to the sound signals to move from one state or phase of consciousness to another. It becomes second nature; on a thought or on a breath you may shift from ordinary everyday consciousness to a state of expanded awareness, a deep meditative state of complete attunement with all that is or a state where time does not exist. Throughout you are in control: the "monkey mind" is closed down and you are free to explore. Your life, if you so wish, is transformed.

There is another legacy for which many people are grateful to Bob Monroe. His books, especially *Journeys Out of the Body,* did much to relieve the fears and anxieties of those—often estimated at approaching 20 percent of the population of the United States—who have experienced the out-of-body phenomenon, many of whom wondered if they were on the point of death themselves or were going mad. The calm, unemotional way he described his own experiences, together with the supporting material included in the book, assured them that there was nothing wrong with their health or sanity and that they were by no means alone in what was happening to them.

An example of this is the experience of a young Scottish woman, Angela, who for several years was tormented by the sensation of being pulled out of her body, sometimes finding herself looking down on it as she lay in bed. She sought help from doctors, psychologists, and psychiatrists, was examined, scanned, and brain-mapped, but to no avail. Then a friend happened to mention the phrase "astral travel." This caught Angela's attention, and she visited Scotland's largest library to see if there were any books on this subject. After some delay a copy of *Journeys Out of the Body* was produced—and there she read a description of experiences similar to her own. She soon learned how to control these experiences and within a year was part of a project studying the out-of-body experience under the direction of an eminent professor.[5]

Yet more significant is the effect of Monroe's work on humankind's greatest apprehension—the fear of dying. Joseph Campbell, talking of the hero's journey, defined the hero as "someone who has given his or her life to something bigger than oneself." Monroe's hero's journey lasted for nearly forty years, almost half his lifetime, from that very first, very tentative out-of-body exploration in 1958 until his culminating experience recorded in *Ultimate Journey*. The message he brought back is encapsulated in his *Lifeline* and *Going Home* programs. It is expressed not in words but in the experiences he made available to others, experiences that do much to take away the fears and anxieties associated with death and dying. No matter what faiths or beliefs the participants in these programs may acknowledge, almost without exception they find that they can accept and, if they so wish, adapt Monroe's depiction of the postphysical death territories that he describes so vividly. Yet, as we have recognized, what he is really describing are not territories at all; they are metaphors for states or phases of consciousness into which you are guided and where you have the freedom to explore, both before and after the death of the physical body.

The programs that Monroe created and the tapes and compact discs that carry Hemi-Sync across the world have one distinctive feature in common—his voice. His wide experience in broadcasting and an instinctive sense of timing contribute strongly to the remarkable effects that are frequently reported. Sometimes peremptory—"Do this now!"—but mostly gently persuasive and always positive, his deep, mellow tones inspire confidence in his listeners, who have no qualms in following his guidance and instruction no matter where they might be led. You do not question what he says. This man, you accept, knows what he is talking about; he speaks from experience and you trust him. No matter where you come from or what your native language may be, he holds you close to him as you listen. The quality of his voice, however, has made him a difficult act to follow. Several of his recordings have been digitally remastered, but other voices have to be employed when new materials are produced. With the increasingly widespread use of Hemi-Sync and the growing number of participants from different nationalities that attend the programs, it is not an easy task to find voices that, like Bob Monroe's, have what could be described as a universal appeal.

Monroe once told of a dream, or it may have been a vision, when he saw from an out-of-body vantage point the world stretched out below him as if on a Mercator's projection. Looking down, he could see points of light—blue light—scattered everywhere, some in or near cities, some simply anywhere. These points of light, he recognized, marked the places where human consciousness was expanding, where a new understanding of life, on this planet and elsewhere, was beginning to dawn. As he watched, a few lights here and there flickered and went out, but more and more began to appear—in Canada, Australia, Japan, Eastern Europe, the Ukraine.

This dream or vision may reflect the spread of his audio technology and his books across the world, with more and more translations of his work and more and more trainers working in countries in every continent, including Brazil, Mexico, Puerto Rico, Switzerland, Denmark, Poland, Slovakia, the Czech Republic, and Japan, as well as France, Spain, Germany, the United Kingdom, and Australia.

Towards the end of his life Monroe accepted that there was no longer any need to seek the approval of the outside world or to insist on the need for validation. In the early days *Gateway* participants tended to be regarded as subjects for research—how they responded, physiologically and psychologically, to the frequencies they were listening to. While Monroe had been willing to expose his scientific collaborators to a wide range of sound signals, he was very careful to use on his clientele only those frequencies that had been tried and tested for long periods of time. The *Lifeline* program broke the pattern, and from then on the emphasis shifted to the subjective experiences reported by the participants. This sent a clear message: that Hemi-Sync needed no further validation. It was securely established as a safe modality. Your experience might be elevating or emotionally distressing, but it was never harmful.

Old age was not kind to Robert Monroe. While he loved reading, especially the work of authors such as Ray Bradbury and Robert Ludlum, and enjoyed current news magazines, including *Time, Newsweek,* and *Scientific American,* his failing eyesight made it progressively more difficult and his refusal to wear glasses compounded the problem. He struggled to complete *Ultimate Journey* and was almost overwhelmed by the emotional turmoil aroused by Nancy's illness and death. He felt that his body was letting him down, and there were times when his frustration became obvious and curtailed his patience. But he never wavered in his assurance that what he had created would provide, to use his own words, "something of value" to humankind.

All this and more is the legacy of Robert Monroe. The courses he designed have proved life-changing for many of their participants, opening them up to the richness of life, to possibilities never before perceived, to depths within themselves they never knew existed. In the hands of others, his discoveries and developments in the field of sound have influenced the health and well-being of countless numbers of people within and beyond the United States. He never set himself up as a teacher—"Don't believe anything I say; go find out for yourself" was his standard response to those who sought enlightenment from him rather than seeking it within themselves. He made no claims to be someone exceptional—"I'm just a monkey who fell out of a tree" was a typical reply to questions about himself or his achievements. He was courageous, always independent, always insistent on being in control, resentful of criticism—at times interpreting suggestions as criticism without being aware of this—single-minded when he needed to be, and deeply emotional, although unwilling, or perhaps unable, to express this side of his nature. His judgment of others was not always secure and he may have misread the motives of some of those he rejected or mistreated, but with hardly an exception they never lost their affection or respect for him.

Monroe's journey was a hero's journey, a spiritual journey, although *spiritual* was a word he very seldom used. He fought his dragons, defeated them, and returned with gifts encapsulated in the programs he devised. On his death in 1995, his old friend Charles Tart, now emeritus professor of psychology at the University of California at Davis, summed up his legacy as he saw it then:

> Bob devoted the last thirty years of his life to sharing what he had learned with others, while he kept experimenting and learning himself. The Monroe Institute and its training programs are as great a testament to his competence and kindness as could be given.

Many people have had deep experiences which have markedly enhanced the spiritual aspects of their lives in these programs. His books have had, and continue to have, an even wider reach. These legacies are not just a great gift to knowledge, but a real service to people who are plagued by doubts and unfulfilled spiritual longings.

True enough. The years since his death have seen remarkable developments in the use of his audio technology in so many ways and in so many countries across the world. And the picture is by no means complete.

After Monroe's death it came as something of a surprise to many of those connected to the Institute that his daughter Laurie was to take over control. For over three decades responsibility for the growth, development, and progress of what had become a highly successful, internationally known educational and research organization had lain in the hands of one man, assisted and sometimes advised by those he allowed to help give form to his vision. His personal experiences had brought it into being, his business skills had enabled it not just to survive but also, in a moderate fashion, to prosper, and his vision had enhanced the lives of the thousands upon thousands who came in contact with what he had created. And he possessed that extraordinary quality for which the only word is charisma. He was, in the well-worn phrase, a hard act to follow.

It says much for Laurie's courage that she was willing to accept her inheritance. To move from the world of real estate in Florida into the less defined areas of consciousness exploration is neither a logical nor an easy progression. Yet the expertise acquired in her business life was put to good use. It took several months for her to sort out her career and relationship issues; once that was done, she moved to live in the vicinity and to take control. Aware that the Institute was ready for expansion, she began to activate ideas for new buildings on the mountaintop. In 1997 work began on Roberts Mountain Retreat, incorporating the Gift House and a second purpose-built Residential Center close by. A control room was installed in the Gift House and comfortable accommodations in spacious units fitted with up-to-date audio equipment was provided in both buildings for a total of eighteen participants and two trainers. It was now possible to run two programs simultaneously, one at the foot and one at the top of the mountain. The reception rooms in the Gift House were retained and a swimming pool was created in the garden. Bob Monroe's log cabin, where so much of his work had been done, was made available for research, and an isolation unit was constructed for individual exploration. While *Gateway, Guidelines,* and *Lifeline* remained the staple fare on the syllabus, in subsequent years several new programs, designed by experienced trainers, have been added. These include inner exploration and personal development, remote-viewing, investigation of shamanic traditions, exploring the possibilities of mind over matter, practicing creativity, and developing new states of awareness. Other programs have been devised to take participants far beyond the bounds of Focus 27, enabling them to explore other energy systems.

Almost all the Metamusic compositions are now created and recorded by professional composers and musicians. In this area, one individual's contribution is outstanding. Barbara Bullard, until recently professor of speech at Orange Coast College, was deeply interested in the effects of music on learning, especially in children and adults with attention deficit disorder (ADD). After investigating current research on the impact of music on the brain, she collaborated with Robert Sornson, a director of special education services, on incorporating beta-harmonic sound patterns, which were shown to increase the level of awareness in youngsters with learning difficulties, with a super-learning musical format that she herself designed. A young composer, John Epperson, was then commissioned to create a piece to comply with requirements that Barbara formulated. *Remembrance* was issued in 1994 and has proved its value time and again. Several more compositions followed, including *Einstein's Dream,* based on Mozart's *Sonata for Two Pianos* and Epperson's *Indigo for Quantum Focus* and *Illumination.*

Another significant development in the use of Hemi-Sync has been in the field of medicine. Brian Dailey, MD, a specialist in emergency medicine at Rochester General Hospital, has been using Hemi-Sync with his patients, including the Surgical Support series and various Metamusic compositions, since the early 1990s. For the benefit of cancer patients he developed an exercise, *Chemotherapy Companion,* first issued in 2001, followed two years later by *Radiation Companion.* With the addition of Metamusic *Sleeping through the Rain* and an earlier exercise, *Journey through the T-cells,* the Cancer Support series, on tape or CD, has proved a valuable adjunct to traditional forms of cancer therapy during and after treatment.

Dr. Dailey also makes use of two more sets of exercises for specific purposes, the Surgical Support series, already referred to, and the *Positive Immunity* program. The latter was the brainchild of the late Jim Greene, a good friend of Monroe and a strong supporter of the Institute. The program was originally designed to help those coping with autoimmune disorders and was first issued in 1990, being piloted by groups whose members were diagnosed as HIV-positive. It has since proved to be a valuable support for improved health and general well-being.

Laurie Monroe's intention was for the Institute to remain a leading force for in-depth exploration and transformation so that participants in its work would be helped to experience, express, and explore their own true nature. In a statement, she added that the

Institute would continue in perpetuity "through the support, dedication and love of those who have had the direct experience of how much more they truly are than their physical bodies." Although at times he seemed to forget this, Monroe maintained that the one constant was change. Since his death, this constant has remained a guiding principle. Under Laurie's management the Hemi-Sync base widened and there are now far fewer restrictions upon its use. Exercises employing Focus levels beyond 21, as in the *Going Home* program, are now available to anyone who wishes to explore them whether they have attended residential courses or not. Among other new releases, a set of CDs entitled *Hemi-Sync Support for Journeys Out of the Body,* described as "a system of training in self-exploration and personal development," was issued in 2004. Another introduction has been an occasional *Gateway* program for teenagers. One participant, coming straight from high school, commented that the program made her realize "that experience is very much dependent on perspective, and that there are no limits to the number of experiences and perspectives one can have." She added, "We were able to strengthen our own states of being, which in turn strengthened the group as a whole because of the shared experience of exploring different states of consciousness."[6]

With Laurie's guidance, in the past ten years eight additional week-long residential programs and four weekend seminars have been introduced, thus increasing the opportunities for further exploration of consciousness and providing incentives for *Gateway* graduates to return to extend their experience. As illustration of the ways in which Hemi-Sync use is extending, the schedule for the year 2006 included nineteen *Gateway* programs, three of them in Japanese, as well as twenty-four advanced programs and five weekend workshops. Outreach trainers have the freedom to develop programs to suit the background and culture of participants according to the countries in which they live. As well as *Gateway,* many advanced programs are available in Canada and France, and *Excursion* workshops are translated into foreign languages as required. Since 1995 the Annwin Institute in Slovakia has been conducting programs in which Hemi-Sync is an important component, and workshops have been held in Poland since 1996. In the following year, Psychognosia, a non-profit center in Cyprus directed by Linda Leblanc and John Knowles, began offering frequent Hemi-Sync programs on the island with workshops, including *Excursion, Advanced Excursion,* and *Going Home.* There is a highly efficient European distribution center for Hemi-Sync materials in Denmark. An outstanding feature of the 2006 Professional Seminar was a presentation by trainers working in Spain, Japan, Puerto Rico, and Brazil, demonstrating the variety of methods of presenting Hemi-Sync and the enthusiastic responses of the participants.

From the beginning, Laurie sought collaboration with organizations and individuals whose missions and goals were broadly similar to those of The Monroe Institute although their methods and approaches were their own. She was delighted when the Institute of Noetic Sciences accepted The Monroe Institute as a strategic partner and offered *Gateway* programs on their campus in Petaluma, California. She persuaded Dr. Norman Sheeley to support and voice a series entitled Network of Light and Mark Macy of ITC to coproduce Bridge to Paradise. She also encouraged further development of Metamusic with ventures into a range of different traditions and styles.

Laurie's business experience proved exceptionally valuable in the difficult period following September 11. For a time, demands for courses fell away and the Institute's finances, like those of so many other organizations, slid into the red. She was ready and able to make the tough decisions needed to deal with the situation and restore the Institute to a solid financial position.

Above all, however, as Darlene Miller expresses it, it was "her personality, vitality, extraordinary generosity of spirit, and her enthusiasm and passion for the work of TMI that endeared her to staff and to the program participants with whom she interacted." Darlene recalls Laurie's "fond and healthy relationship with her inner child, delighting in her impish qualities." She was often heard encouraging someone to lighten up. At Halloween she would disguise herself in costume, usually as an alien, and glide silently through the dining room to see if course participants would recognize her. At Christmas she would dress up as Santa Claus to distribute presents to the staff, "ho-hoing" as she did so. She was, Darlene adds, "upbeat, inspirational, and brought out the best qualities in those around her, motivating them to try harder, to believe in themselves."

Toward the end of 2006 Laurie recommended to the board of directors that they consider appointing an executive director who would be able to take The Monroe Institute "to the next level." It seems that she felt she had achieved as much as she could and was ready to withdraw from the decision-making process and administration. She believed that the time was approaching when the Institute needed to take a significant step forward, to become a major player in the understanding and exploration of human consciousness that was now becoming a central preoccupation in the scientific and philosophical worlds. In the meantime, she would stay on simply to oversee events and maintain a guiding role as chairman of the board.

But events dictated otherwise. A few weeks previously, Laurie had fractured a bone in her shoulder after tripping over her dog at home. She then developed pneumonia. She was treated, but the illness persisted. Then further examination in the University of Virginia Hospital revealed that she was suffering from non-small-cell lung cancer that had already advanced to Stage IV. Chemotherapy treatment was started on November 21. As she was in pain, morphine was also prescribed.

Equipped with oxygen and a wheelchair, Laurie was able to return home. In a letter circulated to staff, advisors, and others associated with the Institute she wrote: "Now I ask for your help, your support, your love, your dedication and your prayers so that I may lean on you during these difficult times that I personally face." It was now time, she added, to search actively for a new executive director; Skip Atwater would act as general manager until an appointment was made.

The end came quickly. On the night of Thursday, December 14, Laurie complained of chest pains. Maria, who was staying with her, called an ambulance as there was no way she could carry both Laurie and the oxygen cylinder to her car. She waited with her until a room was found. The second round of chemotherapy was due, but Laurie's physical condition was deteriorating and before long she ceased to eat or drink. Early in the morning of Monday, December 18, Maria, who had been visiting frequently, called Penny to tell her that Laurie had died around 3 A.M. Two days later, in accordance with her wishes, Laurie was cremated. She asked that her ashes be scattered in the ocean off the Florida Keys, where she had used to swim with the dolphins.

Laurie faced death with the same courage with which she had faced the prospect of following in the footsteps of her father, having been given the task of developing and expanding the work he had been engaged in for four decades. His confidence in her abilities proved well founded. Thanks to her leadership, The Monroe Institute not only continued to survive but flourished as well. She left it ready and prepared to move confidently into the future.

The direct Monroe connection with the Institute ended with Laurie's death, as her uncle Emmett had retired from the board of directors some months previously. The board elected Dr. Al Dahlberg, a longtime member of the advisory board and a good friend of the Monroe family, as its chairman, and Skip Atwater was appointed president of the Institute. The Monroe Institute is now ready to move into its own as a fully independent body.

Notes

1. Peter and Elizabeth Fenwick, *Past Lives* (Headline, 1999).

2. See *Focusing the Whole Brain,* edited by Ronald Russell (Hampton Roads, 2004). Cats, however, seem to create their own healing system, as their purring carries frequencies that are the best for bone growth, muscle and tendon repair, relief and the reduction of edema. These frequencies are 25 and 50 Hz.

3. Recent research projects involving the Hemi-Sync binaural beat technology have included the following topics: treatment for anxiety, relief of insomnia, improving memory recall, relieving postoperative pain, aiding hypnotic susceptibility, improving the functioning and life quality of brain trauma patients, reducing the required amount of anesthesia and intraoperative analgesia, ameliorating the side effects of radiation treatment and chemotherapy, assessing its effect on mood and attention, sharpening concentration and cognitive performance, helping children diagnosed with ADHD, and assisting children coping with severe and moderate behavior disability.

   These projects have taken place or are in progress in eleven universities in the United States, and in hospitals in the United States, England, Norway, and Italy. To date, several have been published in professional journals while many more have been accepted in part fulfillment of degree requirements.

Among the journals recorded are the following: *Anesthesia* 54 (1999), *Anesthesia & Analgesia* 98 (2004), *American Journal of Clinical Hypnosis* 43 (2000), *Alternative Therapies in Health & Medicine* 7 (2001), *Journal of the American Society for Psychical Research* 92–93 (1998–99).

4. *Harsh Lessons & Unexpected Gifts,* by Gail Blanchette (Business Basics & More, 2001).

5. As a postscript to this, a few years later Angela was a witness in a court case that divided her family. Her father accused her of being unreliable, if not mad, as she "went out of her body." The judge rejected this accusation on the grounds that the OBE was well documented and not at all abnormal and declared he was happy to accept Angela's evidence.

6. See *Focusing the Whole Brain,* edited by Ronald Russell (Hampton Roads, 2004).

CHAPTER 13

Robert Monroe and the Exploration of Consciousness

Monroe's exploration, and consequent explanation, of consciousness is grounded on a firm philosophic base. Professor Joseph Felser sums up Monroe's philosophy as deriving from two key principles. "Expressed in imperative form, they are: 'Explore everywhere!' and 'Question everything!'" These, he explains, may be understood as the principles of "radical empiricism" and "radical iconoclasm," respectively. Taking "radical" in its literal meaning of "deeply rooted," Felser affirms that "Bob's philosophical roots are so deeply and closely intertwined as to be practically and theoretically inseparable. Like the Taoist root principles of Yin and Yang, each leads to, and complements, the other."[1]

A working definition of an empiricist is, Felser says, "someone who believes that knowledge is based primarily on experience." He continues: "The more experience we have, the faster our knowledge grows. So it's quite logical and natural that an empiricist is an explorer of new worlds of fact, a patient, but persistent, gatherer of raw data." As for iconoclasm, we have Monroe's own words from *Ultimate Journey:*

> What we need to do, whether in or out-of-body, is
> to ignore or tear down the No Trespassing signs, the

333

taboos, the notice that says Holy of Holies, the distortions of time and translation, the soft black holes of euphoria, the mysticisms, the myths, the fantasies of an eternal father or mother image, and then take a good look with our acquired and growing left brain. Nothing is sacred to the point where it should not be investigated or put under inquiry.

Personal experience uninhibited by belief systems is at the core of his thinking.

The preoccupation of so much of humankind with belief systems was a major concern of Robert Monroe, especially those systems applying to science and religion. He became convinced that belief systems were incompatible with genuine freedom, inhibited personal experience, and hence also impeded the expansion of consciousness.

Through his personal experience Monroe came to understand that, as he expresses it, "the physical universe, including the whole of humankind, is an ongoing creative process. There is, indeed," he continues, "a Creator." Monroe regards the existence of a Creator as a "Known," not as a belief. He takes this "Known" a stage further, adding that the Creator "is beyond our comprehension as long as we remain human." The Creator does not require worship or recognition, does not punish or intercede in human lives, has a purpose that we do not comprehend, establishes simple universal laws, and "is the designer of the ongoing process of which we are a part." In the light of current controversies, there are some who would leap upon that last statement in order to recruit Monroe to the host of contemporary believers in Intelligent Design. At this he would raise an eyebrow, murmur that his statements, however others might understand or interpret them, came not through any belief but through his own personal experience. So, if you want to know, go find out for yourself. It was to help others to find out for themselves that he created the program known as *Lifeline.*

One of Monroe's greatest gifts is his ability to express profundity in language that anyone can understand, an ability that he acquired from his many years in radio. He avoids jargon and technicalities, writing and speaking in straightforward English, never seeking to overwhelm or persuade the reader or listener by displaying his superior knowledge. When it comes to the contentious area of consciousness studies, whose practitioners, with very few exceptions, are not famous for economy or simplicity of expression, Monroe stands out as a beacon of clarity. To describe the various states or phases of consciousness he developed what Felser calls "a neutral terminology"—the Focus states—each accompanied by a number and a simple phrase—"mind awake, body asleep," "a state of expanded awareness," and so on. In so doing he succeeded in demystifying the subject so that his audience required no training in science, philosophy, meditation, or linguistics to understand what he was talking about.

Monroe expresses his own thoughts on consciousness, as evidenced in the philosophy and practice of his Institute, in two paragraphs in chapter 2 of *Far Journeys:*

> Stated simply, the Institute holds to the concept that (1) consciousness and the focusing thereof contain any and all solutions to the life processes that man desires or encounters; (2) greater understanding and appreciation of such consciousness can be achieved only through interdisciplinary approaches and coordination; (3) the results of related research effort are meaningful only if reduced to practical application, to "something of

value" within the context of the contemporary culture or era.

This leads us to the base that consciousness is a form of energy at work. The first step must therefore be to perceive the energy itself—no small trick when you are using yourself to measure yourself, as it were. Once it is perceived in its raw form, you are on the way to understanding how it is naturally used. Such perception will permit a broader and more deliberate control of such energy fields. From control, it is a logical step to apply it in new and expanded forms. This is no more than a circumlocutory way of saying that if you can find the stuff that makes you think and be, you can use it in ways that you are not using it now.

In the epilogue to *Far Journeys* Monroe takes his thoughts further. Here he makes a single positive statement: "Consciousness is Focused Energy." It is, he claims, "a manifestation of a system generated by a form of dynamic energy yet to be identified and measured by mainstream human civilization, a system that is present in all carbon-based organic life." While consciousness is not dependent on time-space, it is, he says, "widely focused into time-space physical matter. This is not the totality of energy consciousness involved, as other forms of the same consciousness are active concurrently in divergent systems of reality." He also comments that, when we are deeply asleep, our consciousness is completely detached from physical reality.

In *Ultimate Journey* Monroe expands on this in a section headed "Consciousness is a Continuum":

In our focused wakefulness, we as Human Minds employ that part of the consciousness spectrum limited to time-space. This is made possible by the device we identify as a physical body, with its five physical senses. This physical body permits us to express externally our mind-consciousness through physical activity and communication.

When this focusing is affected for any reason, our mind begins to drift along the consciousness spectrum away from time-space perception, becoming less aware of the immediate physical world. When this happens, we become conscious in another form. The fact that we often have difficulty in remembering correctly our participation in that other part of the consciousness spectrum does not negate its reality. The problem lies in perception and translation, diffused and distorted as they are by the use of current time-space systems of analysis and measurement.

The spectrum of consciousness ranges, seemingly endlessly, beyond time-space into other energy systems. It also continues "downward" through animal and plant life, possibly into the subatomic level. Everyday human consciousness is active in only a small segment of the consciousness continuum.

Among scientific and philosophical investigators of consciousness, Monroe is almost always confined to a footnote, if indeed he is referred to at all. One of the more dismal features of contemporary consciousness studies is that almost without exception their authors confine their references—and hence presumably their reading—to other academic consciousness studies. The so-called anomalous experiences such as near-death and mystical experiences, telepathy, psychokinesis, and the out-of-body experience itself, seldom, if ever, get a mention, and the same can be said of those novels, autobiographies, and poems where consciousness is examined and explored, implicitly if not always explicitly. With Monroe, consciousness is at the center of his work. The exploration of consciousness is the principal theme of his books, and the ability to move voluntarily into different phases of consciousness is what the participants learn from the courses he devised.

However, when Monroe is referred to in published works—and there are reference to him and the Institute in some two hundred books published between 1965 and 2005—almost all of their titles will be found in the "Metaphysical" or "Mind, Body, Spirit" sections of bookstores. This is where his own books, and the books of other writers on consciousness from a first-person perspective, are likely to be found also. So we need to investigate whether it is possible to relate Monroe's work to any of the current scientific and philosophical approaches to the study of consciousness.

In recent decades, consciousness has come to the fore as one of the great problems confronting Western science and philosophy. The attempt to explain consciousness has developed into a sort of academic business, with professorships and lectureships accumulating and publications multiplying year after year. It has also become a hunting ground for many professionals with qualifications in other disciplines: physicists, neurologists, neurobiologists, geneticists, cognitive scientists, and so on, as well as philosophers, psychologists, and the occasional theologian.

Researchers have come up with a variety of definitions and explanations. We look at just three examples: For clinical neuropsychologist James Newman, "consciousness is a function of an identifiable neural architecture which we have termed the extended reticular-thalamic activation system." For the neurobiologist Gerald Edelman, "consciousness is an outcome of a recursively comparative memory in which previous self-non-self categorizations are *continually* related to ongoing present perceptual categorizations and their short-term succession, before such categorizations have become part of that memory." The philosopher John Searle tells us that "consciousness is a natural biological phenomenon that does not fit comfortably into either of the traditional categories of mental and physical. It is caused by lower-level microprocesses in the brain and it is a feature of the brain at the higher macro levels." These quotations demonstrate a special difficulty: consciousness is a function, an outcome, a phenomenon—but none of these attempts at definition succeed in clarifying what consciousness *is*.

What seems to have happened is that the problem of consciousness (where it comes from, what it is) has been interpreted as "science's last great frontier." It has come to be regarded as if it were one more territory that must be conquered, mapped, and taken into control, using weapons and technologies that have proved themselves in other fields. The philosopher Mary Midgley, however, puts it slightly differently:

> Investigators using this map approach their new problem on the jigsaw principle, armed with puzzle-pieces from various existing physical sciences such as neurology, quantum mechanics, genetics or the study of evolution . . . They try to fit their chosen pieces into the problem. But the problem does not accommodate them because it is one of a quite different kind. It is actually about how to relate different puzzles. It concerns *how best to fit together the different aspects of ourselves— notably, ourselves as subjects and ourselves as objects, our inner and our outer lives.*[2]

In fairness it must be said that not all scientists are confident of finding answers. "I think I can safely say that no one understands human consciousness," wrote the physicist Richard Feynman in *The*

Character of Physical Law (1992). Danah Zohar described it as "one of the least understood phenomena in the world." Nobel prizewinner Brian Josephson declared that "science has as yet made little headway in understanding the phenomenon or even deciding what it is," and the physicist Nick Herbert said, "About all we know of consciousness is that it has to do with the head rather than the foot."

What, then, is this consciousness that Monroe spent so many years exploring? Leaving aside the problem of definition, (because, generally speaking, most of us do have *some* idea of what we are talking about) it may help us to understand more about Monroe's explorations by referring to the well-known statement by William James.

> Our ordinary waking consciousness, rational consciousness as we call it, is but one special type of consciousness whilst all about it, parted from it by the filmiest of screens, there lie potential forms of consciousness entirely different. We may go through life without suspecting their existence; but apply the requisite stimulus, and at a touch they are there in all their completeness, definite types of mentality which probably somewhere have their field of application and adaptation. No account of the universe in its totality can be final which leaves these other forms of consciousness quite disregarded. How to regard them is the question—for they may determine attitudes though they cannot furnish formulas, and open a region though they fail to give a map.

These potential forms of consciousness are what Charles Tart defined as altered states. "A state is an altered state if it is significantly and discretely different from some baseline to which we want to compare it," he says, in *Open Mind, Discriminating Mind* (1989). "Since we usually take ordinary waking consciousness as our standard of comparison, a state like nocturnal dreaming is an altered state." For examples of different altered states, we can refer to meditation, mystical and transcendental experiences, lucid dreaming, out-of-body and near-death experiences. Where mood-altering stimuli are employed, such as drugs or alcohol, altered states can become uncontrollable and sometimes harmful. Monroe's Hemispheric Synchronization, which is neither mood-altering nor physically stimulating, enables those who use it to move freely into different phases or states. Such states may be accessible by anyone at any time, but the Hemi-Sync frequencies can hold you in a particular state for as long as you are listening to them. They act also as training wheels; once you are accustomed to moving into these different states, you can discard Hemi-Sync and do so of your own free will.

These different states are first-person experiences, which Western science has much difficulty in handling. Such experiences are generally considered to fall within the province of those comparatively recently developed disciplines, psychiatry and psychotherapy—or possibly to that much older discipline, divinity—where advice, treatment, or consolation may be administered by professional practitioners.

But this is not the whole story. There are other ways of approaching the matter of consciousness than those currently popular in the West. "Consciousness in the western discourse is a much abused concept," says the Indian philosopher and psychologist K. Ramakrishna Rao in a recent article in the *Journal of Consciousness Studies.* "The bewildering multiplicity of meanings of consciousness left many in the West wondering what exactly consciousness means." He points out that "the phenomena of consciousness appear to have an intrinsically subjective character," and need to be studied from the aspect of the person having the experience, in sharp contrast to the approach of Western science, always happier with a third-person perspective. Only when it is thought there may be something wrong with the person having the experience—he may be physically ill or mentally deranged—does Western science or medicine attend to him. This is what happened with Monroe in the early days of his out-of-body experiences, when he subjected himself to physical and psychological examinations to see if anything amiss could be found in his body or mind to explain what was happening to him. The doctors and psychologists who examined him found him sane with no evidence of physical malfunction. They later went on to evaluate reports from 339 individuals who claimed to have experienced out-of-body travel, of whom 228 had more than one experience and seventy-four had more than ten. No indications of mental imbalance or physical malady were revealed in this survey.

Those well-qualified and experienced researchers who investigated Monroe's Hemi-Sync process are satisfied that it is scientifically valid and can be applied legitimately and helpfully in a number of different situations. Improving sleep patterns, inducing relaxation, accelerating the learning process—these and many more applications have been tested and proved to work. Monroe's personal experiences, however, occurred without the use of Hemi-Sync or any other process or stimulus. Western science, therefore, finds it difficult, if not impossible, to provide any sort of explanation and has paid scant, if any, attention to the content of his experiences.

Turning Eastward, however, we find the approach is very different. Ramakrishna Rao includes the following points in a summary of the scope and substance of classical Indian psychology:

- Indian psychology is study of the person.

- The person is embodied consciousness.

- Consciousness is fundamental and irreducible to brain states.

- Consciousness in the human context appears circumscribed, conditioned, and clouded by a vortex of forces generated by the mind-body complex.

- The mind is different from consciousness. It is a material form, but has the capacity to interface with consciousness at one end and the brain at the other.

He adds that in the classical Indian tradition "consciousness-as-such is essentially non-intentional. It has no content, and consequently is not an object of cognition. It is non-relational and yet foundational for all awareness and knowledge." The quest in the Indian tradition "is for the transformation of the individual and for achieving higher states of consciousness." Yet he is not convinced that the Indian tradition answers all the questions, because it tends to ignore or overlook "what are very pervasive and basic to human nature, i.e. the normal processes."

Rao ends his discussion by comparing Indian and Western ideas on consciousness as representing "two distinct conceptual streams that flow in two different directions." He suggests that the Eastern stream may be too narrow, "with steadfast focus on consciousness-as-such." In contrast, the Western stream is too shallow, "involving only the periphery of consciousness and thus unable to navigate with the heavy weight (hard problem) of subjective and pure conscious states." If there were a confluence between the two, he adds, "we may be in a better position to understand consciousness in its multiple facets."[3]

Viewing Monroe's journeys in the light of Rao's account of the classical Indian tradition, we can see that they accord more closely with Indian thought than with contemporary Western scientific notions. Aspects of his journeys can also be viewed in the light of the Buddhist contemplative tradition. According to this, writes B. Alan Wallace, "the essential stream of consciousness of any sentient being—human or otherwise—cannot be utterly destroyed, nor can it be freshly created." There is "an unbroken continuum of consciousness throughout life, the death process, an intermediate state, and on to the next life." At first this seems to imply that the population must always remain stable, which is manifestly absurd, but this argument is answered by the Buddhist contention that the process of rebirth also occurs between human and nonhuman forms. Moreover, "there are countless other worlds inhabited by human and non-human forms of life: and a being that dies in one world may be reborn in another."[4]

Tibetan Buddhism divides our existence into four continuously interlinked realities: life; dying and death; after death; rebirth. As explained by the Tibetan scholar Sogyal Rinpoche, these are known as the four bardos: the natural bardo of life; the painful bardo of dying; the luminous bardo of *dharmata;* and the karmic bardo of rebirth.[5] Several of Monroe's out-of-body experiences appear to involve visits into one or more of these bardos. The bardo of dying and the karmic bardo of rebirth are realities that are encountered in *Far Journeys,* and the luminous bardo of *dharmata* (defined as "the naked unconditioned truth, the nature of reality, or the true nature of phenomenal existence") is revealed in *Ultimate Journey.* There are also similarities with the concept of all four bardos in elements of the *Lifeline* and *Going Home* programs.

Sogyal Rinpoche points out that most people understand reincarnation to imply there is some thing that reincarnates, traveling from life to life. But Buddhism does not accept an entity such as a soul or ego that survives physical death. "What provides the continuity between lives is not an entity, we believe, but the ultimately subtlest level of consciousness." Although Monroe nowhere expresses anything similar to this concept, it is unlikely that he would disagree with it.

With the above in mind, it becomes clear that many of Monroe's ideas and conclusions, derived from his several hundreds—possibly thousands—of out-of-body experiences, have stronger connections with the philosophies of the East than of the West. Professor Christopher Bache declares "it is not surprising that mainstream philosophers have ignored Monroe's work, as it presents a profound challenge to the materialist vision that rules the modern mind." He comments on Monroe's "sophisticated understanding of the bardo," on his "profound vision of human evolution," on providing "permission to believe that the majority of intelligent life in the universe is actually non-physical," and on his vision of reality that "assumes the concept of reincarnation, and therefore . . . is a vision that sees human beings developing across enormous tracts of time." He adds that, according to Monroe, "all our lives on Earth represent only a small portion of our true existence . . . However, if we begin to understand and integrate the hidden half of our life cycle, the half that takes place between death and rebirth, we can begin to reappropriate the large trajectory of the soul-being that we are underneath our present human identity."[6]

Monroe's three books contain no footnotes, no references, no quotations from other authors. They are simply records of certain experiences obtained in an altered state of consciousness. Some of these experiences may seem banal and in some the reader may suspect a degree of contrivance—as if the material has been trimmed here and there, polished possibly, with the intention of making a point. Many—perhaps most—are fully convincing as they stand, however. In this they are reminiscent of reported mystical experiences such as those of Hildegarde of Bingen or William Blake. Yet Monroe's vision is distinctive in that it owes nothing to the Bible, the

Koran, the Upanishads, or any published text. What is most remarkable is its coherence. It is grounded in logic, not in faith.

We may not share his vision nor may we feel like adopting it as our own. But we have to acknowledge that Monroe's experiences were not inspired—or sullied—by mood-altering drugs, nor were they induced by religious practices, by fasting, or by physical or mental disorder. They simply happened, spontaneously to begin with and later through purposeful contact with what may be described as guidance, at first defined as the Inspec—Intelligent Species—and later understood by Monroe as part of himself. In his final journeys it was revealed to him that his guidance came from his "I There," that nonphysical "I" that contains all previous and present lifetimes and is composed of energy outside time-space—(M) Field energy, as Monroe calls it.[7]

There is an extensive literature describing ventures into nonphysical reality including religious texts, mystical writings, and personal accounts carrying varying degrees of conviction. What distinguishes Monroe's approach is that he not only described many of his experiences occurring over more than thirty years, but that he also sought to devise a means by which others might explore these nonphysical realms. In this he was not seeking to make converts to a particular belief system or to set himself up as some sort of guru. His approach reveals a generosity of spirit in that his main intent was to help those who, aware that they might be more than their physical body, were curious to find out about that "more" and hence were willing to transform themselves.

This was his aim from the outset, reinforced in the penultimate chapter of his last book. "How could I organize all that I had experienced into such a shape that it could be absorbed and put into practice by others?" he asks. "Not only that: how could those experiences, which for me had stretched over years, be compressed into a timeframe which others would find practical and appropriate?" His answer to these questions, to some extent at least, was the *Lifeline* program, whose effect can be measured by the many hundreds of reports in the Institute's records.

Monroe's reading did not include books on the scientific study of consciousness. His conversational approach in his writings and talks is devoid of the weighty vocabulary of academia. He was an explorer, not a theorist, and, certainly to begin with, he had no clear idea as to where his explorations might lead. At the outset of his journeys there was neither planning nor intention. The sharp-suited, left hemisphere–dominated businessman found himself following an uncertain track through a kind of jungle with no guide, no map, and nothing but a torch powered by his own consciousness to light his way. It took much courage to move forward, leaving security and certainty behind.

Christopher Bache points out how these explorations intensified and developed. "The metaphysical vision contained in his first book . . . is primitive compared to that found in his second, published fifteen years later, and his third is more complete still." He adds by way of explanation, "What becomes available in non-ordinary states is always governed by the consciousness one brings to the encounter. Repeated immersion in these states slowly changes one's baseline consciousness, and as one's baseline changes, new levels of reality open around one. Thus Monroe is constantly outgrowing himself."[8] As time passed, Monroe was able to exert more control or management over his experiences so that they achieved a greater degree of consistency. While for many of his readers his earlier journeys raise a number of questions and, in some instances, doubts—that oft-quoted bruise where he claimed to have pinched his friend, for example—the later expeditions into the farther reaches carry strong conviction. So effective are some of his descriptions that it is only too easy to fall into the error of regarding the regions he traverses as actual geographical locations rather than states or phases of consciousness.

We have seen that the theories and conclusions of mainstream Western research into consciousness have little, if any, connection with Monroe's experiences or ideas. This, however, is not quite the whole story. Researchers outside the mainstream, perhaps regarded as mavericks or oddities by some of those within it, have through experiment and observation suggested alternative approaches to the problem. One account of consciousness to which Monroe's concepts and experiences show some approximation appeared in *The Conscious Universe,* by Dean Radin, sometime director of the Consciousness Research Laboratory at the University of Nevada.[9] While Radin does not provide a definition, he suggests a number of properties which, he says, are derived from a combination of Western and Eastern philosophies. Some of these properties are summarized as follows:

Consciousness extends beyond the individual. The strength of consciousness in an individual fluctuates from moment to moment and is regulated by focus of attention. Some states of consciousness have higher focus than others. A group of individuals can be said to have group consciousness, which strengthens when the group's attention is focused on a common object or event. Radin also maintains from the evidence of a vast number of experiments that consciousness can affect the probabilities of events and that it injects order into systems in proportion to the strength of consciousness present.

Participants in the Institute's programs would provide any amount of anecdotal evidence to support Radin's conclusions. Using the term *psi* as a neutral term for all extrasensory perception and psychokinetic phenomena, he includes out-of-body experiences, reincarnation, near-death experiences, remote-viewing, telepathy, and precognition under this heading. Many of these so-called paranormal experiences are reported by these participants and also by

Monroe himself. Radin comments: "What psi offers to the puzzle about consciousness is the observation that information can be obtained in many ways that bypass the ordinary sensory system altogether." These phenomena are all first-person experiences—the type of experiences that the purely scientific approach does not cope with very effectively. The information obtained from these experiences is as subject to scrutiny and examination as information obtained by any "normal" means—from newspapers and journals, television and radio, and so on. Once it has been tested and, if possible, corroborated, then it may well prove to be "something of value" not only to the individual but quite possibly to society at large.

Another relevant observation is a result of research by psychiatrist and neurophysiologist Dr. Peter Fenwick, who has made an intensive study of near-death experiences.[10] Fenwick found that reports of these, along with certain transcendent experiences—a term that applies to many of Monroe's OBEs—appear to give "a subjective view of what lies beyond the physical, suggesting that the very structure of the world is spiritual, that consciousness is primary and unitary and that individual consciousness is part of the whole and survives death." This subjective view is shared by many—probably most—of those who have participated in Monroe's programs, whether they have had previous personal experience of psi or not. The prompting that the program material provides enables the individual to let go of the visible and tangible external world and move quickly and easily into a deep meditative state. This state can be so profound that Buddhist priests who have attended Institute programs say that it resembles the state that had taken them many years of disciplined practice in meditation to achieve.

This meditative state for many program participants is a staging post rather than a terminus. Instances of telepathic communication, precognition, and remote-viewing are occasionally reported and their accuracy has frequently been confirmed. Transcendent experiences, often ultimately indescribable because words are too limiting to express their fullness, are not uncommon. Participants sometimes sense that they have moved into another dimension beyond time and space, or into a different reality that they find themselves able to revisit when on another occasion they move into that same state of consciousness. This ability to move freely and safely into these farther regions, to explore beyond the scope of imagination, and then to return unharmed to the demands and necessities of daily life is a priceless gift that Monroe's researches have made available to anyone who chooses to accept it. In such an altered state you can recognize and perhaps share the vision of the poet William Blake:

> To see a World in a Grain of Sand
> And a Heaven in a Wild Flower,
> Hold Infinity in the palm of your hand
> And Eternity in an hour.

There is also another facet to this gift. Program participants often find that they can tap in to information that they have previously found inaccessible. All information is available "somehow and somewhere" so that moving into an altered state of consciousness—a state of expanded awareness perhaps—may reveal answers to questions or solutions to problems that the usual methods of inquiry have failed to produce. Nor do you need to put on headphones and tune in to the Hemi-Sync material to seek your answer or solution. Once you are accustomed to the feeling of the space—the state of consciousness—created by listening to particular frequencies you are able to re-create that feeling when you need it, no matter where you are and what you are doing. As Monroe often said, the tapes and CDs that carry Hemi-Sync are no more than training wheels, to be discarded when you no longer need them to help you on your journey.

It is appropriate at this stage to look again at Monroe's one formal statement on this very important and topical subject: "Consciousness is Focused Energy." "Energy is in fact the substance from which all elementary particles, all atoms and therefore all things are made, and energy is that which moves . . . Energy may be called the fundamental cause for all change in the world." So says Nobel physicist Werner Heisenberg. Another Nobel prizeman, Wolfgang Pauli, answering the question "What remains of the old ideas of matter and substance?" states simply "The answer is *energy*. This is the true substance, that which is conserved: only the form in which it appears is changing." This relates to what Monroe discovered in his explorations and called the (M) Field, defining it as "a nonphysical energy field that permeates time-space including our Earth Life System."

It so happens that there is a particular theory of consciousness, developed by Professor Mark Woodhouse of Georgia State University, that has some relevance to this. Woodhouse calls his theory "Energy Monism." It is based on his contention that "energy and consciousness are fundamentally understood as aspects of each other," and they share some of each other's properties. Woodhouse, however, would not accept Monroe's assertion that one actually *is* the other. This is how he explains his idea:

> The core foundation of Energy Monism . . . is that energy is, everywhere throughout the universe and up and down the Great Spectrum of Being, the "outside" manifestation of consciousness, and consciousness is everywhere the inner aspect or "inside" of energy . . . Both energy and consciousness parallel each other all the way up and down the spectrum so to speak. Neither grows out of the other.

In illustrating his argument, Woodhouse, whose approach is notably open-minded, makes reference to the out-of-body experience.

> Whatever it is that travels from a body to a target destination and back again has several key features: a sense of self, rudimentary cognitive, emotive and perceptual abilities, location in space, travel through space, and in some cases the ability to create physical changes in a target area. Thus, this traveling sense of self carries with it both conscious and energetic aspects. Something not normally visible to the naked eye, which also occupies space, would have to be energetic or force-like—whether or not it is currently measurable by physics.[11]

Another investigator who uses the out-of-body experience as part of his case for a theory of consciousness is the physicist Amit Goswami. At first his scientific training caused him to regard the OBE as an illusion, but relating it to the evidence of the reality of remote-viewing caused him to think again. "The validity of the out-of-body experience as a genuine phenomenon of consciousness has gained credibility," he wrote in *The Self-Aware Universe,* declaring that it is "the nonlocality of our consciousness" that provides the explanation. "The technical name for signal-less, instantaneous action at a distance is nonlocality," he explains.[12]

Goswami's argument for the nonlocality of consciousness develops from the famous "Bell test experiments" by the French physicist Alain Aspect and his colleagues at Orsay in the early 1980s, which demonstrated that "when two quantum objects are correlated, if we measure one, (thus collapsing its wave function) the other's wave function is collapsed as well—even at a macroscopic distance, even when there is no signal in space-time to mediate their connection." So far, so good; but Goswami still believed that consciousness could be understood by science and that—somehow—it emerges from the brain. It needed a friend—an experienced mystic—to convince him. "Comprehend what the mystics are saying," he was told. "Consciousness is prior and unconditioned. It is all there is. There is nothing but God."

"We do not see it," Goswami writes, " because we are so enamoured of experience, of our melodramas, of our attempts to predict and control, to understand and manipulate everything rationally. In our efforts we miss the simple thing—the simple truth that it is all God, which is the mystic's way of saying that it is all consciousness. Physics explains phenomena, but consciousness is not a phenomenon: instead all else are phenomena in consciousness."

Whether or not we agree with these ideas, they do seem to show that the hold of materialist science on theories of consciousness is beginning to weaken. It may be that in the future more attention will be paid to the significance of transcendent, mystical, and other so-called anomalous experiences, including the well-documented out-of-body experiences of Robert Monroe. In a chapter on the OBE in the comprehensive study *Varieties of Anomalous Experience,* Carlos Alvarado expresses the hope that "future discussion on OBEs will not have to be conducted solely in the context of a psychology of the exotic or the unusual, but in the wider context of the study of the totality of human experience."[13] It is in this context that we should place Monroe's contribution to the understanding of consciousness.[14] Inspired by his personal experiences, he succeeded in designing a means of enabling many thousands of individuals to expand their awareness and explore their own consciousness without recourse to drugs or other stimulants. In addition, he introduced hundreds of thousands of individuals to the perspectives of the altered state defined as out-of-body, enabling them to acquire knowledge and experience thereby. But it would be a grave injustice if he were to be measured in the future only by the number of paragraphs and footnotes devoted to him in publications dealing with research into consciousness. It is his gift to others that is his most valuable legacy.

Notes

1. Quotations are from Professor Felser's keynote address to the 2005 Professional Seminar at The Monroe Institute. His book, *The Way Back to Paradise,* was published by Hampton Roads in 2005.

2. *Science and Poetry* (Routledge, 2001).

3. *Journal of Consciousness Studies* 12, no. 3 (2005).

4. *Choosing Reality,* by B. Alan Wallace (Snow Lion, 2003 [1996]).

5. *The Tibetan Book of Living and Dying,* by Sogyal Rinpoche (HarperSanFrancisco, 1992).

6. *Dark Night, Early Dawn,* by Christopher Bache (SUNY, 2000).

7. Ervin Laszlo (interview in *Network Review* 91 [Summer 2006]) talks of "a field that conserves and conveys information across the universe," which he terms the Akashic field. This has interesting similarities with Monroe's (M) Field.

8. Bache, *Dark Night, Early Dawn.*

9. *The Conscious Universe,* by Dean Radin (Harper Edge, 1997).

10. *The Truth in the Light,* by Peter and Elizabeth Fenwick (Headline, 1995).

11. *Energy Monism,* by Mark Woodhouse, in Scientific & Medical Network, *Network 62.*

12. *The Self-Aware Universe,* by Amit Goswami (Putnam, 1995).

13. *Varieties of Anomalous Experience,* edited by E. Cardena, S. J. Lynn, and S. Krippner (APA, 2002).

14. Justine Owens, PhD, of the University of Virginia, who enjoyed several conversations with Monroe on the connections between academic psychological research and his own independent investigations, commented that "Bob Monroe had deep intellectual ties with the scholarly study of the human mind and his self-taught understanding of the basic principles of learning, memory and self-organizing principles or systems theory was truly impressive." Although there was a certain tension between the academic approach and his own independent investigations, Monroe had no need to see himself as a second-class citizen in this respect.

APPENDIX

The Hemi-Sync Process

F. Holmes "Skip" Atwater, Research Division, The Monroe Institute

Introduction

Robert Monroe developed and patented a binaural-beat technology called the Hemi-Sync auditory-guidance system. The Monroe Institute, a 501c(3) nonprofit research and educational organization, uses this Hemi-Sync system within an educational process. During this process individuals listen to a combination of multiplexed audio binaural beats that are mixed with music, pink sound, and/or the natural sound of surf. Binaural-beat stimulation, coupled with the effects of the other components within the Hemi-Sync process, encourages access to focused, meditative, and alert states of consciousness.

Ancient cultures used the natural power of sound and music to safely influence states of consciousness in religious ceremonies and to promote psychological and physical health. Today, the idea that auditory stimulation can affect consciousness is widely accepted. Hemi-Sync represents the state-of-the-art in the technological application of the natural power of sound and it has a variety of beneficial applications. Studies have shown improvements in sensory integration, relaxation, meditation, stress reduction, pain management, sleep, and health care. Further studies have shown effectiveness in accessing anomalous states of consciousness, reports of peak experiences, a possible antinociceptive effect during anesthesia, and the treatment of anxiety.

Hemi-Sync has also proven effective in producing enriched learning environments, enhanced memory, improved creativity, increased intuition, improved reliability in remote viewing, telepathy, and out-of-body experience. Understanding of the effectiveness of Hemi-Sync goes beyond knowing about the natural power of sound to include the well-known autonomic effects of restricted environmental stimulation, controlled breathing, progressive relaxation, and the psychology of affirmations and visualizations. This paper discusses the brain-mind model, brain waves and their relationship to states of consciousness and the role of the reticular activating system (RAS) in regulating brain waves, and beneficial social-psychological conditioning and educational processes.

Binaural Beats and the Physiology of the Brain

Binaural beats were discovered in 1839 by a German experimenter, H. W. Dove. The human ability to "hear" binaural beats appears to be the result of evolutionary adaptation. Many evolved species can detect binaural beats because of their brain structure. The frequencies at which binaural beats can be detected change depending upon the size of the species' cranium. In the human, binaural beats can be detected when carrier tones are below approximately 1500 Hz. The relevant issue here, however, is this innate ability of the brain to detect phase differences between the ears that enables the perception of binaural beats.

The sensation of "hearing" binaural beats occurs when two coherent sounds of nearly similar frequencies (less than 1500 Hz) are presented, one to each ear, and the brain detects phase differences between these sounds. This phase difference would normally provide directional information to the listener but when presented with stereo headphones or speakers the brain integrates the two signals, producing a sensation of a third sound called the binaural beat.

Perceived as a fluctuating rhythm at the frequency of the difference between the two (stereo left and right) auditory inputs, binaural beats originate in the brainstem within the contralateral audio-processing regions called the superior olivary nuclei. This auditory sensation is neurologically routed to the reticular formation and simultaneously volume is conducted to the cortex where it can be objectively measured as a frequency-following response.

There have been numerous anecdotal reports and a growing number of research efforts reporting beneficial brain-state changes associated with Hemi-Sync's binaural beats. Binaural beats have been associated with changes in arousal states, attentional focus, and levels of awareness leading to sensory integration, improved response to alpha biofeedback training, relaxation, meditation, stress reduction, pain management, improved sleep, health care, enriched learning environments, enhanced memory, creativity, treatment of children with developmental disabilities, the facilitation of attention, peak and other exceptional experiences, enhancement of hypnotizability, treatment of alcoholic depression, positive effects on vigilance performance and mood, inducing propitious altered states of consciousness, and cortico-thalamic adaptation.

Passively listening to Hemi-Sync binaural beats may not automatically engender a focused state of consciousness. The Hemi-Sync process includes a number of components; binaural beats are only one element. We all maintain a psychophysiological momentum, a homeostasis that may resist the influence of the binaural beats.

Practices such as humming, toning, breathing exercises, autogenic training, and/or biofeedback can be used to interrupt the homeostasis of resistant subjects. Naturally occurring ultradian rhythms driven by the reticular activating system and characterized by periodic changes in arousal, may influence the effectiveness of binaural beats. One's first-person experience in response to binaural-beat stimulation may also be affected by a number of psychological mediating factors.

Brain Waves and Consciousness

Controversies concerning the brain, mind, and consciousness have existed since the early Greek philosophers argued about the nature of the mind-body relationship, and none of these disputes has been resolved. Modern neurologists have located the mind in the brain and have said that consciousness is the result of electrochemical neurological activity. There are, however, a growing number of observations that challenge the completeness of these assertions. There is no neurophysiological research that conclusively demonstrates that the higher levels of mind (intuition, insight, creativity, imagination, understanding, thought, reasoning, intent, decision, knowing, will, spirit, or soul) are located in brain tissue. A resolution to the controversies surrounding the higher mind and consciousness and the mind-body problem in general may require an epistemological shift to include extra-rational ways of knowing and may well elude comprehension by neurochemical brain studies alone.

We are in the midst of a revolution focusing on the study of consciousness. Penfield, an eminent contemporary neurophysiologist, found that the human mind continued to work in spite of the brain's reduced activity under anesthesia. Brain waves were nearly absent while the mind was just as active as in the waking state. The only difference was in the content of the conscious experience. Following Penfield's work, other researchers have reported awareness in comatose patients and there is a growing body of evidence that suggests that reduced cortical arousal while maintaining conscious awareness is possible. These states are variously referred to as meditative, trance, altered, hypnagogic, hypnotic, and twilight-learning states. These various forms of consciousness rest on the maintenance of awareness in a physiologically reduced state of arousal marked by parasympathetic dominance. Highly hypnotizable subjects and adept meditators have demonstrated that maintaining consciousness with reduced cortical arousal is indeed possible in selected individuals, either as a natural ability or as an acquired skill. More and more scientists are expressing doubts about the neurologists' brain-mind model because it fails to answer so many questions about our ordinary experiences and evades our mystical and spiritual queries. Studies in distant mental influence and mental healing also challenge the notion of a mind localized within the brain. Nonlocal events have been proven to occur at the subatomic level and some researchers believe that the physics principles behind these events also underlie nonlocal consciousness-mediated effects. The scientific evidence supporting the phenomenon of remote viewing alone is sufficient to show that mind-consciousness is not a local phenomenon.

If mind-consciousness is not the brain, why then does science relate states of consciousness and mental functioning to brain waves? And why does the Hemi-Sync process include a binaural-beat technology that has the potential to alter brain waves? The first question can be answered in terms of instrumentation. There is no objective way to measure mind or consciousness with an instrument. Mind-consciousness appears to be a field phenomenon that interfaces with the body and the neurological structures of the brain. This field cannot be measured directly with current instrumentation. On the other hand, the electrical potentials of the body can be measured and easily quantified. Contemporary science likes things that can be measured and quantified. The problem here lies in the oversimplification of the observations. EEG patterns measured on the cortex are the result of electroneurological activity of the brain. But the brain's electroneurological activity is not mind-consciousness. Therefore, EEG measurements are only an indirect means of assessing the mind-consciousness interface with the neurological structures of the brain. As crude as this may seem, the EEG has been a reliable way for researchers to estimate states of consciousness based on the relative proportions of EEG frequencies. Stated another way, certain EEG patterns have been historically associated with specific states of consciousness. Although not an absolute, it is reasonable to assume, given the current EEG literature, that if a specific EEG pattern emerges it is probably accompanied by a particular state of consciousness.

The second question raised in the above paragraph requires a more complex explanation. The Hemi-Sync process includes the powerful binaural-beat technology because altering arousal states, attentional focus, and levels of awareness allows for an increased repertoire of mind-consciousness experiences. When brain waves move to lower frequencies (lower arousal) and consciousness is maintained (cognitive experience), a unique state emerges. Practitioners of the Hemi-Sync process call this state of hypnagogia "mind awake/body asleep." Slightly higher brainwave frequencies can lead to hyper-suggestive states of consciousness. Still higher frequencies are associated with the alert and focused levels of attention necessary for the optimal performance of many tasks.

Perceived reality changes depending on the state of consciousness of the perceiver. Some states of consciousness provide limited views of reality, while others provide an expanded awareness of reality. For the most part, states of consciousness vary in response to the ever-changing internal environment and surrounding stimulation.

For example, states of consciousness are subject to influences like drugs and circadian and ultradian rhythms. Specific states of consciousness can also be learned as adaptive behaviors to demanding circumstances. Functioning through the mechanism of the extended reticular-thalamic activating system, Hemi-Sync offers access to a wide variety of altered-state experiences for those wanting to explore the realms of consciousness.

Hemispheric Synchronization

The term "Hemi-Sync" was chosen as a trademark because, under its influence, the two hemispheres of the brain appear to function coherently, or in sync with each other. In addition to certain predominant brainwave frequencies, brainwave coherence is an important factor. Brainwave coherence has to do with brain waves from different parts of the brain having the same frequency and amplitude and being mutually entrained so that they operate in a smooth continuous pattern.

The enhanced inter-hemispheric communication encouraged by the Hemi-Sync process sets the stage for brainwave coherence that, in turn, facilitates whole-brain cognition. Whole-brain cognition is not just a lateral concept (left/right-brain) but a vertical notion too. When cortical brain waves are slowed, the filtering function of the cortex becomes less effective and the limbic system (the "emotional" brain) can more readily interact in the cognitive environment. Images, and other sensory data, arising in the limbic system, in the absence of cortical physical-reality judgment, assume an elevated status in one's subjective experience.

Over a period of time, Hemi-Sync users are likely to develop cerebral laterality or less strongly lateralized (left/right) brains. Such a condition may facilitate attention, learning, and mnemonics realms as well as play a significant role in coordination, athleticism, and creativity. Hemi-Sync users may be able to develop specific linguistic and/or mathematical skills, the ability to hyper-focus attention when appropriate, and the remembering of some types of information with extraordinary clarity and detail.

Although synchronized, coherent brain waves have long been associated with meditative and hypnagogic states, Hemi-Sync may be unique in its ability to induce and improve such states of consciousness. The reason for this is physiological. Each ear is "hardwired" (so to speak) to both hemispheres of the brain. Each hemisphere has its own olivary nucleus (sound-processing center) that receives signals from each ear. When a binaural beat is perceived there are actually two electrochemical, synaptic waves of equal amplitude and frequency present, one in each hemisphere. This is, in and of itself, hemispheric synchrony of synaptic activity. The unique binaural beats of the Hemi-Sync system appear to contribute to the hemispheric synchronization evidenced in meditative and hypnagogic states of consciousness. Hemi-Sync's binaural beats may also enhance brain function by enabling the user to reconcile cross-collosal connectivity at designated brainwave frequencies.

The two cerebral hemispheres of the brain are like two separate information-processing modules. Both are complex cognitive systems; process information independently and in parallel; and their interaction is neither arbitrary nor continuous. States of consciousness can be defined not only in terms of brainwave frequency ratios, but also in terms of hemispheric specialization and/or interaction. An individual's cognitive repertoire and, therefore, his ability to perceive reality and deal with the everyday world, is subject to his ability to experience various states of consciousness.

The Hemi-Sync Process Alters States of Consciousness

The extended reticular-thalamic activation system (ERTAS) regulates brainwave activity, an essential element in altering consciousness. The word reticular means "net-like" and the neural reticular formation itself is a large, net-like diffuse area of the brainstem. The reticular activating system (RAS) interprets and reacts to *information* from internal stimuli, feelings, attitudes, and beliefs as well as external sensory stimuli by regulating arousal states, attentional focus, and levels of awareness—by definition, elements of consciousness itself. How we interpret, respond, and react to *information* then, is managed by the brain's reticular formation stimulating the thalamus and cortex, and controlling attentiveness and levels of arousal.

In order to alter arousal states, attentional focus, and levels of awareness, it is necessary to provide some sort of *information* input to the RAS. Hemi-Sync provides this *information* component. The *information* referred to here is the complex, brainwave-like pattern of the Hemi-Sync binaural beat. This unique binaural-beat (neurologically evidenced by the EEG frequency-following response) is recognized by the RAS as brainwave pattern *information*. If internal stimuli, feelings, attitudes, beliefs, and external sensory stimuli are not in conflict with this *information* (e.g., an internal, even unconscious, fear may be a source of conflict), the RAS will alter states of consciousness to match the Hemi-Sync stimulus as a natural function of maintaining homeostasis.

The brain automatically and actively regulates all body functions to maintain homeostasis—an internal equilibrium. In a natural and constant attempt to maintain a homeostasis of the elements of consciousness, the RAS actively monitors and continues the neural replication of ongoing brainwave states (unless, of course, there is reason to make an adjustment due to new *information* from internal sources or external sensory input).

As time passes, the RAS monitors both the internal and external environment and arousal states, attentional focus, and levels of awareness to determine, from moment to moment, the most suitable way to deal with existing conditions. As long as no conflicts develop, the RAS naturally continues aligning the listener's state of consciousness with the *information* in the brainwave-like pattern of the Hemi-Sync sound field.

In objective, measurable terms, EEG-based research provides evidence of Hemi-Sync's influence on arousal states, attentional focus, and levels of awareness. Since the RAS regulates cortical EEG, monitoring EEG chronicles performance of the RAS. There have been several free-running EEG studies which suggest that Hemi-Sync binaural beats induce alterations in EEG. Because the RAS is responsible for regulating EEG, these studies document measurable changes in RAS function during exposure to Hemi-Sync.

But this is only part of the Hemi-Sync process. First-person experience of consciousness is much more than just arousal states, attentional focus, and levels of awareness. The cognitive content of the experience is what gives it meaning. Whereas a specific state of cortical arousal is induced by the Hemi-Sync binaural beats, the content portion of a focused state of consciousness depends on social-psychological conditioning and the mental ability of the individual. The educational application of the Hemi-Sync technology incorporates these dimensions. In terms of social-psychological conditioning, the Hemi-Sync audio-guidance media provide instructions on relaxation and breathing, affirmations for objectifying personal intent, and guided visual imagery. In the Institute's educational programs, skilled trainers—mediators sensitive to the subtle indices of participants' phrasing, body language, and expressiveness—provide counseling and encourage group interaction to insure an environment conducive to enhanced cognitive experience within specific Hemi-Sync generated states of cortical arousal, called *Focus Levels.*

Trainers are experienced in the realms being explored by program participants. Because they have firsthand knowledge of these worlds they can help others alter their own social-psychological conditioning. Trainers encourage introspection on the part of participants to aid in the integration and realization of novel experiences. When appropriate, trainers encourage participants to reframe their experiences into more useful perspectives.

To the degree that mental ability defines one's capacity to experience, cognitive skills can be enhanced through educational processes. Participants are offered materials to read. Informative lectures are scheduled throughout the duration of the programs. The use of multimedia enhances the presentation of educational materials. Planned group discussions provide the opportunity to share and to inspire each other. Development through practice is at the core of the educational process and participants are given numerous opportunities to experience the exciting focused states of consciousness available within the Hemi-Sync process.

Summary

The patented Hemi-Sync auditory-guidance system provides a safe, natural means to alter arousal states, attentional focus, and levels of awareness. The Hemi-Sync process is a unique combination of this powerful brainwave modification technology, coupled with well-understood psycho-physiological inductive techniques (restricted environmental stimulation, controlled breathing, progressive relaxation, etc.), supportive social-psychological conditioning procedures, and conventional teaching methods.

A fully referenced copy of this article may be obtained from The Monroe Institute, 365 Roberts Mountain Road, Faber, VA 22938. Tel: (434)361-1252. MonroeInst@aol.com www. MonroeInstitute.org

INDEX

About the Author

Ronald Russell was born in Croydon, England. He attended St. Paul's School, London, served in the Royal Air Force (1943–46), and then took an Honours Degree in English Language and Literature at Merton College, Oxford. He followed a career in teaching in Newcastle-upon-Tyne, Monmouth and Ely, Cambridgeshire, and examined and lectured for various universities, including London, Oxford, and Cambridge.

Ronald's earlier books were devoted to the history, exploration, and restoration of canals and waterways in the United Kingdom. He was chairman of the National Rally of Boats in 1971. When his wife Jill undertook long-distance swimming for health reasons, eventually raising some £40,000 for charity through sponsorship, he documented her feats in *Swimming for Life,* an authoritative study of the benefits of swimming for disabled people. He also turned to the study of prints, writing two books on that subject. His *Discovering Antique Prints* sold some fifty thousand copies.

After Ronald retired from teaching, he and Jill took the *Gateway* course at The Monroe Institute, following that with several more courses over the years. They joined the Institute's Professional Division and were appointed to the board of advisors. They presented courses in Cambridge using the Monroe Hemi-Sync technology and introduced it also to Slovakia and the Czech Republic. They became close friends of Bob and Nancy Monroe and Ronald edited Monroe's third book, *Ultimate Journey,* contributing a preface to the first edition. He went on to edit two volumes of contributions detailing the many ways of using Monroe's Hemi-Sync: *Using the Whole Brain* (1993) and *Focusing the Whole Brain* (2004).

Now living in Galloway, Ronald has given several lecture courses on states of consciousness for the University of Glasgow. He also wrote his own study of altered states of consciousness, *The Vast Enquiring Soul.* The Russells are both Monroe Outreach trainers, conducting occasional workshops in their home in Scotland, and making annual visits to Cyprus to present the *Going Home* program there.

Hampton Roads Publishing Company

. . . for the evolving human spirit

Hampton Roads Publishing Company
publishes books on a variety of subjects,
including metaphysics, spirituality,
health, visionary fiction, and other related topics.

For a copy of our latest trade catalog,
call toll-free, 800-766-8009,
or send your name and address to:

Hampton Roads Publishing Company, Inc.
1125 Stoney Ridge Road
Charlottesville, VA 22902
E-mail: hrpc@hrpub.com
Internet: www.hrpub.com